DARE
TO
GROW
UP

DARE
TO
GROW
UP

Learn to Become Who You Are Meant to Be

PAUL DUNION

Bartleby Press
Washington • Baltimore

Ellen Bass, "Gate C22" from *The Human Line.* Copyright © 2007 by Ellen Bass. Reprinted with permission of The Permissions Company, Inc. on behalf of Copper Canyon Press.

Printed in the United States of America

Bartleby Press
8600 Foundry Street
Savage Mill Box 2043
Savage, MD 20763
800-953-9929
www.BartlebythePublisher.com

Library of Congress Cataloging-in-Publication Data

Dunion, Paul.
  Dare to grow up : learn to become who you are meant to be / Paul Dunion ; with a foreword by Thomas Moore.
    p. cm.
  ISBN 978-0-910155-87-8
  1. Maturation (Psychology) 2. Self-realization. I. Title.
  BF710.D86 2011
  158--dc23
                    2011040955

To my mother, whose simplicity continues to help loosen my grip upon grandiosity, and who called me away from myself, offering me an opportunity to strengthen my will and claim the uniqueness of my character. And to my father, whose propensity to dream consistently pointed me away from reality and taught me to hold a large vision.

Contents

ACKNOWLEDGMENTS   ix

FOREWORD by Thomas Moore   xi

INTRODUCTION   1

THE LOST ART OF MATURING   3

Mentors, Ritual and Community

CULTURAL INTERFERENCE   25

A New Cosmology ▪ Leaving Home

ANATOMY OF A BOUNDARY   43

How Do Boundaries Work? ▪ Three Types of Boundaries ▪ Quality of a Boundary ▪ Finding Our Love ▪ Receiving Boundaries

SELF-LOYALTY   77

Faithfulness and Devotion ▪ Self-Betrayal ▪ Creating Self-Loyalty ▪ Discernment and Boldness

A PROPER TIME FOR POWER   115

The Nature of Personal Power ▪ The Anatomy of Abuse ▪ Abuses of Power ▪ Abdication of Power ▪ The Challenge ▪ Personal Power and Autonomy ▪ Moving Out of Victim Stories ▪ Death of the Inflated Heroic ▪ A Sacred Reference Point

TIME FOR HEALING   161

The Wound ▪ *Resistance* ▪ *Feeling Vulnerable* ▪ *The Medicine* ▪ *The Wound's Gift* ▪ *Wounding and Healing as Initiatory* ▪ *The Many Faces of Healing*

FORGED BY INTIMACY   209

Emotional Intimacy ▪ *What It Isn't* ▪ *What Is It?* ▪ *A Cornucopia of Proper Times* ▪ *Can There Be Too Much Diversity?* ▪ *Emotional Generosity*

WIND AND BREATH   245

Three Faces of Spiritual Immaturity ▪ *Spiritual Food* ▪ *Betrothed to Life* ▪ *The Novice Mystic* ▪ *Initiated by Life* ▪ *Life Offers Initiation* ▪ *Fate's Assistance May Not Be Obvious*

CALLS TO SPIRIT   273

Abdication of Power or Victimization ▪ *The Adventurous Life* ▪ *Seeking Faces of the Self* ▪ *Circling Back*

Acknowledgments

Much gratitude to Sister Josepha, my kindergarten teacher who honored the proper time for entry into the world by receiving me with delight and great warmth, and also my deep appreciation to Professor William Cobb who introduced me to the world of Existentialism with endless accommodation for my curiosity and the encouragement to live what I found in the written word.

A number of readers offered time, energy and care toward the realization of this project: Gary Blaser, Amy Dunion, Jeffrey Duval, Margaret Harris, Father John Julian, OJN, Alaina King, Gerlinda Lehner, Marie Pace, Walter Van Senbeck, Julie Schweiger and Jim Scherer.

Karen Pergande artistically captured the idea of stewardship for the book cover.

I want to thank my wife, Connie Jones Dunion for holding a vision of possibility when I descended into a Crisis of Faith. And to Elinor Griffith who continued to see a place in the world for my creative efforts and held a light when the way darkened.

Appreciation to Jeremy Kay, my publisher, for his unbridled insistence upon the lucidity of the project. Many thanks to

Thomas Moore who offered time and energy to introduce and bless the work.

Lastly, thanks to Stuart Alpert for pointing the way out of the basement into a larger story.

Foreword

My father once told me that he was slow in maturing. It was a confession that embarrassed him a little, but not much. When I heard it, I wondered if I had inherited this tendency from him, because in many ways I have been slow to grow up and wonder sometimes if I ever will. But as I write, my father is ninety-seven years old and looks not a day over seventy. He is young in spirit, and I often wonder if he had been quick to grow up, could he have aged so well, or even lived so long?

As Paul Dunion says many times in his book, there is a proper time for each of us to mature. You can't push it ahead, and you probably shouldn't let it pass its time. However you do it, it's subtle business. My father's youth floats in him like a plasma. You see it almost all the time, giving him a glow and making him attractive. My wife and I wonder if one of these days he'll find someone and get married again. He seems young enough. My mother, his wife of sixty-three years, died seven years ago.

This is a big year for me. I turn seventy in a few months. I might expect some dreams of passage, and in fact just yesterday,

I had a haunting one. I was driving in my car out in the country and stopped by the side of a road. I liked the feel of the region. I was standing next to a lovely canal and tall, old, protective trees straddled its sides. A quiet village was set apart in the distance. I walked along the canal toward the village. The atmosphere, the architecture, and the natural landscape were nothing like my home, but they were inviting. I just sauntered into a house. I was afraid the owners might think I was trespassing, but I pretended to belong somehow. Two maids greeted me, and then I saw the owners, two friendly middle-aged people who were speaking with friends. They welcomed me, though they didn't seem to know who I was. I felt oddly at home and was surprised at the quiet welcome I got. I had trouble finding my way back to the car, but I made it. As I sat in the seat, I realized that blood was oozing from my pants at my right thigh.

I told the dream to my wife, and she immediately commented that it felt like a rite of passage. Yes, I thought, I've been expecting a dream like this. I'm being welcomed into a new life, although apparently I'm not quite ready for the move yet. Is it death, or is it the next thing, a new phase? Whatever it is, the dream has helped me get ready for a passage.

Shifting from one place in life to another, from a phase that has become familiar to one that is unknown, is not easy. Maybe we don't always cooperate. Maybe sometimes we don't even achieve the necessary movement. Maybe we get stuck, fixated, in the wrong place and time.

Paul Dunion accents the importance of a mentor to help us through these junctions that are crucial but never easy. He has reflected on his own life, the lives of his clients, signals in society at large and rich ideas mainly from psychology. His book is a form of mentoring. He's done at lot of work sorting things out. He's done things I couldn't do for myself, and I appreciate his sensitive and intelligent contribution.

I recognize myself in so much of what he says, especially the challenging dynamic of being both autonomous and social. I err on the autonomous side, easily sliding into the character of a loner. As a writer and teacher I can be outwardly engaged with many people, but inwardly I'm craving the quiet, solitary pleasure of my own home and my own room.

May I say that I have a certain affection for my neurotic tendencies. They make me who I am as much as any gifts or talents I may have. I feel humbled reading Paul's book, because I realize how difficult it has been to mature as a person. I'm almost seventy, but inwardly I'm forty-two. That's the age I feel myself to be. I'm surprised on the street when an old man talks to me as though we share something in common. How could that be? I'm forty-two.

I know that some people have a physical formula for finding your "real" age. To find your psychological age, maybe you can add your actual age to your imagined age and divide by two. That way, I'm fifty-five. Not bad. But it shows how unskilled I am in maturing.

Of course, Paul doesn't mean just getting older. He's talking about being mature enough to handle boundaries, to occupy a decent psychological geography, and to know the difference between moral positioning and ethical engagement. These are real achievements. I would call them soul talents and acquisitions. To make things slightly more complicated, your soul has its own age or ages. Your mind advances through packets of knowledge, but your soul matures through rites of passage that are usually difficult: sickness, loss, ending, separation, failure.

Paul is especially sensitive to the role of relationships in the work of healing. He's interested in shaping workable boundaries, where you're neither remote from nor fused with another person. He understands the importance of your background and early experiences in forging an adult relationship. The way I imagine it, we do not move from phase to phase in life; we pile up childhood, adolescence and everything in between, and then bring this heap of personalities to important relationships. If you aren't in touch with these elements and if you haven't worked them through to some extent, you may find intimacy impossible.

Paul presents a deep and comprehensive view of the human person in relationship with others, and in doing so he doesn't leave out spirit. Intelligence, a vision, a sense of the whole, values that come from reflection and study, reverence—these spiritual qualities are an essential part of the maturing process. Too often psychological reflection turns in on itself and ultimately becomes mechanical. Not so with this book. Its spiritual outlook, never heavy-handed or dogmatic, keeps it open to the mysteries of human experience. After all, traditional rites of passage are marked by spiritual practices and rituals, not by counseling methods. In that sense, this book is a handbook for passages, a spiritual guide full of psychological sophistication. You couldn't ask for more.

Paul writes about the soul, even if he doesn't use the word. He has written a valuable book on dealing with obstacles of maturing. If you don't mature at the proper time, you miss out on the rich life and level of happiness offered in that particular time of life. You get backed up, and then it's difficult to get on schedule.

No one is immune from this process, and therefore everyone can benefit from Paul Dunion's reflections. We need teachers and mentors, people who have the time to study, experience and reflect. We need books to help us get through, especially books like this one that touch on matters of importance and deal with them intelligently and honestly.

—Thomas Moore

Introduction

The birth of the idea for *Dare to Grow Up* was germinated by a conclusion I came to after thirty years of private practice as a psychological healer: nearly all of my clients are significantly confused about living with effective boundaries. This boundary disorientation transcends socio-economic class and levels of education. It appears that the issue of good boundaries is as much a cultural phenomenon as it is a result of any early family experience.

I then asked the question: so what's the big deal about knowing how to live with effective boundaries? The answer came quickly. Boundaries support safety, personal identity and the ability to create meaningful relationships. Without them, the flow of our uniqueness easily gets lost in the ocean of demands and expectations that surround us. We end up neither knowing who we are nor our place in the human community.

It gradually became clear that knowing how to create safety, support personal identity and build significant relationships reflected a deepening of maturity. I decided that the struggles I was witnessing in these three areas reflected a profound truth: human maturation is not natural.

It appears that human maturity, or growing up, is similar to the cultivation of crops; some seed can simply be tossed about and regardless of light, water and nutrients, this seed will prevail and come of age. The rest of us resemble the seed in need of stewardship, where attention needs to be paid to weeding, watering and enriching the ground that holds us.

The culture endorses the spurious belief that maturity automatically accompanies the accumulation of years. However, when we don't get the help we need to identify the *proper time* for learning life lessons, we run the risk of remaining in an adolescent holding pattern well into our later years. In order to attend to the soul's need for deepening, we will need to seek support for our evolving development.

So most of us don't just arrive into adulthood. We do best when welcomed by a community of adults and when the weeding, watering and enriching described in this book takes place. When the welcome is authentic, we are taught that life's masteries are dependent upon a willingness to remain a student of life's mysteries. I remain deeply thankful for the welcomes I have received along the way and committed to pass on what I've learned about those welcomes in the following pages of *Dare to Grow Up*. As you start this journey, let me now welcome you…

1

The Lost Art of Maturing

Initiation represents one of the most significant spiritual
phenomena in the history of humanity. —Mircea Eliade

"**B**oy, it's time for you to die!" proclaims the fictional
chief of an indigenous tribe in the film, *The Em-
erald Forest.* Surrounded by tribal elders, he is announcing that
the time has arrived for a boy's initiation. The boy will not have
to doubt his manhood, what it means to be a man and whether
he will be accepted into the community of men. His native culture will unambiguously inform him when it is time for his boyish ways to die, allowing for the birth of a man.

In the West, we have allowed ourselves to drift away from
cultural norms that guide the maturing process. We have developed a cavalier attitude about maturation that has inhibited our
pursuit of meaning and fulfillment. It hurts us personally and
culturally. We are often more interested in the status of the stock
market and football scores than the depth of our own character.
We are not asking important questions like: How does maturing
take place? How do we know it is actually happening? What do
we need to do in order to maximize its likelihood? How might
maturity nurture a capacity for genuine wisdom?

In our culture, we expect our elders to retire, perhaps engage in endless rounds of golf, topped off with late afternoon cocktails, or maybe just drift off into oblivion with no expectation that we might benefit from the fullness of their years.

Personal fulfillment may ultimately be dependent on our ability to move closer and closer to who we are meant to be, a process guided by a commitment to our own maturation. We can view maturity as a measure of how well we know ourselves, but this does not take place naturally, even as a result of an accumulation of years. Maturation must be directed, supported and encouraged, as the steward attends to the vineyard. However, just as some seedlings find their way to fullness irrespective of unfavorable conditions, some human beings seem equipped to move beyond hazardous circumstances, bearing witness to a seasoned maturity.

One etymological root of the word *maturing* means "happening in the proper time." And so each of us has our *proper time* when physical, emotional, intellectual and spiritual development appropriately occurs. We have our own ways of resisting these *proper times,* either by regressing to an idealized, child-like state of dependency or by pretending to know what we are doing and acting beyond our years. In either case we are out of sync with our *proper time,* placing us at cross purposes with any meaningful pursuit of happiness.

A number of years ago, a friend's daughter was undergoing her bat mitzvah, a Jewish ceremony marking the time of passage into adulthood. At one point during the service her mother stood beside her and said, "My daughter acts only in her own time." My entire body began to shake as I heard her words. It reminded me that in my own life, from when I was seven, I was often asked to act as if I possessed a knowing far beyond my time. I now recognize that this is the condition of a parentified child, one who attempts to meet expectations to be an adult by pretending to possess the abilities asked for. The burdens placed upon me then put me at odds with myself, struggling to accept a version of myself that inevitably fell quite short.

Without paying attention to our *proper time*, we either live from a need to inflate or deflate. I regularly meet bold and over-aggressive people who create a persona much larger than their actual size, which often leads others to see their self-inflation as confidence. I also encounter gentle, sensitive souls who attempt to live smaller than their actual size. In my own experience, I have received messages that instructed me to deflate, learned from my father's excessive emphasis on modesty and frquent reminders not to bring unnecessary attention to myself. But I also received signals from mentors reminding me of my proper size and my *proper times,* giving me permission to inflate by owning my gifts and living them.

Mentors, Ritual and Community

We are not meant to figure out on our own when our *proper time* is taking place. It is supposed to be the responsibility of society to offer mentors, ritual and community committed to helping us recognize our *proper times.* Our culture is barren of all three, leaving us trapped in a constellation of adolescent beliefs and behaviors, where the depths of adulthood quite often go sacrificed.

Mentors

Mentors accept us for who we are, while holding a vision of who we are meant to be. The mentoring relationship is a deeply personal one. In Western culture, the name *mentor* comes to us from the *Odyssey*, where the goddess Athena assumes the body of an elderly man named Mentor who guides and protects Telemachus while his father, Odysseus, fights at the Trojan War.

In the classical Greek tradition, Athena is born of her father Zeus's forehead. From this account Athena is exempt from the experience of gestation and fetal dependency. She is conceived from thought and vision, with the myth attributing wisdom to her divine countenance. She becomes a symbol for a mentor's capacity to advocate for the mentee's autonomy, rather than encouraging a debilitating dependency.

At their best, mentors remain both involved and detached from the young people they serve. Their involvement reflects an investment in youth being able to discover and live their innate gifts. Their detachment allows mentors to guide young people toward becoming their true selves rather than toward fulfilling some agenda of the mentor. Remaining invested yet detached, mentors have a clearer vision of our gifts than parents, who often need us to be something that would address unfinished business in their own lives.

We are told that Athena was both protective and quick to reward and punish. Mentors protect the gifts of their mentees and, at times, protect the gifts even from the mentees themselves. This protection may be experienced as a reward and at other times as a punishment, as mentors push, prod and provoke those whom they guide back to the path.

Mentors vigilantly watch for the *proper times*. Those may be times for learning about more self-accountability, more honesty, more skill-development, more commitment, more responsibility and inevitably, a greater sense of self. This more aware self may be what is intended when we describe development as growing up.

Recently, while facilitating a workshop, I mentioned that one of the most adult utterances we can make is to declare feelings of helplessness and fear. Immediately, one woman cried out, "I don't think that I'm capable of saying I feel helpless." Right on the heels of her declaration, another woman spoke up. "I don't even give myself a chance to feel helpless; I immediately attempt to control the situation, irrespective of my ability to do so."

One of the most significant threats to our maturity is the cultural mandate that real adults don't feel fear and helplessness. Hence, we have large numbers of folks walking around pretending they don't feel scared, but instead comforting themselves with a pretension that not only beguiles others but also places themselves at a great distance from their true selves. We abandon our ability to mature, instead meeting cultural expectations which deny feelings of fear and helplessness.

In his book *The Soul of Sex,* Thomas Moore writes, "Imagine growing by becoming less certain and less informed, getting in touch with your ignorance and foolishness rather than your intelligence, and learning to allow sensation to dim rationality. Imagine personal growth as a matter of becoming more humorous and more earthy, and emotional health as being in touch with the body and given to pleasure."

If we're lucky, this growing-down experience will provide us with necessary provisions for growing up. The more we grow down with the mentor's guidance, the more we shed cultural versions of who we are and learn to honor our uniqueness. By paying attention to our losses, disillusionments and longings, we diminish ourselves. In our *proper time*, we learn to let go of what does not properly belong to our souls.

Mentors can help us identify what might contribute to our maturation and gain the knowledge of what does not work for us.

Where are we troubled? Is it friendships, intimate relationships, work, vocational issues or financial concerns? Maybe we are feeling lost or confused about who we are or struggling with the loss of a loved one. These struggles will likely be an indication of an emerging *proper time* for learning and healing, guided by a mentor.

During the Renaissance, a mentoring relationship was a common way to learn and develop skills. But today, most people would be shocked at the notion that we can actually get our maturity mentored. In a time when mentoring rarely exists outside the office, it can be challenging to find and solidify a mentor relationship. However, it can be done. The first step is to announce to friends, relatives, neighbors and co-workers that you are looking for a mentor and the specific kind of skill that you are seeking to develop. This may be a difficult task because it calls for permission from yourself to ask for and acquire help. We need to feel deserving and believe that receiving help does not make a disparaging statement about our characters. The next step is to interview two or three of the people whose names come up, attempting to confirm that they actually possess the competency we are seeking.

It's important to create time to get to know one another and decide whether a good rapport is possible. The power of a mentoring relationship happens when mentor and protégée choose one another. The choosing occurs when both individuals trust one another and hold the faith that they belong together, and that they are capable of collaborating creatively. This is especially important if the relationship is intended to be long-term.

There are many inspired spiritual and psychological teachers but still, inspiration is often accompanied by deception, so there are also plenty of charlatans. This may also serve as a *proper time* for deepening our discernment regarding authentic guides. Genuine teachers understand that their charisma is analogous to a large bell that can be used to gain a student's attention. Since charisma is held in high esteem in an extroverted culture, we can be mesmerized by bright and shiny expressions of exuberance and charm. Speaking with soul and meaning is subordinated to simply speaking a lot. We can find ourselves admiring that which entertains us and quells our own social anxiety. People with charisma may have us believing that we are in the presence of someone who is highly evolved, rather than understanding that we are simply being charmed, which may or may not reflect real substance.

Credible teachers call us to evolving beliefs, values, dreams, longings and imagination. Their goal is to bring our attention to our *proper time* for learning and healing. They do not attempt to convert us to an ideology or their own personal worldview. The faithful mentor accepts us for who we are and where our journey has so far taken us, while at the same time, holds a vision of who we were meant to be. If we are lucky, the mentor will be vigilant about noticing an imbalance between acceptance and expectation, and will correct accordingly.

Much like seeds in the vineyard, where some grow no matter where they are thrown and others require care and attention, many if not most of us will need our maturity to be nurtured. It is the mentor's responsibility to identify a *proper time* for learning and bring it to our attention. The mentor's guidance may include identifying resources necessary to augment our learning experiences. This becomes especially true if it is our emotional or spiritual lives that are being shepherded.

Community

A community is not a gathering of people who get together in order to watch a ballgame or ride on a train to a particular destination. After all, when the gathering or the journey is over, the group disbands. Nothing holds them together. In a genuine community, the people are committed to a common purpose that transcends their individual goals. A group of neighbors could be a community dedicated to bringing peace to their neighborhood or a group of co-workers committed to maintaining safe working conditions.

The depth of community evolves best when its purpose is inexorably connected to the process of getting there. For example, the community striving to generate a climate of accord discovers that the more each person takes responsibility to build a trusting rapport with neighbors, the more likely it is that they realize their common purpose. In an authentic community, individuals actively participate and remain accountable for one another's health and prosperity regardless of purpose.

It may very well be true that it takes a village, a community or a clan to raise a child. When children are raised in the collective, several important dynamics take place. The first is that children are offered multiple role models, affording them a more diverse and extensive map to adulthood. In moving outside the circle of the nuclear family, children can find adults who possess interests and gifts that resemble their own, offering perhaps more fitting scripts for adulthood.

A community also offers an abundant supply of social dynamics, where a child can witness and learn about trust, loyalty, betrayal, cooperation, conflict and other essential expressions of the human condition. Most importantly, they can feel comfortable, knowing that their care and guidance is being directed by the best collective wisdom.

Children know they can manipulate parents. However, they experience a deep sense of relief when their limits are made clear by a larger group. The aspiration of dividing and conquering is put to rest.

A Calling

Anything in life can call us to a *proper time*. If we're listening much can be gained. One such call came for me in February 1991. It was a beautiful day for skiing in central Vermont, packed powder, winter sun and a gentle breeze at our backs. By noon, my former wife Amy and I were ready to head toward the lodge for some lunch and a brief rest. Upon entering the lodge, we were greeted by an avalanche of hungry and tired skiers, with no available seating in sight.

I flopped about in my ski boots, carrying my hat, mittens and goggles. I began to feel like a child of five returning home from a morning of sledding with friends. I made my way from one end of the lodge to the other, seeking a place to land, regain my composure and my rightful age. Surely, most of New England had convened at this lodge on this particular Sunday. I watched people of all ages as they laughed, ate and told their favorite alpine tale. I felt as if I had crashed a party and was desperately wishing for a last-minute invitation.

As I stood helplessly in the middle of the lodge, I spotted Amy waving her hands and gesturing to a couple of available seats. An immediate sense of relief descended upon me as I plodded along, lifting each ski boot in an exaggerated fashion so as not to stumble. Catching an aroma of hot chocolate began to further soothe my feeling of being displaced.

Dropping into the chair, I removed my jacket and boots as Amy placed fruit and cheese on the table in front of me.

Feeling like my adult self again, I looked around and was startled to see a white-haired man, perhaps in his early sixties, sitting directly across from me, sporting a red flannel shirt with a live monkey attached to a leash sitting in his lap. Astonished, I couldn't keep from staring. They appeared as out of place as a skier standing behind the bars of a monkey cage at the zoo.

My gaze must have acted as some sort of tractor beam. The monkey made its way across the table and positioned itself comfortably on my lap. It was my first ever physical encounter with a monkey and the setting made it all the more jolting. My befuddled reaction must have been obvious.

"Don't worry, she's got a diaper on," the monkey's escort explained, reassuring me of actions that I had not considered.

I forced a smile. I wasn't quite sure how I felt about this monkey's choice to seat herself. She seemed harmless enough. The situation was still bizarre, but also somewhat intriguing and I decided to relax.

Without introduction, the gentleman on the other end of the bench began to tell us the story of his monkey. "Rosie stays with me for the first two years of her life. At that point I will bring her to Boston University where she will undergo intensive training." He addressed me as if we had scheduled this tutorial on the education of the monkey.

"What kind of training?" I asked.

"She will be trained to become the companion to a person who is quadriplegic. Her assistance will afford that person an opportunity for privacy and some autonomy by helping with eating, drinking and tasks such as turning the pages of a magazine."

Amy and I were amazed. As I ate my lunch, eye contact between me and the monkey became more fixed, like two children observing one another. Our gaze prompted me to wonder just how different this creature and I were from one another.

I reached for more cheese, while folks gathered behind me and began asking questions. Rosie and I were quickly becoming an unusual alpine item. Talk of trail conditions and the challenge of the moguls was quickly replaced by inquiries regarding my relationship to the monkey.

"You'll need to ask this gentleman." I responded to the mounting curiosity regarding the primate on my lap.

The monkey began preening my shirt by removing pieces of lint. "What is she doing?" I asked.

"Well, I think it might be your facial hair," he responded, obviously withholding something.

"What about my facial hair?"

"I think Rosie is exploring you as a possible mate," he suggested, maintaining a serious expression.

I have always enjoyed and felt open to a wide range of female attention, but this was a bit much. I wanted to remain respectful of this animal, yet I didn't want to do anything that might encourage her romantic interest.

My face must have reflected my turmoil because suddenly everyone around me burst into laughter. This provided a welcome break which I saw as an opportunity to disengage from my new friends and head back to the slopes.

"Well, we better get going," I announced, hoping the monkey's handler, whose name I still did not know, would graciously help end my encounter with this precocious anthropoid.

"He's leaving with this woman, come Rosie," he instructed.

The monkey once again peered into my eyes with a look that seemed to say, "Last chance, big guy, is it going to be me or her?"

Rosie proceeded to move from my lap, crossed the table and returned to the man. We gathered our belongings, thanked him for sharing his story and bid him and his friend goodbye.

I walked away from the table eager to return to skiing, when the gentleman yelled, "Hey, there're two things you should know about this monkey."

The demand and urgency of his voice stopped me. I turned and faced him.

"Did you know that if this monkey's mother had died while giving her birth, the other female monkeys would have offered the care that the baby needed?"

"No, I didn't know that."

"And did you know that when Rosie is assigned as the companion to a person who is quadriplegic, she will remain with that person until one of them dies?"

"No, I didn't know that either," I turned quickly to walk away, not knowing whether my determination to leave was due to a desire to get back to skiing or feeling overwhelmed by his questions.

"Let me ask you something else!" cried the man, his voice commanding that I again stop and pay attention.

I turned one more time, compelled to hear what this guy wanted to say, annoyed that this exchange was continuing.

"Do you believe the kind of loyalty and commitment exemplified by the monkeys was passed on to us in evolution?"

"I don't know. I don't think I've ever considered it." A little dazed, I was now eager for this discussion to end. I waved and briskly moved away.

I walked out of the lodge disoriented, not sure I even possessed the necessary composure to effectively negotiate the slopes. I had walked into a ski lodge for a brief respite and was introduced to a primate whose capacity for loyalty and commitment might surpass my own. And that was the question that haunted me over the coming weeks: Did I possess the depth of commitment and loyalty exemplified by this monkey?

I started to admit that I lived with no meaningful connection to my community. My allegiance was to my own immediate family. Wasn't my responsibility to care for my children and make sure they got to basketball practice and horse-riding lessons, and all the other varied privileges and entitlements fitting to suburban, middle-class children? After all, I was meeting my duties as financial provider and chauffeur.

That monkey made me look at myself as I had never done before. I began to call my values into question and experience a crisis of identity. A sensation of nausea was brewing within me that I could not quell with some antacid. The antidote lay somewhere in my soul. I decided to trust the sickening feeling that wrapped itself around my guts. I asked it to show me the way. With the help of my own mentor, it became clear that

what ailed me would not be subdued by an interesting theory
or altruistic intentions. Action would have to be taken.

In the fall of 1992 I created a mentoring community for
teenage boys called Boys to Men. A dozen men met every Tues-
day evening for six months, building trust and cohesiveness
and then welcomed twenty 14-year-old boys into what we had
created. Most of these boys had no men in their lives, never
mind twelve men who were committed to working as a team.

It became obvious these boys were waiting to be welcomed by older males. We began to understand the power of
gang membership, which offered the boys the inclusion and
acceptance of older boys. We realized that our purpose was
to offer the boys an opportunity to participate in an authentic
male community, and that left us with the challenge of creating such a thing.

This community was not to be built upon a vision that the
boys were troubled and in need of our remedial efforts. No, that
kind of thinking would have simply reduced us to a group of
guys attempting to offer a social service and could alienate the
boys more than they already were.

We needed our beliefs, values and purpose to be captured in a philosophical statement that would inform the boys
about who we were and at the same time remind ourselves of
our vision. We were also giving voice to where we believed
both responsibility and power lay. The following was read at
the beginning of each meeting:

> We hold the vision that men have allowed the death of
> community, so our boys join gangs. Men have abdicated
> their right to initiate boys into the mysteries of adult-
> hood, so our boys attempt to initiate one another. Men

no longer take responsibility for the boys in their neighborhoods, so our boys turn to males trapped in their own adolescence, who are available in playgrounds and on local street corners. Men have forgotten what they might die for, so our boys are willing to die and kill in random drive-by shootings. Men have forgotten about the ancient power of being committed to a path with a heart, so our boys are drawn to the shadows of power: greed, violence, intimidation and reckless behavior. Men are confused about what it means to be adult, so our boys pretend they are men. We believe by walking consciously through these shadows, we will ignite the flame of our manhood and illuminate the way back home for our boys.

The story of our community became a story of men determined to deepen their own maturity, not a story of offering correction to misbehaving boys. We saw youth who were acting out as heralds announcing a clear and poignant message: They no longer could tolerate the absence of men in their lives and they were willing to kill themselves and one another, rather than live outside the community of men.

Our paradigm shift offered us a new way to see young people and a fresh perspective on the problem. We also had a new way to see ourselves and redefine what it means to offer support to the boys. We gradually defined our community as a place where its members could be heard, a place to hold people accountable for their behavior, a place for truth-telling, a place to learn and a place for fun and celebration. We learned to help boys clarify their problems, help them discern what was in and out of their control and, when appropriate, offered them guidance and direction.

No matter how much acting out they did, we refused to define the boys as damaged goods. We constantly reminded them that they possessed the power and the responsibility to support their own lives. We became very effective at communicating our distaste for a boy's tendency to define himself as a victim of his past or of the system.

We need communal support in order to track our *proper times*, process them, and identify what we need to learn and how others can play a pivotal role in our learning. Community offers an opportunity for belonging, where we embrace the faith that our individuality or autonomy has a place with others. Within a context of belonging, we become more willing to lean into the unknown, believing that we will be supported when we venture to a place we have not been before. *Proper times* inevitably include some form of separation from old ways, ways that constrict our deepening and expanding.

It can be extremely difficult to participate in authentic community in a culture that encourages rugged individualism. The initial challenge is not to succumb to the temptation to accept alienation as a normal way of life. Community must be fought for. There are several worthwhile starting points. One approach is to begin bringing more truth-telling to a single friend. The seeds of community may be planted by two people sharing their losses, their challenges, their fears and longings. The strength of that bond is enhanced when they are clear about what they want from one another and willing to hold each other accountable for broken agreements. Others can be welcomed along the way.

Another course is to join a group that appears to share our interests and values. Of course, this doesn't guarantee there will be an interest in truth-telling, but we might be able to find at least one person who wants to go beyond mere social engagement and that can lead to the birth of community. The key is to refuse to succumb to isolation and to rekindle the desire to be seen for who we are, rather than acknowledged for the contingent, social personalities we invent.

Ritual

My wife and I recently attended a summer evening event in Providence, R.I., called Water-Fire. After hearing dozens of folks speak highly of this event, we enthusiastically attended. We stood on a walkway overlooking the Providence River where some one hundred buckets of logs were distributed approximately twenty feet apart floating on the river. Just after sunset the logs were set afire while music played in the background.

After standing there with 7,000 other people watching aquatic blazes for some thirty minutes, I turned to my wife and asked, "What the hell are we all doing here?"

"It's romantic," Connie responded. She seemed to admonish me for my insensitivity to the romantic extravaganza, enhanced by warm temperatures, a gentle breeze out of the northwest and a full moon.

I understood the romantic aura of the event, but my best intuition was that with 7,000 people of different backgrounds and ages staring at logs burning on a river and listening to music piped in, something else was transpiring. And this happening occurred every other Saturday evening throughout the summer. At the very least, we were all participating in a relatively primitive ritual, maybe a blessing of the river.

The next morning my mind continued to be riddled by the

activities at the river. Could this be an example of just how hungry we are for ritual? Is there some need to bless our waters? And then it dawned on me: we had been watching two elements normally in an antagonistic relationship to one another—water and fire—move beyond their typical antipathy into an expression of harmony. Perhaps this could be a symbolic gesture of our own internal worlds where oppositional forces dwell, seeking resolution between love and hate, acceptance and rejection, freedom and bondage, control and surrender, determination and resignation, independence and dependence, etc. The entire experience became a vivid depiction of our need for ritual that addresses the odyssey of the soul's maturation as it attempts to bring into balance the polarized expressions of the human psyche.

The loss of cultural support concerning our maturation is evidenced by the absence of meaningful rites of passage. Even the rituals we do have, like those found in today's organized religions, are used to serve the institution, not the individual. Our culture has become somewhat barren of rites, leaving us with little or nothing to work with as we attempt to recognize and acknowledge our *proper time.*

Ritual is essentially a theatrical production where a story is translated into a set of actions. When a ritual is done with reverence, or as Mircea Eliade suggests, "For a thing to be done well, it must be done as it was done the first time," the service will likely resonate with ancient voices. When it is a story about a central expression of the human condition, and the actions we are exercising have been taken throughout the ages, it is likely we will feel ourselves being called to the sacred.

A Latin root for the word sacred is "inviolable". An authentic ritual has the power of making a declaration unalterable, fixed and permanent. Within a ritual context, men's learning is sealed, acknowledging a passage or the emergence of a proper time.

Rituals are meant to be symbolic, and as such, they are telling stories as well as offering participants the opportunity to step into a story. In our mentoring community, our rituals were designed to tell a story about death, birth, mystery and the revelation of lessons about gender and adulthood. Our rituals were initiatory in nature, because, after all, the word *initiate* means "to begin or to be born," but with a firm understanding that all beginnings are accompanied by something ending.

Our initiations or rite-of-passage rituals took place after one year when a boy could demonstrate a commitment to support himself, the other boys and the philosophy of the community. At a farm owned by one of the mentors, we created a sweat lodge from saplings covered with blankets and built a fire pit in the center. Then to the beat of a drum we marched the boys a quarter of a mile to the lodge, gave an orientation to the ritual and provided safety guidelines.

The mystery of the evening was meant to remind them that maturity is a great deal about making peace with uncertainty. Once in the lodge, a leader requested that they quietly focus upon what needs to end or die in their lives. Inevitably, the boys started telling stories of abuse and violence, narratives we typically did not hear at our regular meetings. It was as if the ritual demanded a deeper level of truth. After listening to the boys, the men pushed the boys to let go of self-pity and self-destructive behavior, of blaming others, and of following ineffective leaders and bullying.

As the heat built in the lodge, the boys were asked to call to mind what they wanted for their lives, what new expressions of life they were willing to welcome. Again, adult men strengthened the process by adding suggestions like self-accountability, self-respect, compassion, clarity and perseverance.

The next phase of the ritual included stories told by the men that demonstrated some foolish choice made in the name of being real men. We believed that tales of our buffoonery and self-aggrandizement and what we learned from it, helped the boys to discern false bravado from genuine expressions of manhood.

Before exiting the lodge, men took turns uttering what we called lessons of manhood: Learn what's in your control and what isn't. Learn who is truly a friend. Learn to be creative with your aggressive energy. Learn to gently laugh at yourself. Learn to know and accept your limits. Learn to ask for help and learn to take responsibility for yourself and your community.

The experience ended with leading the boys to the farmhouse where other mentors had prepared a feast. Each new initiate was asked to stand while the mentors acknowledged strengths, skills and gifts possessed by the boy. Aided by fatigue, the power of the ritual helped the boys experience the words of the men as believable. Even the toughest of the boys opened to these blessings. Their cheeks and jaws softened, shoulders dropped, eyes moistened and body armor dropped away as the pronouncements of the men entered their hearts. It was like the new dawn light moving through the last shadows of night, illuminating the landscape.

We never knew how many lessons stayed with them; however, it was deeply gratifying to hear a boy make reference to an example months later. We also never knew for certain what had died for the boys in that lodge. Our hope was that at least some secrecy and shame about something perpetrated long ago had disappeared.

In the absence of cultural norms for acquiring mentors, building community and integrating ritual, we are stripped of any viable mechanisms for guiding what's to happen at the *proper time*. However, the hunger for community, mentors and ritual will persist. I recall asking a colleague, who worked with teenagers, how it came to be in vogue for young people to wear their trousers below the hip. He explained that in a lockdown situation in a prison the belts of inmates are taken away as a precaution against suicide, thus causing their pants to drop. Young people will identify with any group that appears to offer mentoring, community and ritual, no matter how precarious the subculture.

If left on our own to find our way, we begin to believe that compulsive self-reliance is an indication of maturity. In actuality, we grow accustomed to denying we are lost, pretending we are adults.

2
Cultural Interference

To know what you prefer, instead of humbly saying "Amen" to what the world tells you you ought to prefer, is to keep your soul alive. —Robert Louis Stevenson

Beyond the failure to provide mentors, ritual and community in support of maturation, there are a number of cultural mores that interfere with maximizing our *proper times* for appropriate learning. It behooves us to become aware of these hindrances in order to exit from adolescent holding patterns, but also to make a valued offering to others, especially the young.

A New Cosmology

A cosmology based on consumerism is a major deterrent to maturation. It suggests we can make purchases that will diminish the inherent insecurity of life. A corollary to this thinking is that products are available that can augment self-love, and make us feel good about ourselves. If we procure the right commodities, we can ward off feelings of powerlessness that accompany the mystery and unpredictability of the human condition. With plastic in hand, we prop ourselves up while consumed by the paralyzing grip of financial debt.

The primary lesson taught to initiates in many societies

is the teaching of the *Mysterium Tremendum* (Great Mystery). The belief behind such education is that young people cannot pass into adulthood unless they learn to make peace with life as mysterious, insecure and unpredictable. Creating a dynamic relationship with life is a radically different journey than pretending life can be made secure by making acquisitions.

Recently, I heard a philosopher speak on a radio program. She suggested that if it's true that life is mysterious then maybe the idea that life is mysterious is itself a mystery. I was struck by her willingness to engage in such intellectual frolic. I couldn't help but wonder if she would continue to playfully approach life's mystery and insecurity if she awoke to find her daughter dead in her bedroom from an overdose, or her husband on his way to the hospital following an automobile accident, or if she were told she needed a double mastectomy. Of course, we don't wish any of those things, but it behooves us to be willing to understand life the best we can, not losing ourselves in a kind of intellectual recreation. So much of our maturation depends upon having an authentic understanding of life that is reflective of our experience, and then making peace with that understanding.

Consumer cosmology becomes a paradigm aimed at denying the essence of life, spinning formulas geared to overcome the insecurity of being alive. Canons about the right education, the right financial investments, the right job, the right spouse and the right neighborhood are all illusions offering us security in the face of an impenetrable mystery. It is a doomed blueprint for life. It will neither make us secure nor help us to grow up. It's a lie.

We do young people a tremendous disservice by not introducing them to the "Great Mystery of Life." The consequences are devastating. They often believe there is something wrong with them because they feel insecure or anxious. They come to my office with the belief that the rest of world is doing fine and they want to know why the application of cultural formulas isn't working. They become disoriented when it comes to creatively coping with insecurity. They fear loss, abandonment, failure, confusion and change. They understand neither life nor themselves, and yet still expect to feel okay in the process. They are ill-equipped to live life on life's terms, which keeps them trapped in adolescence.

Learning to Accept Death

Another major obstruction to maturity is the culture's inclination to deny death. We magically remove death from life. Yet, to separate death from life is to make it nearly impossible to be fully alive.

One consequence of denying death is the creation of an adversarial relationship to change. Since nothing is static, life is essentially about change. There is something beginning and something ending (dying). To deny change is to deny life, hence death and life are inexorably connected.

Living at odds with change causes us to remain ignorant about how to grieve. We don't know how to let go and move on. We don't know how to die well and thus don't know how to live well.

By denying death we lose gratitude and appreciation for life. We take each breath for granted, pretending that today could not possibly be our last. This childish vision of a life without end sets us up to live with a cavalier attitude, often driven by a need for immediate gratification. The *proper time* for com-

ing into the age of stewardship passes us by, leaving us with a
juvenile understanding of our life's purpose. We have no understanding of what we have come to the planet to give and remain
confused about the nature of our offering.

Refusing to accept death predisposes us to diminish the
value of the present and over-invest in the future. With the illusion of endless tomorrows, the present becomes easily avoided,
and we comfort ourselves with thoughts of unending possibility. However, real choices and real decisions can only be made
in the present. We sacrifice a great deal of power by leaping
beyond it to the future. Unlike children, adults are devoted to
discovering the meaning of authentic personal empowerment.

When we deny death, we shroud the end of our lives in
irreverence. We no longer know how to bring truth, grace and
compassion to death and dying. In the process, we surrender
many expressions of personalization and adopt the protocol of
some funeral home.

Men seem especially disoriented when dealing with someone's death and are commonly relegated to the tasks of driving
vehicles, delivering food and making phone calls rather than
being allowed to infuse the grieving experience with meaning
and richness.

The Territorial Imperative

A major impediment to the process of maturing is an over-
bearing cultural directive to divide the outer world and the inner world and allocate to each gender, with everything outside
of us belonging to males and everything inside of us belonging
to females. Although sexism and its oppression of women existed long before the Industrial Revolution, the latter part of the

19th century was a pivotal time for the dichotomizing of the two worlds. Men migrated to factories, losing their connection to the earth and nature, and in doing so, watched the responsibility and power they once shared in the home be transferred to the women of the household. A strong line was drawn between the home and the workplace, with men doing whatever was in their power to protect the turf of the latter.

During the Industrial Revolution, the process leading to the mechanization of men had begun where men started to look at themselves as automated. It hindered their ability to connect with emotions and intuition. Performance, not wisdom, was the goal.

The home became a female sanctuary as well as a metaphor for the inner world of emotion, imagination and intuition, while the marketplace became a male haven and a metaphor for the outer world of business, higher education, religion and politics. These images would constellate with enough energy to drive women out of places of commerce and ban men from the interior world of emotion and intuition.

Sabotage of Female Development

Cultural mandates that drive women out of the outer world and prohibit men from entering the inner world have strong injurious impacts upon maturation. Females quite often remain unconscious of their innate gifts; hence, they ignore the development of talents and competencies that would easily result in being manifested in a worldly vocation. When the outer terrain is defined as off limits for females, their inner world diminishes as they hold a limited vision of themselves. They often see their gifts only as the ability to offer nurturance and emotional support, skills compatible with the inner region.

The use of logic and reason, especially as applied to world-ly endeavors, is defined as belonging in the male domain. This can leave women deciding they are intellectually inferior. In her book, *In A Different Voice*, Carol Gilligan depicts what it means for females to leave themselves: "The dissociation of girls' voices from girls' experience in adolescence, so that girls are not say-ing that they know and eventually not knowing it as well, is a prefiguring of many women's sense of having the rug of experi-ence pulled out from under them, or of coming to experience their feelings and thoughts not as real but as a fabrication."

Teenage girls watch older females vigilantly shepherd men's egos. Gilligan goes on to say, "For girls and women, is-sues of femininity or feminine identity do not depend on the achievement of separation from the mother or on the progress of individuation. Since masculinity is defined through sepa-ration while femininity is defined through attachment, male gender identity is threatened by intimacy while female gender identity is threatened by separation."

Women take on the impossible task of making sure that the men in their lives feel good about themselves, thus protect-ing themselves from the possibility of abandonment. They are expected to pay homage to the paternal ideal.

It's correct to point out, as Gilligan does, that males get the cultural okay to achieve and separate. However, males are also often condemned to compulsively achieve in order to support a fragile and conditional state of self-approval. Male separation from family, the home, or place of origin is typically a bravado expression of compulsive self-reliance, rather than genuine au-tonomy. Real separation from the mother is seldom convincing for men, since it is predicated upon a strong paternal attachment, which is seldom available. In this way men and women have much in common; they are both searching for their fathers.

Authentic individuation is the ongoing unearthing of our uniqueness, revealing personal values, beliefs and preferences. Females are taught to become an extension of males, affording them some sense of attachment and a more ambiguous sense of self, since their identity is a reflection of those around them. Males experience the terror of potentially violating some cultural mandate of manhood, which leads them increasingly away from their true selves, sacrificing uniqueness for a fabricated expression of adulthood.

Not all women allow their development to be dictated by cultural injunctions. For some, their liberation is a result of role models, older women who were pioneers in areas normally limited to men. In other cases, females possess a drive and a learning style that makes them more comfortable with the utilization of logic and reason.

The benefits of authentic feminism have been enormous. It has offered women greater consciousness of restrictions inflicted upon them by a patriarchal culture. Many women have responded favorably by combating the cultural definitions of womanhood. Just as important, women are now free to openly address their own development. However, the work of feminism is a long way from complete and our culture still places limitations on women's opportunities. Luckily, more and more women in our society protest whatever oppression they may face, even at the risk of their attachment to men.

Driven by fear, men collude with women's self-oppression. It creates a turf war that becomes increasingly intense. Men abdicate their authority in the home and instead establish control over the workplace. When fathers return after work, they defer to a woman at home. Sons learn very quickly that their place is out of the home and a legacy of holding little or no power and responsibility in the home is perpetuated, even while they attempt to remain dominant in the workplace.

Men are often unaware of how it hurts themselves when they participate in the oppression of women. Women become lost to them as collaborators working toward a common goal. They compete with women rather than co-create with them. When the power and entitlement of women in any institution is marginalized, a valuable resource is lost. And when men have life partners who are under-sizing themselves, these women are unable to call men to the best in themselves. These women end up either idolizing the men in their lives or becoming significantly dependent upon them, neither of which fosters authentic mutuality and intimacy.

Sabotage of Male Development

This excerpt is from a talk I gave not that long ago to a group of about eighty men:

> Gentlemen, you're not complaining! The culture has told you that your interior world is off limits, that in order to be real men, you are to sacrifice an intimate relationship with yourself and with those whom you love. Gentlemen, you're not complaining! You were told that real men act self-destructively. You are encouraged to ignore your losses, become numb to your grief and forget about what you love. And gentlemen, you're not complaining! You were told to

get a job and forget about a vocation, to pretend that you are not being called. And while you're at it, work a lot and ignore your gifts, gifts that your people are waiting for. Gentlemen, for God's sake, you're not complaining!

At the end of my talk I wept, thinking about my grief from witnessing countless men turn against themselves by adopting destructive cultural mandates of manhood.

There are two major distinctions between the cultural injunctions leveled against female maturation and those directed at males. The first is that most men have calmly accepted the cultural prescription that *real* men abandon their interior worlds. But no one is talking about how women collude with male immaturity, as if men, all by themselves, could stay trapped in an adolescent holding pattern.

Burger King aired a commercial some time back that begins with a young man having lunch with a young woman on the patio of a restaurant that serves trendy fare. In disgust, he launches himself out of his chair, and while singing, "I am Man; hear me roar," he runs across the street to order a Whopper. Men from all walks of life, striking macho poses, begin to follow him and sing, demanding their proper macho meal. They assert their masculinity, doing things like chopping cement blocks with their bare hands.

In another spot, for a popular cell phone company, a father passes out new phones to his teenage children, excited that this will allow them to stay more in touch with him. The kids' expressions communicate just how little they want to get on the phone with their father. The mother intervenes, reminding the children that the phones will be best used for calling friends. The father is portrayed as ignorant to the real needs of his kids—all done to promote a product. Imagine a commercial where a woman is depicted as making irrelevant or ludicrous remarks at a company board meeting!

A local radio station plays the following ad: "It's my co-coon—my new BMW is the place I go to laugh, sing and talk to myself. It's a place where I can agree or disagree with the likes of Don Imus. It's the place where I can be myself more than anywhere else. It's my personal rocket ship to the stars."

"It's the place where I can be myself more than anywhere else." It's obvious that all the laughing, singing and talking to himself is not happening in the presence of others. Real men drive real cars and only get permission to be themselves when they are alone and isolated. We have not advanced much from the solitary image of the "Marlboro Man," disconnected, alone and pretending not to need anyone.

One afternoon, I started watching a broadcast of a college basketball game between Villanova and Syracuse. As one of the Villanova players checked into the game, one of the commentators pointed out he was suffering from the flu. The other announcer piped up: "The greatest panacea is adrenaline! Once a player starts playing and playing well, he won't even know he's sick!"

The message is that real men don't let illness get in the way of competing and competing well. In fact, such determination might be just what the doctor ordered. Would anyone dare suggest that this sick young man ought to rest and maybe take something to boost his immune system instead of engaging in harmful activities? If males remain confused about their own self-care, they will likely remain ignorant about the genuine welfare of children, women and the elderly.

Our culture defines manhood as both being in a male body and out of touch with being emotionally isolated from others, and inclined to act self-destructively. We have come to simply accept that men will not make their way out from the emotional grip of adolescence. Indeed, we expect men to be emotionally immature, unable to define the *proper time* for their emotional development. Men remain confused about their emotions, unable to feel and consequently, unable to communicate effectively about what they feel.

Due to the works of Howard Gardner (*Multiple Intelligences—The Theory In Practice*, 1993), Peter Salovey and David Sluyter (*Emotional Development and Emotional Intelligence*, 1997) and Daniel Goleman (*Emotional Intelligence*, 1995), we know that emotional immaturity can manifest itself in several distinct ways. Self-awareness is diminished and the ability to manage emotions and support motivation is weakened. The ability to exercise empathy and general effectiveness in relationships can be seriously impaired.

Men are trained to ignore their emotions and live as if there is nothing emotional to be aware of. As their awareness is dulled, they run a high risk of somatic illness where emotional energy shows up as a physical symptom. These symptoms can be everything from ulcers to back pain. Bernie Siegel, the holistic oncologist, has suggested that a high percentage of his lung cancer patients also carry unresolved grief.

As self-awareness lessens, so does men's capacity to experience the uniqueness of their individuality. The waters of their emotional lives dry up, leaving them parched by the loss of what they truly love. Without the ability to live closely to the seat of their own souls, they become more and more susceptible to cultural definitions of manhood. They sacrifice deep personalized versions of what it means to be a man. They become generic men, borrowing society's prescription to bolster a sense of male identity. And so the cycle continues.

Because the inner world of men has been deemed taboo by the culture, men often are poorly equipped to manage their feelings. They ineffectively deal with distress and this often shows up as depression and anxiety. Since they neither recognize nor creatively respond to these conditions, it diminishes their resiliency to cope with life's challenges. An inability to manage their emotions leaves men prone to acting out their feelings in violence, rage, ridicule and blame, never understanding what drives their behavior. They also direct violent behavior toward themselves in the form of addiction and other reckless actions.

Emotional mismanagement also leads to passive-aggressive behavior. Men internalize anger leading to procrastination, forgetting about promises, violating commitments and agreements, and sabotaging projects with others. Men who have either a gentle persona or one characterized by intellectual reflection will commonly manifest their suppressed anger in passive-aggressive behavior.

True motivation is not simply an impulsive act toward some arbitrary goal, but rather action guided by discernment. Without emotional vibrancy, men also lose the ability to self-motivate, to understand what truly feeds their hearts and moves them into action. Questions like what to do, how to do it, when to do it, who does it serve and even do I love what I am pursuing are all part of mature motivation.

Emotional immaturity is also expressed in an inability to exercise empathy, the capacity to feel the sadness of another, instead of just sympathy or sensitivity for another's sadness. This empathy may only come when we explore the depths of our own pain and step across emotional chasms that separate us from one another. Exercising empathy is fundamental to building trust and deepening intimacy.

Effectiveness in relationships is a direct reflection of our level of emotional maturity. What are characteristics of emotional maturity? Look for the capacity to creatively approach diverse values and beliefs, as well as the ability to create rapport, manage conflict, solve problems and make effective decisions.

Because men are supposed to remain strangers to their own losses, they easily become immune to the suffering they encounter. Equally harmful is the tribulation women experience when they attempt to build meaningful relationships with immature males. Regardless of the cultural imperatives that lock men into diminished maturity, they would not be preserved without the help of women.

Female Collusion

In decades working with couples in psychotherapy, I have seen women conspiring time and time again to sustain the immaturity of males. One example occurred while working with Doris and Rob, a couple in their early fifties. Coming to see me alone, Rob reported that his wife was troubled by his inability to communicate his emotions and effectively work through problems. After eight sessions and having attended a men's gathering, Rob asked if his wife could join us for a few sessions. I agreed.

I initiated the session by asking Doris how she felt about communication in their marriage and their attempts at problem-solving.

"Oh my, I am delighted! Rob is telling me how he feels and he actually listens to me when I'm talking!" Doris almost came off the edge of her seat.

"Sounds like you see some desired change. I'm assuming you would like to stay on this path and continue to deepen your relationship to Rob," I suggested, anticipating her agreement.

"Oh no, I'm quite satisfied," said Doris.

"Don't you want to see Rob continue to strengthen his connection to his emotional life and to you?"

"No, I don't. How would I know where that would take him, and us? For all I know, he might decide to leave me. He might decide that he doesn't need me any longer. As long as Rob doesn't insult me or ignore me, I'm fine."

"Rob," I asked, "do you feel at all insulted by what Doris just said?" I hoped he might come to his own defense.

"Insulted? No, I don't feel insulted at all." Both he and Doris cast a gaze in my direction that seemed to dare me to attempt to disrupt their arrangement.

I still feel indebted to Rob and Doris for voicing what so many couples only imply. It helped me to let go of any denial I had been carrying regarding female complicity with male immaturity.

I was recently interviewed by a female journalist writing an article about male friendship. The topic of men and emotional intimacy came up. She asked, "Do you think that they are simply not wired for it?"

She was wondering out loud what society readily believes, that men are incapable of a genuinely intimate emotional relationship. I held my irritation in check. "No, I don't think the issue is faulty wiring. We simply tell males that if they want to be real men, they must remain strangers to their own inner emotional landscape, and therefore appear impoverished in an intimate relationship. They are simply trying to be the kind of men they were told to be."

Many women have little experience of feeling love from a significant male, including their fathers. Girls protect their father's inability to express love and often internalize its absence by concluding that they themselves must be unlovable. These girls live with a deep "father hunger" and grow into women who continue to see themselves as undeserving of love. Without the option of receiving a man's love, they settle for just being needed instead. And the greater the immaturity of men, the more they need women for nurturance, emotional support and even guidance. This dynamic sets the stage for unease and bitterness between men and women, as dependent relationships leave men feeling resentful and women feeling burdened and angry.

Women often form a false sense of security, believing they will not be abandoned as long as the men in their lives depend upon them emotionally. There are unfortunate implications to this alleged safety. Women are not actually being chosen by love when it is pure need that they are receiving. Hence, these women live with the gnawing emptiness and a quiet form of abandonment.

The process where men depend upon women for their emotional well-being maternalizes their relationships, leaving them feeling more like sons than husbands. These "sons" are prone to adolescent behaviors, often an affair.

A beer commercial depicts a young couple sitting on a sofa together when the phone rings. The man answers and then relates to the woman that his friend Pete needs to vent. The young woman encourages him to go to his friend in need. In the next scene Pete opens the door of his apartment, and is greeted with high-fives and hollers of "let's vent!" In the following scene both men are watching football and drinking beer while the young man phones his partner to explain that it will be a while before he returns home... Pete is still venting.

This ad is filled with the kind of messages that sabotage male and female development as well as mature heterosexual relationships. It reinforces the idea that males will not emancipate themselves from adolescence and that it is fine for them to lie to their female partners in order to join their pals for fun. In fact, the commercial exploits the woman's concern for Pete's emotional welfare as a strategy to go play without getting any flack. It also suggests that both the male and the female are locked into roles that will preclude any significant expression of mature intimacy, thus preventing their relationship from becoming a setting where each can access deeper levels of maturation.

In another beer commercial, three young males are gathered in a pub with an attractive, young female bartender. "Guys, let's talk commitment," she says.

At once, the three men recoil, showing signs of anxiety and resistance. The young woman encourages them to relax; she simply wants to tell them about this particular beer's commitment to satisfy. The men reclaim their composure.

The message is that it is appropriate for males to fear commitment, unless of course, it is about the taste of a beer. But why would males fear commitment? Could it be that we have communicated to males that faithfulness involves a loss of freedom?

The idea of being dedicated is typically linked with being obedient. It is not a man's values, needs and desires driving allegiance to a relationship, but rather a woman's. From that perspective, the male can only comply or rebel. Hence, there is no *proper time* for males to define their commitments and own them, in order to enhance their freedom and their personal power. The loss of the power to commit is a serious violation to the souls of men.

There is a great deal of reinforcement for males to remain the sons of their wives or partners. We often see them, these sons, wander off in search of girlfriends, abandoning their wife-mothers. Women have openly insisted on a political voice and socio-economic opportunity, but have not demanded an opportunity to be emotionally intimate with men. Women frequently report to me that they listen to women who gather together, complain about the immaturity of the men in their lives and then, quickly lapse into resignation.

We have been looking at some of the ways that our society interferes with the process of maturing. A number of cultural injunctions significantly plague our attempts at growing up. However, we can dare to grow up and support ourselves by accessing a mentor, reintroducing ritual back into our lives, participating in an authentic community, and responding favorably to the *proper time* for learning life lessons. We can experience relationships with the opposite sex as a *proper time* to interrupt any participation with the other's immaturity.

In order to raise consciousness about how we sabotage our own maturation, we need to visit the challenge of leaving home. Let's think of leaving home as what it means to separate from cultural beliefs and values that comforted us and eventually situated us into a story that is not our own.

Leaving Home

The theologian Paul Tillich described maturing as the willingness to leave home again and again. Leaving home can be a metaphor for the ending of some level of dependence and separation from the familiar. A Latin meaning for the word *dependent* means "danger," and so we know that resistance to leaving home can be dangerous. We are caught in the quandary of a home being a place to feel comfortable and secure but also as a physical and psychic space where our individuality and essential uniqueness can die.

Under the domain of our parents, we easily can maintain a vision of their strength, remaining ignorant of our own. We believe we are under the care of the benevolent parent who remains vigilant in protecting our best interest, so there is no need to take such responsibility for ourselves.

Leaving home often occurs in very subtle ways. It may be a practical idea about where to live, where to work, what to eat, how to handle money and what kind of spiritual practice to incorporate into our lives. Sometimes leaving home is a story about how to relate to a boss at work, or how much of our individuality we are willing to sacrifice in the name of job security. Other times it's about how much of our uniqueness we will allow ourselves to maintain in our relationships. Ultimately, leaving home is about learning to honor our autonomy, learning to be who we are meant to be rather than adapting to what others would have us be. Supporting and protecting who we are meant to be calls for employing sophisticated and effective boundaries.

3
Anatomy of a Boundary

Nothing but the fire of separation can change hypocrisy and ego. —Rumi

There are a number of personal dynamics which injuriously impact our capacity to employ effective boundaries. Boundaries separate us from others and let us know where we begin and end. Boundaries offer us safety, identity and create the possibility of true union with others, yet they continue to be the most misunderstood of all psychological dynamics. Each *proper time* we encounter offers us a chance to learn about the use of boundaries and their contribution to our needs for autonomy and belonging.

Inevitably, forces outside of us and also within pull us away from what we believe and value. Thus, learning to fight—without being unnecessarily destructive—creates a warrior-like energy essential to allowing the powers of maturity to take hold within us. These outside forces may be expectations of others as well as social and political influences. However, it is the interior forces that we will most need to reckon with. Seeking the approval of others, fear of abandonment, fear of being alone, fear of ridicule and other needs of dependency are examples of what we face. Confronting these energies requires that we fight the "good fight" and will ultimately determine the quality of our boundaries.

For many of us, maturation suffers due to ineffectual boundaries, yet there are very few places to learn about good boundaries. A family simply cannot offer us a perfect balance between our need to be a separate, unique self and our need to belong. Life in an enmeshed family, where belonging is prioritized and autonomy discouraged, often yields an adult whose boundaries are very weak. In families where estrangement is the rule, people learn to live with excessively strong boundaries, which allow them to live with the alienation they have grown to know. We can conclude that every family has some expression of either enmeshment or estrangement, making it important that we never stop learning lessons about boundaries.

Especially in case of parental neglect, sibling bonding becomes a prized strategy for surviving. This often leads to the regular use of weak boundaries. The children believe that they must have as much access to one another as possible in order to survive. People raised in such families either continue to live with very weak boundaries with family members, while securing strong boundaries with the rest of the world, or implement deficient boundaries everywhere.

There are, of course, a number of other parental dynamics that injuriously impact our capacity to employ effective boundaries.

Poor Modeling

Parents who are confused about good boundaries will inevitably pass that confusion on to their children. Parents cannot teach a skill they do not possess and their children run a high risk of transferring their limited understanding to the next generation. Consequently, terrible boundaries become a generational dynamic.

The dilemma is that unless a person undergoes a crisis and possesses enough determination to get help, there is practically no way to learn about good boundaries and interrupt the legacy. It is quite common for bright, educated and professionally successful people to come into my office knowing little or nothing about employing effective boundaries. Much of the challenge lies in the fact that ignorance about boundaries is not limited to our families. We, as a culture, remain relatively oblivious when it comes to good boundaries.

Emotional Incest

Nothing will twist and contort a child's understanding of good boundaries like an experience of what could be called "emotional incest." It occurs when a parent, surrogate parent or trusted authority figure brings a child into a mutual emotionally supportive relationship.

In non-mutual relationships, such as the ones with parents, teachers, and clergy, people in the parental role supply strong boundaries, which help supply encouragement and direction for the child or protégé. They are also the boundary-makers in the relationship. The emotional support in these relationships flows one way—in the direction of the child. In an emotionally incestuous relationship, support flows both ways, meaning children are expected to give as much as, if not more than, the adults. In these relationships boundaries are significantly more limited, making the needs of adults more accessible to children and children more responsible for those needs.

Predictably, where adults employ excessively weak boundaries with children, in order to get their own needs met, there will be issues regarding power. When adults believe they are incapable of gaining support from another adult or are too scared to take the risk, they are likely to take advantage of the children over whom they hold authority.

Parents, teachers, clergy and coaches are all in positions to engage in emotional incest. The more children trust adults, the more power adults possess to influence and control. They can teach children to have permeable boundaries, which gives them greater access and control. Children learn that power is to be used to serve whoever possesses it.

Sexual Incest

It may surprise you when I refer to the use of weak boundaries used by adults as "incest." Yet, sexual incest shares many of the same characteristics as emotional incest. It too is perpetrated by trusted authority figures who violate the sexual boundaries of a child. There are similarities in both forms of incest. Both are violations of trust, and an abuse of power leading to a violation of boundaries. Typically there is not a specific sexual variety of emotional wounding. A sexual incest survivor may be prone to living either with inadequate sexual boundaries (promiscuity) or highly restrictive sexual boundaries (sexually walled off). In either case, the damage can be viewed as a boundary issue and treated as such.

Sexual incest survivors run a high risk of perpetuating the violation of power and boundaries. Survivors often carry their own shame as well as the shame of their perpetrators, which makes it necessary to find compassion for their stories before they are able to carry power without violating the boundaries of others or allowing their own boundaries to continue to be violated.

Narcissistic Parents

Parents who are still waiting to be seen and heard by their own parents are likely to exercise poor boundaries, allowing them to remain self-absorbed, demanding attention from their children. Narcissistic parents will not allow their self-focus to be disrupted by the unique needs and wishes of their children. They are perfectly content to have their children be extensions of themselves.

Children raised by narcissistic parents learn to fear intimacy. It is simply another opportunity to be absorbed into another's individuality, jeopardizing their autonomy. As adults, they are inclined to employ unyielding boundaries in an attempt to safeguard their individuality.

Controlling Parents

Controlling parents send a confusing double message about boundaries to their children: "My rules are rigid, but my relational boundaries are excessively indistinct." This allows the controlling parent to have greater access to the child, while discouraging autonomy and promoting compliance.

Under these conditions, children learn not to trust themselves and instead accept the appropriateness of being influenced. Poor boundaries maintain the will of the parent in their need to be influential. The children grow up employing either very feeble boundaries as they depend upon an authority figure or a loved one to define them—in the spirit of

their parents—or they live with strong impenetrable boundaries, aimed at preventing them from being controlled. In
either case, the ability to utilize the power and creativity of
effective boundaries is lost.

Permissive Parents

Permissive parents commonly had very controlling
parents who were not especially available, either physically
or emotionally. They are determined not to reproduce the
restraint and regimentation of their childhoods, and so they
exercise extremely undependable boundaries with their
own children. The idea that their children will benefit from
the freedom afforded them by a high permeability of their
boundaries is illusionary.

The excessive permeability of their boundaries will prevent these people from effectively exercising their authority and
sabotage their capacity to clearly define and administer what
they believe to be acceptable and what isn't. Teenagers typically
define themselves by reacting to the boundaries established
by those in authority. Their reactions to authority offer them a
sense of identity during a very confusing time.

When boundaries are weak, children become anxious and
confused. Their natural reaction is to act out in search of a much
needed boundary. Firm boundaries become the context in which
teenagers can craft their own identities. Adolescents discover
who they are because parents are clear about who they are.

Permissive parenting is routinely motivated by a desire to
be liked. Parents like this often do for their children what their
children can do for themselves, leaving young people confused
about competency and being responsible.

By the time they become adults, people raised in a highly permissive environment often carry a severe general disorientation regarding good boundaries. They may find it difficult to hear "no" as a response to their requests and problems honoring boundaries of others. They literally don't know where they end and others begin.

Parentification of Children

"My parents were divorced when I was seven," George, a thirty-nine-year-old massage therapist explained when he came to me complaining of feeling alone in his relationship. "My three-year-old sister and I lived with my mother who was depressed. Of course, we didn't know that at the time. She spent a lot of time in bed, missed work regularly and had problems keeping the house clean."

"What was life like after the divorce?" I asked.

"Well, it was quieter around the house. You could say that I raised my sister. We were supposed to spend every other weekend with my father, but he and my sister, Lorie, didn't have a great relationship. She would complain of not feeling well when we were scheduled to be with him."

"Did your mother have friends or family that supported her through the divorce?"

"Not really, she spent a lot of time in the house."

"Wasn't there anyone she could confide in?"

"Yeah, I guess me," he blurted out.

"You look surprised that you describe yourself as your mother's support," I said, hoping he would be willing to explore his revelation.

"I didn't realize that my mother really didn't have anyone else. Plus, I was just a kid."

"Being just a kid means that you didn't really know how to support your mother. The roles were reversed; she was supposed to support you,"

George soon realized how little he expected from his relationships. Similar to his relationship with his mother, he found himself giving a lot and receiving very little. He began to glimpse the source of his aloneness.

"Parentified" children are prematurely yanked out of childhood and asked to play a parental role for either a sibling and/or a parent. They are often plagued with deep feelings of inadequacy since they were assigned duties that they were not prepared to undertake. As adults they are prone to continue to find themselves in a parental role. They exercise extremely unsubstantial boundaries in regard to giving, excessively and obsessively, as if fulfilling a permanent mandate to do so. At the same time, they live with non-permeable boundaries expecting little or nothing. They demand of themselves to give regardless of their desire to do so.

They see most acts of dependence as a setup for deep disappointment, so they safeguard by employing weighty, non-permeable boundaries. This prevents them from depending on anyone.

Without being exposed to good boundaries in our families of origin, it can be difficult to establish them later in life. Since the single most debilitating element of most relationships is inadequate boundaries, learning the qualities of good boundaries and how to employ them will support our development and our capacity to create intimacy with others.

How Do Boundaries Work?

Boundaries work for us when they help us attain and protect what we want. One way we learn to maintain our autonomy and become the individual we are meant to be, is by separating from the ideas, emotions and behaviors of others.

How much separation we need or want will vary from situation to situation. It takes constant practice to develop the kind of discernment that will guide us in determining how much separation we need in each particular circumstance. Of course, there are obvious cases: if a truck is bearing down on us as we cross a street, we will want a great deal of separation from the truck and the impending harm.

Knowing what we want will greatly aid our attempts at discerning how much separation we need. In the above example, we want safety and only safety, so we move away from the truck as swiftly as possible. But what about living with an alcoholic spouse? How much separation do we want then?

We probably don't want much interaction when the spouse is intoxicated. At those times, a good deal of separation is desirable. Do we want to attempt to sustain some semblance of family life? Do we want to live in the hope that the spouse will come out of denial about the addiction and seek help? Do we want to attempt to maintain some form of emotional and sexual connection to the spouse? How much depth and emotional intimacy do we want for ourselves? How much do we want to be seen and heard by a partner? Getting clear and honest with ourselves about what we want goes a long way toward helping us discern how much separation we need and therefore the quality of boundary we need.

Another important question can help guide us: Do we

have any control over what is happening? Without any control, we will likely want to employ significant separation, since our involvement will likely have no meaningful impact.

Since we cannot be responsible for what we have no control over, how much responsibility do we really want to take? If we choose not to take any responsibility, then we will benefit from a great deal of separation. If, however, we decide that we do have some control after all, and we do want to take responsibility, then we will need to exercise less separation and identify what type of boundary we want to use. We shall see how the flexibility of a semi-permeable boundary will allow us to take some control and responsibility for our choices. Before we look at the qualities of a boundary, it will be useful to identify the types of boundaries available to us.

Three Types of Boundaries

There are essentially three types of boundaries. There are intellectual boundaries that separate us from the ideas, beliefs and values of others. Emotional boundaries separate us from the emotions of others, and behavioral boundaries separate us from the behavior of others and from destructive acts of nature.

Intellectual Boundaries

I have heard people state a number of arguments for why being single just isn't good. One woman expressed a number of them all at once. "For one thing, people think that there's something wrong with you. I mean you just look weird sitting and eating alone in a restaurant. Plus there's the endless loneliness that will either drive you to drink or eat too much. Before you know it, you're either significantly overweight or attending AA meetings, which fortuitously might help with the loneliness. And then there are all the friends and relatives who feel sorry for you and are constantly trying to fix you up, which leads to a lot of really bad blind dates."

If you are single and happen to be listening to this woman talk about the headaches associated with being single, you better acquire some good intellectual boundaries before you're convinced that your own situation is hopeless. Most folks who get into arguments probably don't want to argue, but they need a boundary, so they offer a counter argument as a way of securing a boundary. Rather than expel excessive amounts of energy in a heated argument, it would serve us to suspend competition and simply ask the speakers how their positions serve them and benefit their lives. By understanding the emotional benefit for the intellectual position each participant takes, we can be much more co-creative and collaborative than the average intellectual joust will allow. Or we can formulate an intellectual boundary.

Constructing Intellectual Boundaries

Intellectual boundaries are constructed when we can separate our ideas from the ideas of another, either by acknowledging that we have a different belief than the one being expressed or that we haven't formulated an opinion on the topic. The issue here is bigger than simply being confident in your beliefs, since confidence could still lead to claiming you're right while another is wrong. By establishing intellectual boundaries, we preserve a diversity of opinions.

There are many ways in which we can obstruct or sabotage our intellectual boundaries. In conversation we might have great respect for the person speaking and feel that we are not entitled to declare a differing belief. Or we might simply judge ourselves as intellectually inadequate, causing us to feel confused and even scared to suggest what we believe. In some cases, we might decide that someone would feel offended by hearing a diverse opinion. We remain silent, taking responsibility for another person's possible negative reaction.

There's often the natural desire to avoid an argument. We resist giving up the comfort inherent in the illusion that we share the same belief system. But if we don't employ at least a quiet boundary within ourselves (either having firm thoughts of a different opinion or of a not yet formulated position) we run the risk of taking on the speaker's belief. When this is an isolated incident, it's no big deal to take on another's position. However, over time, such an act can be injurious to our autonomy. We can become deeply uncertain about who we are, what we believe and what we value.

It is common for families and other social groups to demonstrate a low tolerance for intellectual diversity, instead favoring uniformity of thought and opinion. People holding authority often feel more secure when they are surrounded by intellectual homogeneity. Parents feel more in control when their children think like they do.

It can be extremely challenging to develop good intellectual boundaries while promoting disparate thinking between ourselves and others.

"That's crazy!" "You've got to be kidding me!" "I've never heard anything so irrational!" "Do you really believe that?" "That makes no sense to me whatsoever!" These are all attempts at boundary-making aimed at preventing the thinking in question from influencing us, but fail to accommodate diverse thought.

We learn very early in life either to be adaptive and take on the thinking of another or employ hard and fast boundaries that seriously inhibit collaborative thinking.

The words *agree* and *disagree* are the most used terms when people are exchanging ideas. The word *disagree* sends a message loaded with challenge and a competitive edge that says, "I'm much more interested in proving I'm right, rather than exploring and understanding how you came to hold your belief." The word *agree* often communicates a kind of comfort and security stemming from shared beliefs.

I asked my friends and colleagues if they would be willing to stop saying they either agree or disagree with me. I explained how I was putting a moratorium upon the use of those terms. After expressing some initial puzzlement, they were willing to declare that they either liked or disliked what they heard me saying. Very quickly, more grace entered our conversations and we became more curious about one another's preferences and biases.

Avoiding excessive adaptation (no boundary) or exercising extreme boundaries, which repress divergent thinking, is especially important in an intimate relationship. A meaningful relationship critically depends upon participants feeling that their unique thinking will be invited by their partners. When such an invitation is absent, people inevitably begin to withdraw intellectually, emotionally and physically.

Emotional Boundaries

Emotional boundaries separate us from the emotions of

others. How we experience our emotions is probably the most poignant expression of personal uniqueness. There are a number of reasons why we would want to separate our emotions from the emotions of others.

We set the stage for preserving the unique nature of our emotional lives when we disconnect from the emotions of others. No one feels anger, fear, grief and joy quite the way we do. The employment of such a boundary can be challenging when we have legitimized our emotions based upon a common emotional response with another. We are often ready to surrender our unique emotional experiences in order to secure the emotional company of another person.

Couples often define the quality of their relationship as a reflection of their common emotional reactions. But really, this tendency is indicative of fusion and not intimacy. Fusion occurs when one or both people are willing to sacrifice the uniqueness of their emotional experience in order to soothe themselves into an illusion of oneness. Intimacy happens as both people honor the uniqueness of their emotional responses even if it prompts a level of tension in the relationship.

Good emotional boundaries protect us from ridicule and unnecessary shame. It is common for people to have adverse reactions to our emotions and when they do, it serves us to separate our emotions from theirs.

The need for emotional boundaries is most obvious when we take responsibility for another's emotions. This occurs when we define ourselves as responsible for another's happiness. When a person is distressed or sad, we try to fix them, saving them from the upset. It's easy to live guided by heroic attempts at saving others and ignoring our limitations. We often live under the illusion, not only that we can, but also that it is appropriate to rescue people from the inherent calamities of the human condition.

Most friendships and intimate relationships suffer from bad emotional boundaries. The tendency is either no boundary or excessive boundaries. Bad boundaries either lead to fusion or estrangement, but hardly ever intimacy.

When we have no emotional boundaries, it becomes almost impossible to tolerate negative reactions to our behavior. We live under the axiom: "If you're mad, I'm bad." Many of us experienced parental anger as children and viewed it as an implication of the removal of love, rather than a reaction to specific unacceptable behavior. We continue living this belief in our adult relationships. "You're mad, then I'm bad" means that in the presence of your anger, I cannot support my personal value.

So we cope by either pushing back the person who is angry with us in order to interrupt the "you're mad, so I'm bad" dynamic or we withdraw physically and emotionally in order to regroup and reclaim our personal sense of worth. Either choice offers us little or no hope of feeling good about ourselves and our partner while we communicate.

I am often asked if it is ever appropriate to feel any responsibility for the emotions of another person. Yes, it is fitting to feel responsible when we either say something or do something that violates our own value system and evokes a hurtful or angry response in someone. Clearly, we need to know our own values in order to decide when and how we want to take responsibility. If we have not violated one of our own values, then it is crucial not to be responsible for the emotions of others. However, achieving this requires successfully learning how to construct an emotional boundary.

Constructing Emotional Boundaries

A great way to focus our attention when we need to construct an emotional boundary is to ask the question, "Whose emotional story is this?" We can identify whose emotional story is being discussed by simply noting who first introduced an emotional reaction into the conversation.

By thinking about "whose emotional story is this?" we not only focus our attention, it also helps us to avoid simply attaching our own emotional reaction to the emotions already introduced by someone else. Here are a few examples of someone reacting without an ability to focus on the emotions of the speaker due to poor boundaries:

"What the hell is wrong with you? This is the third time that you are late!" (reaction) *"No it isn't. This is only my second."*

"I can't believe you." (reaction) *"What did I do now?"*

"You're very selfish." (reaction) *"I've been doing a lot around here."*

"Can't you see what I need from you?" (reaction) *"Don't tell me I messed it up again."*

"I'm really sick of worrying about money." (reaction) *"Maybe I should get a job."*

In each dialogue the listener enters the story by saying something about him or herself. Without sound emotional boundaries, the likely result is poor communication. The boundary can be constructed completely in thought or combined with the use of language, in which the speaker must remember that he or she can only speak about his or her own experience. Let's take a look at six similar dialogues, with the difference being that the listener in each case will keep the emotional story about the speaker.

"What the hell are you doing? This is the third time that you're late!" (new reaction) *"What time did you expect me?"*

"I can't believe you!" (new reaction) *"Tell me what it is about me that surprises you."*

"You're very selfish." (new reaction) *"Tell me how you concluded that about me."*

"Can't you see what I need from you?" (new reaction) *"I want to hear more about what you need from me."*

"I'm really sick of worrying about money." (new reaction) *"Sounds like money has become a real issue for you lately. Tell me what's going on."*

Notice how the listener does not directly enter into the speaker's story even when the story is in some way about the listener. Remember that speakers can only articulate what they perceive, think or judge about the listener, and their thoughts, their perceptions and their judgments make up their story. With a bad boundary, listeners are sure to slip into the speaker's story; with a good boundary, they might stay out of it.

Imagine what happens when listeners jump into the conversation with their own stories and speakers respond by adding even another topic. Chaos ensues. No one knows exactly what's being talked about and everyone soon feels angry, helpless and hopeless. When these kinds of exchanges become routine in marriages, spouses begin to feel deeply alienated at best and, at worst, the termination of the relationship becomes quite appealing.

Let's look at the kind of conversation where the boundaries are so weak that one person's story leaks into the other's story. The result is an avalanche of topics with no one feeling understood.

"You never come with me to visit my parents." (topic 1)

"I've been to visit them in the past." (topic 2)

"I always take the time to be helpful with your mother." (topic 3)

"You never appreciate what I do anyway." (topic 4)

"Of course I don't appreciate what you do, because you do so little." (topic 5)

"Who cuts the grass, trims the hedges, walks the dog and changes the oil in the car?" (topic 6)

"You do just what you want to do, with no interest in making the small sacrifices that make a marriage work." (topic 7)

This is a typical marital exchange with both people having such weak boundaries that they allow themselves to be defined by the other, and then feel compelled to defend themselves. Below is the same conversation with good boundaries, with the focus upon the original story of the speaker, or, in this case, on the wish to have the listener visit her parents.

"You never come to visit my parents."

"I didn't realize it had been a long time. What do you want me to do?"

"Oh, I don't know. How about coming with me some time to see them?"

"When would you like me to come?"

"I would like you to come in either October or Christmas."

"Is either time as good as the other?"

"Yes."

"Okay, then I'll come with you at Christmas."

Simply put, good communication is the result of good boundaries. Bad communication is a symptom of bad boundaries.

There are several obstacles that often interfere with the

construction of good emotional boundaries. A need to please can easily move us quickly into the speaker's story as we attempt to justify, explain and do our best to minimize some negative impact our behavior might have had. A need to take responsibility for others will quickly vault us into stories that don't belong to us. Low self-esteem also can create a knee-jerk reaction, hurling us into the speaker's story as we scramble, attempting to discredit the speaker's issue.

Behavioral Boundaries

Behavioral boundaries separate us from the behavior of others or from acts of nature. These boundaries can be as easy to identify and employ as driving on the right side of the road, or as demanding as removing ourselves from a friend or loved one because we feel mistreated by them.

Constructing Behavioral Boundaries

Several challenges face us when we construct behavioral boundaries. First, we must possess enough self-awareness to accurately identify the need that requires a behavioral boundary. It may be a need for quiet, for privacy, for rest or a host of other personal requirements, which call for little or no interaction with others. These boundaries also call for us to recognize our right to be self-serving and to act in behalf of our needs. And because these boundaries call for specific action, they are readily witnessed by others and open to their scrutiny.

How much action to take is a common problem when attempting to employ an effective behavioral boundary. It's only too easy to do too little or too much, resulting in undesirable consequences. The more discerning we become, however, the more our behavioral boundaries will serve our purposes.

Quality of a Boundary

There are essentially three levels of quality pertaining to boundaries. There are permeable boundaries, semi-permeable boundaries and non-permeable boundaries. Permeable boundaries allow for little or no separation. Semi-permeable boundaries allow for some separation and non-permeable boundaries maximize separation.

As you might expect, permeable boundaries allow for a great deal to pass through. They minimize separation. It may be helpful here to identify some permeable emotional boundaries, as well as permeable intellectual and behavioral boundaries.

Permeable Emotional Boundaries

Permeable emotional boundaries typically occur either when we allow ourselves to take on the emotions of others or when we take responsibility for their emotional states. We begin to actually experience the emotions they experience. If they're depressed, we're depressed; if they're scared, we're scared; if they're happy, we're happy; if they hate their boss, we hate their boss. It is as if there is a direct line of emotion flowing from the other to us, causing us to be fused. Our emotional identity is created by what is flowing into us from the other.

Typically, when there are excessive permeable emotional boundaries in a family, the children are taught to lie. When a family is willing to sacrifice saying "no" to one another in the name of taking care of one another's feelings, they are agreeing to live with poor boundaries. Once that norm is in place, the only option for family members is to offer fraudulent responses of "yes", when a "no" is much closer to the truth. Replacing the response of "no" with a "yes" can easily broaden the scope of lying to entail both subtle and gross misrepresentations of what people feel and believe.

Emotional fusion is quite different from either empathy or sympathy. Often people believe that emotional fusion is intimate, when actually it denotes a loss of intimacy. True intimacy calls for the presence of two unique people, often supported through empathy and sympathy. Empathy is an ability to identify with the other because of a similar experience we have had. We feel with the other, from a place of our own experience. Sympathy is the capacity to feel for the other, because we view their situation as unfortunate in some way.

There are times when we can take responsibility for another's emotions, and it will not necessarily suggest that our emotional boundaries are excessively permeable. If we believe that something we did or something we said has caused pain or distress for another, and we deem our behavior as a violation of our own values, then we very well may want to take responsibility for the other's emotions. In this situation, it is not simply the emotional state of the other person that dictates our responsibility, but rather the role our values play in determining our course of action.

Permeable Intellectual Boundaries

Permeable Intellectual Boundaries occur especially when we take on the beliefs, opinions or values of another. While attending a seminar on fiction writing, I heard the instructor declare, "When a character is single-dimensioned, the story isn't large enough to capture some realistic expression of the human condition."

I heard her words with an extremely permeable boundary. It felt just right to incorporate what I heard into my own belief system.

The permeability of an intellectual boundary may not be a problem when we are hearing an idea that is quite compatible with an already established line of thinking. However, permeability does suggest openness and receptivity to being influenced. So the question naturally arises whether or not it is in our best interest to be influenced. The over-arching guideline when applying boundaries is to remain discerning. This is especially true with permeable boundaries, because we are allowing so much to come in.

While working in couples counseling with Frank and Amy, a couple in their 50's who've been married for fifteen years, the permeability of Amy's intellectual boundaries became an obvious issue.

"I can't believe how terrible your record keeping has been with our finances," declared Frank. He looked away from Amy and shook his head.

"I don't know what you mean. All the bills get paid on time." Amy cast her eyes toward the floor.

"You don't even let me know how we are doing, whether we're behind or caught up."

"I tell you when I'm going to do the bills," Amy said. "But you always say you're too busy to get involved."

"I'm working! I make sure this family eats!" Frank yelled.

"Well, maybe I could get a part-time job and keep you better informed," Amy said tearfully.

Amy's permeable emotional boundary allowed her to abandon her satisfaction in handling the family finances and accept responsibility for Frank's discontent. After she adopted Frank's emotions as her own, Amy ended up agreeing to Frank's opinion of her, even though she initially saw herself as doing a good enough job. Her intellectual boundary became increasingly permeable as she sacrificed her own beliefs and adopted Frank's. The permeability of Amy's emotional boundary led to her excessively permeable intellectual boundary.

Permeable intellectual boundaries certainly allow us to be influenced and learn from the ideas of others. There is nothing wrong with employing them as long as we eventually make the beliefs we hear our own. However, applying such boundaries routinely will leave us with a serious identity crisis, not knowing what we believe or what we value. We run the risk of attempting to live life from borrowed beliefs and values.

Permeable Behavioral Boundaries

Through the years I have often heard couples report frustration because they asked their spouse to stop yelling and the spouse would then scream louder. In this case, the request to stop yelling is ineffectual, a permeable boundary that stops little or nothing as the rampage continues. The boundary here may need to be less permeable, like leaving the room or the house.

Obviously, if we want to be impacted by another's action, it makes sense to employ a permeable behavioral boundary. People who want to develop a great rapport, generate a sense of team, heighten a capacity for collaboration, deepen emotional intimacy or even have sex will do well to exercise some level of permeability with their behavioral boundaries. Because permeable behavioral boundaries allow so much to happen, being critically discerning will be extremely important.

Semi-Permeable Boundaries

The second quality we can apply to boundaries is semi-permeability. A semi-permeable boundary has the power to allow certain elements (emotions, ideas, behaviors) to pass through while blocking and separating others. It might be simply compared to a screened window that allows light and air to pass while blocking insects and outdoor debris. The effective use of semi-permeable boundaries may be the single most significant resource when building a serious relationship.

Semi-Permeable Emotional Boundaries

Emotional boundaries that are semi-permeable allow for the passage of warmth, compassion, love, support, encouragement, nurturance and affection while blocking and separating what is harmful or simply unwanted. Examples of what might be considered an emotional violation include sarcasm, ridicule, shame, blame and unsolicited advice.

The skillful application of semi-permeable emotional boundaries is a strong indication of emotional maturity and an indication of our ability to learn boundary formation at the *proper time*. We will need to know what to allow to flow freely, and what to block. This not only calls for a sophistication of discernment, but also a measure of resiliency. After all, some people are sure to have unfavorable reactions to our boundaries.

We can ask ourselves several relevant questions to help to build semi-permeable emotional boundaries. The first is:

Whose emotional story is this? This may lead to several other questions that might keep us mindful about the dangers of our boundary becoming too permeable: Do I want to rescue or save the other party from their own emotional dilemma? Am I too quickly inclined to hear the speaker's story as being about me? Do I feel the need to justify or explain my behavior? Am I anxious to provide the speaker with a quick solution?

Conversely, there are questions we might ask ourselves to help us to remain more conscious about making the boundary too non-permeable, not allowing for much or any contact at all. How eager are we to end a conversation abruptly? Do we feel restless with the need to just run away or distance ourselves?

Semi-Permeable Intellectual Boundaries

Semi-permeable intellectual boundaries allow us to be open to the views of others while avoiding capitulation. We are able to collaborate, co-create and brainstorm, yet at the same time continue to hold authority over our own beliefs. Like in other levels of boundaries, the primary question is: Whose intellectual story is this anyway?

Semi-Permeable Behavioral Boundaries

The value of semi-permeable behavioral boundaries is that it allows us to have meaningful social contact and offers opportunities to create alliances and coalitions with others. Thus, we allow ourselves—and our bodies—to give and receive affection, nurturance and love. We can be in the presence of others without feeling physically dominated, intruded upon or bodily violated.

In the process of constructing this level of boundary, we can ask ourselves several discerning questions: Is the person I'm with too physically close or too physically far from me? Do I want to continue to hear what this person is saying? Is there something I want that calls for more or less physical contact with this person?

Non-Permeable Boundaries

When your desire is to prevent engagement with others, non-permeable boundaries are needed. They are most useful when we are engaged in a task that calls for little or no outside interference and critical when there is a direct threat to our safety.

Non-Permeable Emotional Boundaries

Non-permeable emotional boundaries do not allow us to be impacted by the emotions of others. These boundaries are extremely useful when we do not want to be in someone's emotional story, where our desire to remain emotionally separate is absolute and firm.

One of the vital roles of the family is to provide emotional safety, but in families where emotional safety is neither honored nor talked about, children grow up with no understanding of non-permeable emotional boundaries. Threats to emotional safety include: ultimatums, moralizing, blaming, stereotyping, ridiculing, sarcasm and offering unsolicited advice. In families where mistreatment is commonplace, family members are not emotionally safe and non-permeable emotional boundaries will not be tolerated.

It also can be helpful to practice these non-permeable boundaries in situations where we are prone to either rescuing or attempting to fix people when it is out of our control. Before being able to act with a semi-permeable boundary that allows for empathy or sympathy, we may need the emotional pendulum to swing to the other side where we can remain caring but appear quite detached. We may have to be able to risk being perceived as unloving, at least for awhile, until we become more flexible and agile with our boundaries.

Non-Permeable Intellectual Boundaries

Non-permeable intellectual boundaries protect us against thinking that is dangerous or toxic, and from beliefs we want nothing to do with. However, discerning whether or not we are hearing an idea worth our attention calls for a good deal of emotional maturity.

Opinions that are small-minded, excessively rigid, or lead us away from our humanity should not be given the power to influence us. We need to be clear about thinking that supports our humanity, expanding and facilitating thought with real vision and creativity rather than limiting and contracting.

Along the way, we will inevitably be fooled. At times, we will trust in ideas that are small and rigid and distrust thinking aimed at strengthening and empowering us. The key is to maintain a sense of wonder. Try to understand the part of us who has been gullible enough to accept beliefs that do not serve us well and who refuses to acknowledge when new ideas might contribute to our well-being. It's similar to describing a character in a story. We may describe one aspect as naïve, attached to some idyllic outcome or desperate for the approval of others. Focus on specific ways we sabotage ourselves. It's more important to simply remain curious rather than judging ourselves harshly for not getting it right.

Ann Marie is a forty-eight-year-old high school teacher

who after a few months of working with me explained how she had heard a local New Age guru talk about the importance of relying upon her own thinking. I recognized that she had also discovered the source of her non-permeable intellectual boundaries.

"Several years ago I heard this woman talk about how we need to depend upon our own beliefs and not those of others," she explained enthusiastically. "We need to honor our own path."

"Tell me, what does honoring your own path look like?" I said.

"Well, I almost never ask anyone for advice. I think through a problem and come up with my own answer. It's important to have your own answers."

"I'm wondering if what you heard from the teacher at the workshop was something you might have believed to some degree already."

"Yeah, I think so. She confirmed what I kind of thought," Ann Marie added.

"It sounds like others have little or nothing to offer you."

"Well, they really don't. I mean they can't really know me anyway."

"Tell me, what kind of guidance did you receive from your parents as you grew up?"

"My father worked a lot of hours and my mother was usually depressed. My mother was fundamentally useless when it came to offering advice," she said. "But she sure knew how to dress us up for church on Sundays," she added with disdain.

"So I'm hearing that your mother certainly was not a viable resource when it came to guidance. I can't help but wonder if you decided that the whole world was like your mother."

This was the starting place for Ann Marie's reliance on

non-permeable intellectual boundaries and the beliefs that supported them. She gradually took a risk. She accepted the idea that the whole world was not like her mother and viable guidance could come from others. She began to expand her story and the world became much larger for her.

Many factors influence our appropriate employment of non-permeable intellectual boundaries. Our willingness to remain small is one that is worth noting. An attraction to small, reductionist thinking is one way to remain childlike. It is possible to escape the anxiety that inevitably accompanies ambiguity and uncertainty by adhering to basic intellectual recipes. These formulas for right-thinking are equipped with the power to direct us errorlessly and serve as a temporary balm for life's angst.

One such blueprint is positive thinking. The prescription is as long as we think positively, we will be maximizing self-care and handling any problematic situation. The dilemma is that when we apply positive thinking whenever we face some quandary, we run a very high risk of moving into denial. We are no longer able to see inherent danger, cruelty, pain, sadism or even our own self-destructiveness.

Another example of reductionism is the philosophy promoted in the New Age film, *The Secret*. We are encouraged to believe we can create whatever we wish by remaining mindful of our intention. Of course, the seduction here is the offering of a quick and simple path to self-empowerment.

We can be easily seduced by offers of a fast path to human development. Buying into a McDonald's-type brand of personal growth, however, will leave us wanting, lacking the depth of authentic maturation. We stay small, believing that the lack of results is simply because we haven't gotten it right.

Here are some questions that can help us judge how non-permeable our intellectual boundaries should be:

Is the thinking inviting you to neither give nor receive much?

Are the opinions you are hearing inviting you to make peace with uncertainty or deny it?

Are the beliefs encouraging or discouraging you to remain curious?

Do the opinions claim to offer you some kind of guarantee?

Does the thinking invite you to effortlessly become a better person?

Do the views suggest that the source of truth and healing lie somewhere outside of you? Does the thinking encourage you to know and live what you love?

These questions can help identify whether or not a proposed set of beliefs might actually be helpful. However, the real work is to find the part of us that wishes to remain small and childlike and tries to achieve that end by employing bad boundaries. We either allow ourselves to be influenced by unsound thinking or prevent ourselves from being impacted by promising beliefs. We will explore the idea of remaining small in the following chapter.

Non-Permeable Behavioral Boundaries

Julie was a twenty-eight-year-old mother of a two-year-old girl and had been battered by a live-in boyfriend for eight years. She spoke of the shame she felt each time he beat her and the shame she experienced because she couldn't leave him.

It is only too easy to see the appropriateness of Julie applying a non-permeable behavioral boundary to prevent the perpetration of her abuse at the hand of her boyfriend. In order for Julie to generate the power to create that kind of boundary, however, she would need to become more mindful and more compassionate toward the part of her that continued to rely on a permeable boundary.

During the next eight months of counseling, Julie admitted that she had been raised in an alcoholic family where semi-permeable and non-permeable boundaries of any kind were unacceptable. The bathroom door was not to be locked, and there was no door to her bedroom, reflecting the family's attitude toward boundaries.

She also discovered that love in her family meant loyalty and loyalty meant making choices that met the expectations of others. Julie became acquainted with the little girl in her who would strive to maintain control of her chaotic world by seeing herself as responsible for anything painful or traumatic. The same loyal child, convinced she was the cause of all unfortunate happenings, was keeping her in a battered situation.

Once Julie could embrace the little child in her with compassion, releasing her from responsibility for the pain caused to her by others, she was able to move herself and her daughter into her mother's home. That move, along with a court-ordered restraining order, gave Julie the non-permeable behavioral boundary she deserved.

Non-permeable behavioral boundaries are meant to protect us from anyone or thing we deem dangerous or potentially injurious. Like Julie, however, we may need to face a demon or two from the past.

Discernment is also required. It is common to find people using non-permeable behavioral boundaries when they don't really need them at all. This is especially common when old wounds and old ways of coping continue to direct our lives. When we experienced some form of violation as a child without addressing it as an adult, it is only too easy to view life as a calamity causing us to take refuge behind a non-permeable boundary.

Finding Our Love

Our boundaries will not be clear, vital and organic without heart. When our lives are guided and lived by what we love, we come to understand what we must protect, what we must honor and what we are willing to be touched by.

Schools and religions often turn us away from the pursuit of what we love. Children are rewarded if they can successfully negotiate their way through abstract scientific and mathematical concepts, and set religious scripture to memory. Instead of knowing what we love, we are subjected to a cultural mandate to conform and perform. We are encouraged to betray what lives at the core of our soul.

The late Leo Buscaglia told the story of Jimmy and his primary education experience. Jimmy is told to draw a tree in kindergarten and he enthusiastically grabs a variety of colored crayons and begins to draw. His teacher stops him and draws a tree on the blackboard that he can reproduce.

Similar experiences continue to happen for Jimmy, as teacher after teacher insists upon showing him what a tree looks like before he starts to draw one. Finally, one day in the fifth grade, his teacher instructs the class to draw a tree, whereupon, Jimmy sits quietly. The teacher asks him why he isn't drawing.

Jimmy responds by saying, "I'm waiting for you to show me what one looks like."

Buscaglia ended his tale by declaring, "Who do they think they are? They're going to show this child what a tree looks like, he who climbs trees, eats in them, pees out of them, imagines himself fighting dragons in them and falls out of them! Do they really believe that they can show him what one looks like?"

Buscaglia's anecdote shows how the threat of being seen as unacceptable wears on us and leads to a disruption of our self-loyalty. The resulting weak boundaries inevitably reflect the fatigue and the fear we feel when the price of self-loyalty is paired with the threat of being culturally marginalized.

When we remove ourselves from what we love, we instead become absorbed into what is popular or culturally endorsed. If we're lucky, we will have an experience that will make us shake with anxiety, reminding us that we have walked a long way from our core self.

The more we live oblivious to what we love, the more we fall victim to self-betrayal. In the midst of such duplicity, our boundaries are at best vague and arbitrary, lacking the sharpness that only our love can bestow upon them. Bad boundaries are inevitably a reflection of the confusion we have regarding whose story we are living in.

Receiving Boundaries

Being the ready recipient of the boundaries of others calls for us to trust our intuition about the motivation of those boundaries and to maintain good boundaries ourselves. We will have a particularly difficult time hearing someone say "no" to a request, if our own family lived with poor boundaries. When our own emotional boundaries are too permeable we will be inclined to hear another's boundary as a personal rejection, a statement of our lack of deservedness. This can often make us angry, and we attack those employing boundaries with charges like: "You're insensitive," "After all I have done for you, you're really selfish," or "You're not very cooperative."

When we encounter the boundaries of others and our own emotional boundaries are not excessively permeable, we can accept the boundaries of others as a story about their needs and desires and not about us. We may be disappointed but we do not allow ourselves to be defined by the story contained in their boundaries. The challenge is to learn to bear our disappointment, trusting that our need will be met.

There are exceptions. If someone we know finds it necessary to regularly resort to non-permeable boundaries, where we frequently hear "no" to our requests and invitations, it is critical to allow ourselves to trust our intuition about the motivation of others. If we see a theme of excessive use of non-permeable boundaries, then prudence dictates that the severity of the boundaries will result in hard obstacles to intimacy and belonging.

We have explored how boundaries separate us and protect us. In each type of boundary—emotional, intellectual and behavioral—there is varying degree of permeability or how much they allow through. Deciding what we desire and what we love will determine whether we need a boundary that is highly-permeable, semi-permeable or non-permeable.

Finally, we examined the task of receiving the boundaries of others and how a degree of non-permeability on our part will allow us to hear their boundaries as a story about them rather than a story about us.

Employing effective boundaries is a way to remain loyal to ourselves. Now let's explore what it means to develop and live with a personal faithfulness, heightening our awareness of the role of self-betrayal in our lives.

4

Self-Loyalty

There are people who hate themselves because they haven't come to terms with their helplessness. They feel threatened by helplessness itself, not by those who caused or reinforced the feeling, and this is what produces their boundless rage. Therefore, they repress their helplessness, which has made them feel rejected and despised, at the same time internalize their oppressors' contempt for them. In this way they commit betrayal of the self. —Arno Gruen

Faithfulness and Devotion

Good boundaries are a measure of our ability to support the uniqueness of our unfolding humanity while preventing unwanted material from defining us. Our identities are cast with the stories we create during the dynamic process we call *defining a self.* There is, perhaps, no theme more pervasive in all of literature than that of loyalty and betrayal. And not only is it of prime importance in our relationships with others, this same motif is paramount to our relationship with ourselves and our stories. Each *proper time* holds the opportunity for deepening self-loyalty. How do we remain faithful to ourselves, devoted to what is in our best interest?

In order to remain faithful, we must be committed to unearthing the truth about our origins and remaining conscious of what we find there, no matter how frightening or disturbing, with as much compassion for ourselves as possible. In fact, remaining compassionately self-examining will be a central theme in our quest for self-loyalty. However, as in any good story about loyalty, we must begin by focusing upon betrayal.

Self-Betrayal

We came into the world completely dependent upon others for our survival. Our parents held power over us that was used to some degree or another to abuse or neglect us. We were then left to cope with the ensuing helplessness, which created our predicament. We had three strategies to endure our fear and vulnerability, and help us to cope with the strain of our situation. The neo-Freudian psychologist Karen Horney identified them as a submissive pattern, a domination pattern and a distancing pattern.

The Adaptive Victimization Strategy

I recommend renaming ideas and concepts we are learning. Renaming helps us to claim the thinking for ourselves and allows us to weave our own inspiration through the thinking. It is how we bring new meaning into our lives. In considering Horney's first pattern, a submissive pattern, I have recast it as an *adaptive victimization strategy* because we are colluding with the perpetrator by making it appropriate to be victimized and fitting to remain in a victim's position.

Simply put, it's a strategy based upon thinking, "if you can't beat them, join them." It unfolds like two boxers who get into a clinch and begin hugging each other, as a way to rest and protect themselves from receiving the next powerful punch. It is as if we think, *it's safer for me to be closer to you and farther from myself, so merging with you is how I will make myself safe.*

As children this particular technique is one of the few options available in our struggle to cope with feelings of helplessness. What is initially an act of loyalty, however, will over time become a significant act of self-betrayal. Arno Gruen's *Betrayal of the Self* identifies the eventual depth of betrayal caused by adaptation:

> The disturbing thing about our adaptation is not only that to some extent we all live involuntarily in accordance with the will of other people, what is really dangerous is that the moment we live outside the bounds of our body, so to speak, we begin to fear the freedom suddenly revealed by the breakthrough of our original sense of self. While it is true that we all long for freedom, in many ways we are simultaneously dependent upon power, desiring recognition and praise from those who hold it. This condemns us to an eternal search for approbation from those very people who deny our real needs.

Gruen tells us that in the midst of adaptation, our lives are directed by the will of others, so our devotion to ourselves becomes seriously impaired. Even when we are exercising our own will, and willing to jeopardize the favor of others, we can easily fall back to this strategy.

I often hear people ask why shabby leadership is tolerated in a particular organization or on a national level. Our tolerance may very well be a reflection of our adaptive inclination and our fear of becoming alienated from people in more powerful socio-political positions. This excessive tolerance of poor leadership can be seen as a result of not being able to rely on our faithfulness to self. We will accept a duplicitous connection to others, rather than fight for the freedom to be who we are meant to be.

When we are not conscious of our victimization strategy, we cannot interrupt it, and may very well live it out for a lifetime. We constantly wonder why we have been suffering at the hands of others, all the while soothing our quandary with a stroke of self-righteousness. We confine ourselves to a very small story about injustice and cruelty directed toward good people like us, crafting a lifestyle that is reflective of an abdication of power.

Sometimes our victimization stories become ways to memorialize those we love. We remain loyal to those who may have hurt and neglected us by maintaining the appropriateness of our helplessness and the accompanying trauma. The message we declare is, "I will live the way you treated me as a testimony both to you and to me not deserving anything better." Of course, the implication is that if we deserved better treatment, a lost loved one would have offered it. We end up focusing our loyalty on someone who perpetrated abuse upon us.

In childhood, an adaptive victimization strategy was an act of self-loyalty helping us survive the trauma of helplessness and fear. Slowly, it became a major act of self-betrayal. Adults guided by this script of victimization are capable of easily selling their souls. They survive by merging and fusing with others. They take on the beliefs, the values and the desires of others as they, over time, drift away from everything they might call themselves.

They live with very permeable boundaries, ones incapable

of supporting any real sense of autonomy. They remain confused about how to really take care of themselves and are usually waiting to be saved by another. Their wait usually ends in bitterness and cynicism; they turn away from life as they perceive
life as the ultimate perpetrator, insisting upon doing them in.

We don't simply lose ourselves through an adaptive victimization strategy. We tend to aggrandize others, diminishing
ourselves while we merge with them. This begins in childhood,
when we lose the ability to see our caregivers' true humanity in
their shortcomings and wounds. It is simply not advantageous
to acknowledge the limits of those who are supposed to save us.
It is easier to believe that others will be more receptive to our
needs if we ignore their flaws.

It serves us well to live close to our adaptive victimization stories. Keeping these stories close allows us to remain
conscious of our propensity for self-betrayal. We remember the
ways we have coped with our needs for survival. It is, after all,
easy to forget when we confront change, which represents the
possibility of moving away from what has always worked for us.

I recently experienced an event that evoked my own adaptive victimization strategy. While attending a conference, the
speaker was lecturing on something called "archetypal meaning." His point seemed to be that images have a particular meaning and if we are evolved enough, then we can understand the
true meaning of a specific image. He went on to introduce the
images of a small table with two chairs, two glasses and an un-
opened bottle of wine on the table. The presenter asked, "What
is the meaning we can attribute to this image?"

I was hurled back into fifth grade where I felt perpetually
challenged—and often defeated—by the teacher posing some

question. There I sat, feeling not a day over ten years old, hoping that I could at least silently come up with the right answer. Or at least not be identified as someone with the wrong answer.

Several participants offered possible answers, all quickly rebuffed by the facilitator. A heavy silence enveloped the room. I noticed that I neither wanted to be the person who spoke the wrong answer nor sit silently with some mistaken interpretation.

I began to notice that my high, shallow breathing dropped to somewhere closer to my belly. Had I actually accepted this idea that the image in question has one bona fide meaning? This thought no sooner settled in my mind when a woman from the back of the room yelled out, "Potential, the meaning of the image is potential!" Our speaker enthusiastically endorsed her response.

I raised my hand with the fervor of one bidding at an auction. "I would want to include possibility, absence, death, closure and loss as other possible meanings," I said, realizing I was speaking considerably louder than necessary.

The instructor said, "Well, okay," casting his eyes downward and moving on with a new focus. I assumed he already knew the absurdity of attempting to ascertain the proper meaning of the image. However, it occurred to me that he may have simply found it more appropriate to ignore my suggestion. In any case, I sat there and welcomed my truth, considerably less concerned about what an authority figure might think of it.

In this situation, my emotional boundary was non-permeable. I didn't want to be polite; I simply wanted a boundary that would deflect the sarcasm I heard.

When accustomed to using an adaptive victimization strategy, we naturally have an excessively permeable boundary. This particular tactic loses its usefulness as we practice employing more non-permeable boundaries and notice that there are no dire consequences.

The adaptive victimization strategy is meant to generate safety and acceptance, and unless interrupted, we will attain neither safety nor love.

The Domination Strategy

When we have either been dominated or dominated someone else, we can employ the domination strategy and take on the more appealing role. Essentially, we either behave the way we were treated or act like the person who is dishing out the treatment.

The domination strategy is often celebrated. We have high praise for business executives who push and shove their way to the top. Add success at generating a significant profit margin and these power-wheeling entrepreneurs approach deification. However, recent choices by financial tycoons may get us to reevaluate some of our values.

James Hollis refers to this power dynamic and its implications in his book *The Eden Project—In Search of the Magical Other*:

> One such strategy derived from the unconscious but controlling idea that I am powerless would be to devote my life to having power over others. In professional arenas I might simply appear ambitious, perhaps driven, and almost certainly rewarded for my productivity. But the driven person is never at peace with the

soul, for the productivity is a defense against the angst of powerlessness.

Self-Betrayal through Domination

The tentacles of self-betrayal are considerably more subtle in domination than in victimization. When we take up a domineering posture, we strive to hold power over others, communicating to them that we are disinterested in being collaborative, co-creative or working in concert in any meaningful way. We exhibit a disinterest in others, investing little or nothing in knowing others or supporting them and their personal and professional development. The typical reactions to our attempts at domination are retaliation, sabotage and distancing. We soon discover that our alleged power over others is short-lived.

Efforts toward domination eventually place us at odds with ourselves. We find ourselves running away from helplessness, fear, and ultimately all experiences touching on vulnerability. To move away from our core being by trying to dominate moves us away from life, possessing neither an awareness of ourselves nor even of life itself.

Contrary to the cultural myth that suggests that if we have the right education, right financial investments, right job and live in the right neighborhood, then life will be secure and predictable, the reality is the opposite: life remains mysterious, insecure and unpredictable. The only way to make peace with an insecure and unpredictable journey is to allow ourselves to feel vulnerable and learn to sustain ourselves when we do so.

Pretending to be impervious to feelings of vulnerability forces us to create a contingent personality, one lacking in truth and authenticity, only aimed at responding appropriately to situations. We try not to allow our experience to make us look bad. We construct a small story based upon false bravado, and this investment in looking good rather than authenticity compresses the fullness of our humanity into an impoverished psychological narrative.

To achieve this, our hearts must be closed, lest we run the risk of feeling loss, longing, desperation, fear and even love—all which create opportunities for us to feel helpless. We gradually lose touch with what we cherish, what we value and even what we might be willing to die for. After a while, we live either in a state of numbness or with low grade anxiety as our psyches protest the parts of our souls we have sent into exile.

When we lose an understanding of what is in our control and what isn't, it places the very control that we revered into jeopardy. External agendas, projects and socially approved enterprises now own our souls. Our identities are no longer flowing from the deep well of our inner lives, but are now reflections of whatever states we have competitively driven ourselves to. Emotionally separated from ourselves, we are condemned to emotional estrangement with others.

A domination strategy, with its accompanying self-betrayal, was mostly exemplified by men. That is, until recently. An unfortunate result of feminism is that women to some degree now prefer domination to victimization. Women have become more inclined to live under the illusion that self-loyalty and power come from dominating others.

The culture has shown no sympathy for men who dehumanize themselves by trying to survive by dominating others. Hence, there is no hope that women will receive any compassion for betraying themselves by using domination as a way to success.

The Distancing Strategy

The distancing strategy, the third attempt at dealing with our helplessness, I often refer to as the "I'm taking my ball and going home" strategy. The objective here is to simply not play the dominance game, neither dominating nor being dominated. This strategy employs non-permeable boundaries in the hope of minimizing the impact of anothers' will in order to limit feeling helpless.

Distancing from others will not exempt us from experiencing helplessness. Life offers enough opportunities to undergo helplessness. Illness, death and accidents are just a few of a long list of possible losses.

When we employ rigid boundaries as a way to reject the influence of external forces and protect our own needs and values, it seems that we have found an effective way to support our autonomy. We imply that we are willing to sacrifice our belonging in order to remain loyal only to ourselves. However, what typically goes missed is that autonomy and belonging remain in a significant dialectical relationship. Our experiences of belonging add to our individuality as we create ourselves as social beings. We decide how to love and be loved by others, how to make decisions with them, how to solve problems and conflict and collaborate with them. Also, our beliefs, values, imagination and desires craft how we relate to others. In such an association, autonomy and belonging depend upon one another for their virility.

The non-permeable boundaries associated with distancing stunt our individual capacity to love and be loved, resolve conflict, engage in collective problem-solving, and inhibit various forms of collaboration. The distancing strategy often takes place on a level where we withhold our emotional lives. We eliminate the angst of possible judgment and rejection by vigilantly insulating our emotions, keeping them guarded behind strong non-permeable boundaries. We soon become insulated emotionally from ourselves, however, as a ubiquitous numbness engulfs us. Once again, extreme boundaries interfere with our relationship to ourselves as well as our relationships to others.

When we attempt to protect ourselves from helplessness utilizing one of the three strategies—victimization, domination or distancing—self-betrayal is inevitable. When we use an adaptive victimization strategy, we try to secure belonging at the cost of our autonomy; a domination strategy works toward safeguarding autonomy, but sacrifices belonging; and the distancing strategy operates with the same intention as the domination tactic, championing autonomy.

Each strategy attempts to offer some level of protection when facing feelings of helplessness and fear. The objective is not to simply eliminate these strategies. The accommodation inherent in each strategy has an appropriate place. No, instead, betrayal ensues when these coping mechanisms operate unconsciously and are not limited to dealing with isolated incidents in our lives, but rather are used automatically with no consideration of each strategy's shortcomings. Because they rely upon extreme boundaries (permeable and non-permeable), they lack the discretionary strength needed to sustain autonomy and belonging.

Creating Self-Loyalty

The creation of self-loyalty may be the most honorable and demanding undertaking we can embark upon thus deepening the maturation process. It is the kind of devotion and faithfulness reflective of good boundaries and an interest in learning about good boundaries, as self-loyalty requires us to take care of our own needs rather than compulsively attending to the needs of others. In our journey to create self-loyalty, it is helpful to examine what we need to learn in order to achieve our goals.

Feeling Helpless and Scared

If we go about thoughtlessly feeling helpless and scared, we will inevitably employ one of the three strategies that keep us confined by self-betrayal. Without thinking we experience these feelings until one of the strategies automatically kicks in, determined to defend us. This process happens as quickly as it takes to close our eyes, protecting us from a bright light.

Acknowledging that we are feeling helpless and scared is half the battle; the other half is accepting that it's fine to have such feelings. Men have been acculturated to see such emotions as inappropriate, and subsequently, they run a higher risk than women of getting stuck in patterns of self-betrayal. Acceptance is a very powerful way to lead us into greater self-loyalty. Powerful emotions show us more about the basic insecurity of life rather than make a statement about us. From this perspective, we are simply having an appropriate response to the vulnerable nature of being alive.

Once we have accepted this, the next step is to seek help by identifying who might be an ally. The best allies are often those who know something about our particular challenge, have some competency in the area and enough maturity to help us accept our limits. Our allies may help draft new approaches to empowerment and efficacy, and sometimes we see that we are not as helpless as we thought. On other occasions they facilitate the strengthening of our internal resiliency for feeling scared and helpless.

Recently, in one of my men's groups, a young man was wrestling with feeling overwhelmed and started expressing his situation as a calamity. Another man turned to him and said, "Boys feel overwhelmed and then catastrophize their experience. Men feel overwhelmed and ask for help." The ensuing silence was filled with the truth of the man's remark.

Mindfulness of Self-Betrayal

It is critical to stay mindful of how and when we betray ourselves. Introducing deeper levels of devotion to ourselves takes time and it can be very frustrating to see ourselves fall prey to our own duplicity. Mindfulness is typically undermined by deciding that we can shame ourselves out of these acts of disloyalty. It will not happen. We are simply treating ourselves the way our parents did when they deemed our behavior unacceptable.

To stop denying how we betray ourselves is not easy, especially if we have been practicing adaptive victimization, where we see our predicaments as the result of the choices of others. It means moving into self-accountability where we define ourselves by our decisions.

With effort, we see how we are disloyal to ourselves and what we might need to create more devotion.

A tendency toward betrayal by victimization will call for more self-focus and accountability.

A propensity to betray ourselves through domination will mean a willingness to feel vulnerable and let go of a need to control that which is beyond our control.

If betrayal expresses itself through distancing, we can practice self-disclosure where we take the risk to come forward, revealing something relatively meaningful about who we are. When "distancers" become more comfortable with semi-permeable boundaries, they don't have to be so inaccessible.

As we track how we betray ourselves in an attempt to become more faithful, we can recognize how we often unconsciously employ either excessively permeable or non-permeable boundaries and begin to explore the power of semi-permeable boundaries. Slowly over time we can integrate the understanding and skillfulness of using semi-permeable boundaries to support our need to belong and to be autonomous.

Living Close To the Interior World

Living close to our interior worlds lies at the heart of a life characterized by self-loyalty. It is probably the oldest and most pervasive axiom of all mystical traditions. The expressions of self-betrayal (victimization, domination and distancing) do just the opposite; they pull us out away from our interior worlds. In order to be loyal to anyone, we must be willing to know them, appreciate them and accept them. And so it is with ourselves, we must be willing to live close to the person who dwells within us.

This call to self-intimacy carries several significant challenges. We must develop a capacity to accept the anxiety that will inevitably surface when we delve into the mystery of ourselves. We won't know what awaits. There will be times when we may not even know who we are. While feeling that kind of fear, we will have a choice. We can either move into one form of self-betrayal or attach ourselves to some role as a contingent personality, allowing our role in a situation, such as teacher, parent or student, to define us.

These contingent personalities are meant to offer an escape from the tension caused by being uncertain about who we are. Roles such as spouse, partner, child, provider, employee and employer are attempts at augmenting a sense of self. Joining organizations is another way, especially religions that not only help ease the angst of our uncertainty, but also offer enough dogma so we don't even have to think about who we are. We are who we are told to be. We sacrifice maturity and become child-like, excusing ourselves from serious ethical considerations by remaining obedient to external authority.

Tension also happens when what we discover in the interior world is distasteful or disdainful. Now rather than wrestling with uncertainty, we must deal with what is unacceptable. When we find parts of ourselves that we deem objectionable, we respond with denial, projection, self-righteousness and shame.

We wish away traits such as arrogance, insensitivity, a propensity to lie, jealousy and greed. Of course, they do not magically go away, but rather become the raw material for projection, which is commonly accompanied by self-righteousness. Suddenly, we see arrogance, insensitivity and jealousy all around us.

If we cannot purge ourselves of the undesirable, then shame is likely the order of the day. And since most of us do not care to inhabit a place where there is violence and trauma, the challenge is to create a large enough story to include compassion and kindness, so we can learn to generate peace in our inner world.

Sometimes shame can be helpful. Some years ago I decided to organize a block party as a way to rally my neighborhood out of the grip of alienation. A large crowd left the confines of their homes and spilled out onto the streets in celebration. Children and adults alike seemed to rejoice in their deliverance from isolation.

At the end of the day a boy approached me and said, "Mr. Dunion, can we do this again?"

I understood the boy's words went beyond his appreciation for the day's merriment. I believe that the spirit of community vibrated somewhere in his DNA. Unfortunately, it would be a long time before we would do it again.

Within the following year, my own family would be fractured by divorce and my communal efforts would be constrained under the weight of the shame of a failed marriage. How could I be a voice organizing neighbors when I couldn't keep my own family together?

As the years passed I was met with a new shame. I believe that children need to be raised in community and yet I did nothing to infuse cohesion into the neighborhood. The shame of my own displaced family sat side by side next to the shame of lacking the integrity to do something about the ever-increasing alienation in the neighborhood. Eventually, the former humiliation diminished while the latter grew to agonizing proportions.

Time after time as I made the turn down our street, the gnawing throb of embarrassment reminded me that I was not living my values. I hoped that one of the neighbors would take up the task of bringing the neighborhood together or that we might move to a fresh location, offering me a reprieve from violating my own values. Knowing full well that redemption through relocation was not about to take place, I anxiously decided to take action.

I identified a couple who I thought might be receptive to the idea of creating a neighborhood event. When I went to phone, I discovered their number was unlisted. It meant I needed to walk across the street and enter a home I had never been in. The very act felt like a violation of a sacred taboo. Besides, these folks were at the original function and I knew they would likely blame me for failing to maintain the tradition of the block party. My only solace was the knowing that tomorrow I could drive down the street less of a hypocrite.

I walked to the neighbor's home and knocked. They greeted me warmly, which temporarily put me at ease. Harry and Maggie introduced me to Sammie, their vibrant and engaging four-year-old daughter. I was struck nearly speechless with humiliation and sadness when I realized that I had not even known that Sammie existed. Within moments, the enthusiasm of Sammie's parents to the idea of a neighborhood gathering reignited my ability to speak.

As the months passed I appreciated the shame that had grown while I resisted taking the actions called for by my beliefs and values. A simple walk across the street allowed me to step away from hypocrisy and toward integrity. We now have had several more successful neighborhood gatherings and the momentum builds. But what I cherish most is watching Sammie move about the neighborhood with an ease and comfort that conveys the clear message that she is at home.

Living close to the interior world calls for a deepening of

our willingness to walk with our truth. These truths are typically characterized by a simplicity that attest to their credibility, such as: I'm scared, I'm angry, I'm lonely, I'm sad, I'm grateful, I'm lost, I'm joyous, I want...

The more we embrace what we discover in the interior world, the greater the chance for genuine loyalty to flow through our lives. Employing good boundaries to a great degree will depend upon our affinity with our interior terrain. We must know what we value in order to know what we need to protect. We must be familiar with what we love and desire in order to effectively identify what should be allowed through our borders. Unless we know what we value and love, we won't know who or what to allow into our life.

Self-Trust

We don't teach people to trust themselves. In fact, the only cultural paradigm for trust is founded on how we relate to others and not to ourselves. Much of the research about how we trust other people utilizes the operative definition of trust as a belief, a belief that we will be told the truth and be treated kindly. However, it may be appropriate to apply this same definition to self-trust. If we trust ourselves, we believe that we will allow ourselves to know the truth about us and treat ourselves kindly.

Coming to know our truths means interrupting the misguided loyalty characterized by each of the adaptive strategies. Rather than protect our parents, we are called to continue to deepen and broaden our understanding of how we were both wounded and granted gifts by our original caretakers. Most of us treat ourselves the way we were treated as children. Neglect leads to more neglect and abuse begets abuse; such awareness places the focus upon the choices we make, opening us to the possibility of breaking with the past.

We will inevitably turn away from our truth, if we don't learn to hold it with compassion. It is not easy to see what we deem socially unacceptable and, quite often, it's not so easy to accept what is brilliant about us. Only through a continued commitment to extend compassion to ourselves will we become resilient enough to continue to bear witness to the wonder and the darkness of our essential uniqueness.

Much of contemporary thinking about worthiness suggests that we must listen well enough to the voice of affirmation and when we don't listen well enough, we won't feel good about ourselves. There may be another perspective worth our attention. There is a way in which we become comfortable with the level of love, attention, support and acknowledgement that circulates through our lives. When there is a sudden expansion and intensification of life resources, we are challenged to be larger than we are accustomed. It may occur as simply as an unexpected compliment.

We often need time to reconcile how we see ourselves when another of life's offerings come our way. We may need to first experience what it's like to have a capacity to hold these new gifts. We are preparing to live in a larger story. We are stretching the size of our deservedness. It means letting go of the old paradigm of either being worthy or unworthy. Rather, we are growing comfortable with this new size of personal value and we may feel unworthy as we do so.

Staying With Boundary Lessons

Nothing shows more devotion to ourselves than a commitment to continue to learn about good boundaries, especially as the *proper times* present situations for such learning. Our self-loyalty rests upon our interest in developing an ability to exercise boundaries that work. We don't need to be perfect at boundary-making; we simply need to remain students of boundaries.

In learning about boundaries, our goal is to employ boundaries that support our autonomy and our belonging. It takes a combination of maturity and foolishness to pursue both autonomy and belonging, as authentically strengthening the former often seems to fortify the experience of the latter. And so, it appears that the tenor of our humanity depends upon both of these pursuits.

The most common message I have heard from clients over the years is: "If I am too much myself, and not up to the business of pleasing others, I will be alone." Fair enough, but the second most popular statement has been: "I got so involved with him (or her or them) that I lost myself." The inherent contradiction in these messages is that we will either have ourselves (autonomy) or we will have others (belonging), but not both.

Semi-permeable boundaries are meant to allow us to have ourselves without cutting us off from others. They allow us to be touched, influenced and chosen by others without completely losing ourselves. However, semi-permeable boundaries are never perfectly employed. They are simply an aid as we meet one of life's greatest challenges. Bringing our autonomy and belonging needs into some sense of balance will inevitably call upon our best creative efforts.

We spend our lives living in hundreds of stories that do not really belong to us but rather to others. We live in the beliefs, values, emotions and expectations of relatives, friends, lovers, teachers and clergy. Their stories are both an opportunity to discover who we are as well as a chance to get lost in their narratives, stepping away from our own. We find our way back to our own saga by living very close to the question: Whose story is this?

Typically, the story belongs to the first person who speaks, even though they might use language that sounds like the story belongs to the listener. Here are a few statements that can be challenging to clarify whose story the speaker is describing.

Each statement is a story about the speaker followed by description in parenthesis of the nature of the story:

"What the hell are you doing?" (The story is at least about the speaker's confusion and possibly anger regarding what the listener is doing.)

"I can't believe how selfish you are." (The story is about the speaker's belief that the listener is selfish or the speaker might want more control over the listener's behavior.)

"Why didn't you put the milk back in the refrigerator?" (The story is about the speaker's curiosity about the listener leaving the milk out, or more likely, about the speaker's anger regarding the non-refrigerated milk.)

"You told me that you would pick me up at 7:00." (The story may be about the speaker hearing the listener make an agreement to be picked up at 7:00 p.m. or the story may be about the speaker feeling angry with the listener for being late.)

"You know better than that!" (The story is likely about the frustration, disappointment or anger of the speaker.)

"You take everything too personally." (The story is likely about the speaker's unwillingness to address how he or she is communicating.)

It can be challenging to employ good boundaries when

speakers use language that implies that they are largely describing the listener. Most speakers we encounter will likely not be using language that clearly depicts their own stories. We learn quite young how to speak in a code that keeps our real stories hidden and protected from possible ridicule and shame. This leads to serious breakdowns in communication as adults. In order to communicate more effectively, as speakers, we need to learn how to represent our stories directly and clearly. How can we as listeners, however, take care of ourselves and our communication when speakers are not clear about their stories?

Two benefits occur when we ask the question: Whose story is this? The first is that it can be easier to hear the story being communicated as belonging to the speaker. Second, we have an opportunity to construct a boundary to support our autonomy, which separates us from the story of the speaker.

When the boundary is excessively permeable we step into the speaker's story and attempt to make it about us. We know when that has occurred because we either begin defending ourselves by attacking the speaker, defending ourselves by explaining ourselves, or shutting down and distancing.

It's easy to step, jump or crawl into the speaker's story. When we are children, authority figures almost always make their stories about us, so we are well-conditioned to accept invitations into the speaker's story. This story easily ignites a need to step into their narrative when we hear a derogatory remark, which in some ways reflects the shame we are already carrying.

Perfectionism will get us into the speaker's story when we hear an utterance that seems to portray us as less than perfect, and we launch into an attempt at vindication. A history of employing the adaptive victimization strategy can quickly place us into the speaker's story as we engage in merging. Conditioning, shame, perfectionism and the adaptive victimization strategy all carry very permeable boundaries leaving us susceptible to entering into stories that don't belong to us.

Once we are clear about whose story we are hearing and we are holding onto our autonomy with some force, there are several ways we can connect to another. The first is to simply ask the speakers what they want from us. Soliciting another's wishes keeps the focus on their stories and shows that we are interested in their needs as well. We can also express empathy, acknowledging the story we hear from them or by simply asking them to tell us more. Sometimes, empathy can be communicated by a gentle touch or listening with undivided attention.

It is important to note that an emotional or an intellectual boundary aimed at strengthening our autonomy alone can be done quietly, within the confines of our own thoughts. However, a boundary meant to support both our autonomy and our belonging requires language or a behavior that expresses a need for connection to the other.

Sometimes we stroll into the speaker's story because we want to save or fix them. An inclination to fix or save almost always carries very permeable boundaries and often comes from finding the other's situation unacceptable to us or that we are failures if we can't rescue them from their plight. Learn to accept the mystery of another's journey and admit that we don't know what they are healing and learning. It can also be advantageous to learn to understand our own limits, recognizing that another's quest lies beyond our greatest efforts to

aid them. Try to recall when others tried to rescue us and the
inevitable emptiness that resulted.

Discernment and Boldness

The creation of boundaries that will support self-loyalty
requires discernment and boldness. Discernment is the capacity to see, to be clear-sighted and be able to discriminate.
Boldness is daring to enlarge ourselves by way of our thoughts,
words and actions.

Right-Sizing Ourselves

There are at least three conditions that are critical to the
development of discernment. The first I call being right-sized,
which is acting with an authentic assessment of our strengths
and limitations. When we are not right-sized, it becomes very
difficult to see and accurately determine what we should allow
in our lives and what we should keep out.

The domination strategy tends to inflate us or over-size us.
We act as if we are larger than we really are. We hold a grandiose
vision of ourselves that often denies our limits and ignores what
needs to be learned. Being over-sized often is accompanied by
a bravado composed of false confidence and covert insecurity.

From this inflated posture, it becomes increasingly difficult to realize the things that are too much for us to handle.
Guided by aggrandized self-expectations, boundaries become
too permeable, causing us to take on tasks and projects that get
us overwhelmed, often resulting in burnout. This is especially
true because over-sizing typically precludes asking for help.

It is relatively easy to see how over-sizing would skew our
vision, hampering effective discernment and making it very dif-

ficult to determine the appropriateness of a particular boundary. Considerably more subtle, yet equally troublesome to favorable judgments of discernment, is under-sizing ourselves.

The adaptive victimization strategy and the distancing strategy tend to leave us under-sized. This is a natural outcome since both strategies are aimed at increasing our anonymity and invisibility. The cultural expectation is that men will often over-size themselves, while under-sized men simply go unnoticed. And although feminism has offered some permission for women to be right-sized, it remains relatively unpopular in the culture at large and we still expect to encounter *under-sized* women.

When under-sized, we speak and act with less power and competency than we actually possess. Under-sizing skews vision, leaving us with a propensity for non-permeable boundaries as we see ourselves as incapable of a wide range of experiences. Our life's possibilities are limited as to keep our choices congruent with a small perception of ourselves. To under-size is to keep ourselves and our lives much smaller than necessary.

I have noticed that men who are overly sensitive to their inner worlds are susceptible to under-sizing themselves. Men's movement activist Robert Bly once described this population, "In my travels I have encountered a new male. This man takes his spousing and his fathering very seriously. It's important to him to be actively involved with his community. He has a large heart and he would create war on no one. This man will change little or nothing in his lifetime." Bly's quote captures the kind of impotency indicative of under-sized men.

Right-sizing our souls reflects a genuine curiosity and acceptance of our gifts, our wounds and our limits. Because we are not objects, it is not possible to actually be right-sized. However, we can remain in the process of right-sizing as we maintain an attitude that is both vigilant and restorative.

Those people who are over-sized experience a sense of danger as they loosen their grip on being inflated, since it calls for a willingness to step away from using a domination strategy. People prone to under-sizing will also feel vulnerable as they let go of merging, feeling the threat of separation and distancing with the anxiety of them becoming more visible.

Right-sizing sharpens our vision. It becomes easier to discern what tasks, experiences and people to allow in and what ones to keep out. We have a better idea about what risks and challenges are compatible with our abilities. Those over-sizing often need to confront their arrogance and their fear while making their way to their rightful size. While those under-sizing will need to confront their false modesty and be bold enough to become who they are meant to be.

We also sharpen our discernment as we live nearer to what we desire. When we know what we want, we begin to see what may need to be kept out and what is to be allowed in. When we either don't know what we want, or are afraid to act off of our desire, our boundaries tend to be excessively permeable. Our lives are more likely defined by the desire of others rather than our own.

People who claim they simply don't know what they want have been practicing under-sizing themselves. When I hear them complain about someone in their lives, I often ask if they like the person whose behavior they disapprove. The normal reaction I get is a look of disorientation. After some discussion it becomes clear that they didn't realize they were entitled to decide whether they either like or dislike someone.

We act as if we don't know what we desire as a strategy to avoid conflict and indulge our illusion that we can control the acceptance of others. If we don't know what we want, then others certainly won't find our wishes to be disruptive.

A commitment to focus on being right-sized can go a long way toward contributing to the soundness of our discernment. However, life often presents us with complex situations making it challenging to see what kind of boundary would best serve us. Hence, the third condition, ethical engagement, rounds out our ability to develops mature discernment.

Ethical Engagement

Ethical engagement is the willingness to honestly seek and understand our values and live with them clearly in sight. We discover and rediscover the principles identified as our priorities for living. The exploration about why we hold a particular value, the curiosity about what serves us and others, and the reasons that emerge constitute our ethics.

Developmental psychologist Lawrence Kohlberg established six stages of moral development. Stage one, the most basic, establishes what is right or moral based upon whatever authority deems rightful behavior. Stage two prioritizes individual claims of what is important, moving away from authority to establish what is considered to be good. Stage three emphasizes the role of helpful intentions and motives. Stage four stresses obeying laws for the benefit of the society as a whole. Stage five is exemplified by asking questions about the values and principles that will benefit society with emphasis upon the democratic process. Stage six calls the nature of goodness and justice into question in the most objective way possible with social disobedience being an option.

Kohlberg did not see the evolution of these stages as a product of maturation, although it does appear that there is a *proper time* for moral thinking or ethical engagement to become more sophisticated. Kohlberg saw our social experiences as having the power to promote the deepening of our capacity for *ethical engagement.*

He believed that two specific occurrences supported our development. The first he referred to as cognitive conflict. This happens when we believe our moral positions are either challenged by the views of others or our circumstances make it difficult for us to hold two different values. We then may feel the need to expand our thinking in order to address new perspectives. For example, a man could believe that people should not engage in homosexual behavior and because of that, it is okay to discriminate against gays. The same man may discover that in fact his son is gay and may want his son to be entitled to be treated fairly and justly and with the same respect as heterosexuals. The conflict in his thinking may bring him to a new dimension of ethical engagement, offering a chance to generalize his love for his son to an entire population of men.

Another developmental stimulus was identified as role-taking opportunities, which are simply chances to take the views of others into consideration. These opportunities appear to occur when we are presented with diverse views. If we permit ourselves to remain curious about the values and positions of others, we may allow the diversity of thought to provoke a deeper understanding about our own values.

Cognitive conflict and role-taking opportunities are expressions of some level of belonging or connection to others. In turn, this has the power to strengthen our autonomy by causing us to reexamine our beliefs and values. Our interactions with others have the power to deepen our interaction with ourselves when we employ semi-permeable boundaries that both allow us to be touched by the thinking of others without simply adopting their positions. Such a reexamination offers the opportunity to actively advance our individuality.

Our values are ultimately driven by deep feelings like respect, reverence, devotion, loyalty and love. These feelings usually result from life-altering experiences where we may have felt loss, defeat, desperation or overwhelmedness. We inevitably search for beliefs and the kind of thinking (ethics) that will support the legitimacy and application of our values. The more intense our reflections, the more we will strive to share them with others. What this means is that we won't simply believe that some value serves only us, but also wish it for others, trusting that it will serve their lives as well.

Our ethical engagement reflects a sense of maturity when we are able to ask whether our moral positions reflect our best wisdom or instead feel compelled to hold a view as a consequence of some early wounding. In such a case, our values may simply be the result of having felt mistreated or neglected in some way instead of holding a moral vision that may affect an entire community.

We deepen our capacity for ethical engagement when we tenaciously take ownership of the values we recommend to others, and at the same time are open to understanding the values held by others. In order to be open to diverse views, we must move away from an adversarial relationship by dropping our tendencies to compete or attempt to convert the other. We can hold the faith that we may be in the midst of an engagement with the other, in which co-creative collaboration can reveal possibilities not previously envisioned.

Taking a moral stance can be difficult, especially when we know that there may be unpleasant implications for one or more people. It can be tough. The more complex the issue, the more we realize that no single position is unequivocal. Ethical engagement reflects a growing maturity where we learn to allow our values to guide us to a particular position while remaining mindful of the size of the moral task, and tempered by curiosity about varied perspectives.

Authentic ethical engagement is characterized by ongoing passionate and evocative inquiry into our values while remaining humble about our exclusive hold on truth. The key is not to succumb to indifference no matter what the size of the task or rigid and uncompromising tension that arises. We see this kind of humility and faithfulness to ethical curiosity in Plato's *Dialogues*. Socrates is asked by Meno if virtue is acquired by teaching or by practice:

> I literally do not know what virtue is, and much less whether it is acquired by teaching or not. And I myself, Meno, living as I do in this region of poverty am as poor as the rest of the world; and I confess with shame that I know literally nothing about virtue; and when I do not know "quid" of anything how can I know the "quale?"... Then, Meno, the conclusion is that virtue comes by the gift of God to those to whom it does come. But we shall never know the certain truth until, before asking how virtue is given, we set ourselves to inquire into the essential nature of virtue.

In the Socratic tradition, we can be guided by questions taking us closer to what we truly hold to be important to us:

- Will I or someone else be concretely injured by the employment of my boundary?
- Can I tolerate disapproval as a response to my boundary?
- Would I recommend this boundary to anyone else in a similar situation?
- How would I feel about being the recipient of such a boundary?
- Is this boundary congruent with what I believe?
- Will I be in integrity with the employment of this boundary?
- Am I making an exception of myself through the employment of this boundary?
- Are any of my values violated by acting on this boundary?
- Does this boundary support my self-loyalty?

Right-sizing, living from personal desire and remaining ethically engaged contribute greatly to enriching our capacity to be discerning. Without effective discernment, we are forced into the utilization of extreme boundaries, ones that are either too permeable or excessively non-permeable. Our discernment guides the creation and application of semi-permeable boundaries as we judge what to allow in and what to keep out.

Before leaving a discussion about discernment, we should address the importance of judgments. It is customary for judgments to get a bad rap in most personal growth circles. But really, good discernment is the result of thoughtful and balanced judgments. Typically, judgments that make someone, some group or ourselves feel bad and undeserving of love are not creative and make no meaningful impact on our ability to be discerning. Judgments should identify real sources of danger and the nature of effective protection, clarify what we are receiving from others, what we want to give, what needs to be done to generate more clarity and compassion, and make a significant contribution toward reliable discernment.

Ethical maturity calls for a capacity to be touched by deep feelings, moved by instinct and capable of in-depth reflection. We do not achieve a permanent state of ethical engagement; at best we get opportunities to renew it by loosening rigidity and allowing ourselves to be touched by new information and perspective. Recently, I received such a chance.

On an ordinary Sunday morning I was leaving the local supermarket, pushing my shopping cart toward my parked vehicle. I noticed a couple behind me wheeling their carriage of groceries down the middle of the driving lane. A car pulled up behind them, and the driver made a derogatory remark about the inappropriateness of obstructing his advance. As I placed my groceries in my car, I noticed the driver parking his vehicle adjacent to the car occupied by the couple he just chastised.

Starting my car, I noticed both men chest to chest daring the other. I slowly backed up, hoping the incident would simply subside, allowing me to go on my way without having to make a decision of whether or not to get involved. The man who had just arrived turned to make his way into the supermarket. When he had walked ten feet away, his adversary blurted out, "Faggot!" The man immediately turned to reengage his antagonist.

Remaining in my car some thirty feet away, with my head hanging out of the open window, I began to yell, "Hey! Cut it out! There are children all around here! That's no way to show kids how adults settle disputes. Grow up!"

With my voice echoing off the grocery store walls, both men looked in my direction, a bit stunned and surprised. One man responded sheepishly, "Okay," and walked in the direction of the store.

I would have preferred that my intervention was not necessary. As I drove away, however, I was glad about the action I took, which prevented any escalation of the conflict. There had been no real time for reflection. Emotion and instinct were guiding me and, at least for now, I was satisfied with the choice and the outcome. Similar to most values dilemmas, the consequences of my intervention were not predictable. The conflict could have intensified or the men could have turned against me as the common foe.

I also wondered how these men might remember that morning. Would they simply see their encounter as the result of the other man's ill-behavior? Would they learn anything important? Would they change their behavior in the future? Ethical situations are inevitably laced with the unknown.

The essential challenge of remaining ethically engaged, moving into the depths of ethical maturity, is that we must be willing to step into a psychological disposition that by its nature is antithetical. On the one hand we need to remain curious, open, receptive and respectful of the complexity and vastness of issues pertaining to values, and on the other hand, we must be prepared to decide. The best we can do is to remain flexible as we assess whether we are in need of more receptivity or more decisiveness. Typically, the behavior we need will be the one we have the most resistance to adopt.

We likely have to cope with some level of tension, no matter our chosen position. If we remain curious, we may face the tension of making a wrong decision. Impetuous decision-making causes a tension created by ambiguity and confusion. If we're honest, though, we will likely see clearly the source of our tension.

The Introverted Challenge

Self-loyalty presents a specific challenge for people who are introverted yet live in an extroverted culture. Introversion is a propensity to focus inwardly in order to ascertain what is believed or valued. Unfortunately, our extroverted culture encourages us to focus outwardly in order to discern who we are. This extroverted social mandate directs us toward a myriad of external events, products and ideologies aimed at augmenting a fledging sense of autonomy, but the mandate is more interested in sales than the development of authentic autonomy.

Introverts have come to my office reporting years of shame and self-loathing because of their shyness, yielding natures and lack of enthusiasm for large social events. In order to cope with the existing culture, they turned against themselves, living with a gnawing sense that their very natures were flawed.

The self-betrayal of an introvert is often played out as an attempt to pretend that they are extroverts, condemning them to a deep feeling of inadequacy. Or they simply withdraw more, distancing themselves from opportunities to make friends and develop relationships. They often report feeling lonely their entire lives.

Introverts begin to engender self-loyalty when they can understand and accept the gifts of their introversion. They usually need very little external stimuli in order to identify how they feel and what they believe. They are rarely verbose, allowing them to offer clear and succinct statements. They have a natural inclination for listening effectively. Their quietness is often testimony of their ability to remain close to themselves, not easily being pulled away from their core by external conditions. I have yet to meet an introvert with an attention deficit.

One of their greatest strengths is their capacity to generate depth and meaning in their relationships. They tend to look inside of themselves, even while interacting with others, which helps them avoid more superfluous encounters having little or no relevance to their lives.

An introvert would do well to remember that it is natural for them to maintain the distancing strategy, which hampers good boundary development. This awareness can allow an introvert to feel at home even in an extroverted culture. They can deepen their allegiance and loyalty to their own souls as they learn about their natural strengths and how to employ them creatively.

The Extroverted Challenge

In the pursuit of self-loyalty, extroverts face quite a different challenge. The culture blesses their tendency to seek and engage external stimuli. Extroverts naturally focus on the external to discover what they believe and value. Hence, they typically feel quite comfortable in a culture where they can utilize the external environment to help define themselves. The views of others become a cognitive smorgasbord, allowing extroverts to select different appetizers and entrées to assemble their belief system.

There are several significant hazards facing extroverts. They easily fall prey to over-identifying with what lies outside of themselves and often internalize these external values and beliefs without adequate scrutiny. Self-betrayal ensues.

Because extroverts rely deeply upon the opinions and views of others for their view of themselves, their boundaries are often excessively permeable. They often hastily adopt what sounds good. The immediate benefit to them is a reduction in the tension accompanying the uncertainty of who they are.

Extroverts are prone to getting lost. The culture defines a rich experience as one infused with endless stimuli—an extroverted extravaganza! Extroverts can easily be pulled from one impulse to the next, until their capacity to focus is overwhelmed by a myriad of external attractions. Extroverts are seduced into believing that an abundance of stimuli will eventually lead them to more clarity. However, they find that they cannot navigate the maze and become lost, further and further away from their core.

In order to produce deeper self-loyalty, extroverts need to employ boundaries that prevent the environment from overloading them. They can become more discerning, look inside, and put a stop to any further information beyond what has already been gathered. This makes most extroverts feel anxious, because it removes the outside stimuli they need for further self-definition.

We have been exploring the idea of maturation as a commitment to remain mindful of our tendency to step into self-betrayal, noticing the employment of the survival strategies of victimization, domination and distancing. These strategies, however, are unable to sustain our increasing need for both autonomy and belonging. We must give ourselves permission to feel helpless and scared, if we wish to move from self-betrayal to self-loyalty. We must remind ourselves of the way in which we betray our true self.

When we have a faithfulness and devotion to our need for *autonomy* and *belonging* we expand self-loyalty. We develop this self-trust by learning how to employ effective boundaries, remaining discerning and bold, committed to pursuing our rightful size, no matter whether you are an introvert or extrovert.

Nothing has been more bastardized by our culture than personal empowerment. We are presented with profoundly distorted depictions of power, leaving us confused about how we may exercise our own power when the *proper times* arise. So now we turn to exactly what it means to cultivate and steward personal empowerment.

5

A Proper Time for Power

For no human being can stand the perpetually numbing experience of his own powerlessness. —Rollo May

Our thinking about power is often split, leaving us either naively believing that the pursuit of power is a bad thing or deciding that anything that brings us immediate satisfaction is a power worth possessing. The former often leaves us either feeling victimized or excessively dependent upon others, while the latter leads us to seek power from sources outside of ourselves. In a culture that often sells us quick solutions for fulfilling our needs and desires, we are willing to seek these external sources, even though authentic empowerment only exists within.

We are a culture fixated on external expressions of power. We hold great reverence for physical power, economic power, social and political power as well as power of role or position. There is very little opportunity to learn about personal power. Its pursuit is either ignored or considered a waste of time and energy.

Our focus on external power may be a reaction to our neglect of internal or personal expressions of power. Manifestations of personal power tend to be deeper and more suited to the life of the soul. Our society usually offers illusions of power in the name of wanting to sell us something. Hence, there are countless claims to personal power in everything from automobiles to religious opportunities.

A number of years ago I joined a speakers' organization that billed itself as an opportunity to develop my public speaking skills. It quickly became apparent that the group had little or no interest in fostering speaking expertise. The order of the day was marketing, and specifically, how to market oneself as an expert.

The inherent philosophy of the organization was that success was a matter of image and perception. We were taught to see ourselves as the CEO of our own company, even if there were no employees. We were encouraged to get friends and relatives to write letters of endorsement, as if they had benefited from our alleged expertise. The idea was to do whatever it would take to create an image of success. I listened to endless appeals to the creation of image with little or no attention given to skill development; and after a while, I found that my participation was in violation of my integrity.

I recall being told at one session that a very successful motivational speaker would be offering a presentation at our next meeting. I had arrived at that meeting with great anticipation of the benefits from hearing a man who had risen to notable heights in the speaking profession. Once the gentleman took the stage, he immediately began to run from one corner to the next, speaking quickly enough to be completely inaudible. His dashing about was only interrupted by an occasional spin, resembling a novice ballerina.

His gyrations finally came to an abrupt halt, some sixty minutes later. I had been completely unable to decipher his message and just wanted to exit the auditorium. The display I had witnessed got me wondering if we had become a society easily seduced by exhibits of speed, size and sound that signify little or nothing. Could it be that much of what we consider powerful had more to do with how big, how fast or how loud? Such a view of power seems littered with adolescent debris.

The Nature of Personal Power

One way we can define personal power is as an evolving and deepening capacity to evoke life and to receive life. We can expand our ability to gain personal power by developing our autonomy. This includes learning to be clear about personal values and beliefs, the knack of knowing what we want and then being able to express our desires. Further, we need an understanding of our skills and talents, the ability to know what we want to learn, the ability to feel and express emotions and to cope with disappointment. It serves us to hold a vision of a vocation and pursue it. Finally, we have to have the ability to employ effective boundaries.

We deepen our competency to receive life by addressing our need to belong, by noticing to whom we are attracted, identifying and asking for what we want, fighting and resolving conflict, giving and receiving love, coping with diverse values and beliefs, generating emotional intimacy, collaborating and co-creating, making collective decisions and offering as well as receiving leadership.

Our adeptness at sustaining our needs for both autonomy and belonging is a measure of the maturity of our personal power, a growing capacity to be fully alive. Defining ourselves as victims has a significant negative impact on our ability to develop personal power. Creating stories about ourselves as victims literally sacrifices our potency, and we create such narratives because we don't know how to creatively carry our experiences of suffering and loss. There is almost no cultural encouragement to deepen our relationship to suffering.

If suffering is only seen as something in need of elimination, then we are left prone to victimization, especially when the elimination isn't quick enough. If we are socialized to define power as social, economic or political, there is little chance to deepen our learning about personal power.

Having personal power that is underdeveloped is like driving a six-cylinder vehicle with only five cylinders working. We buck and jerk our way along, feeling frustrated and anxious, as we long for a smooth ride, one that might restore joy and peace to our lives. Diminished *personal power* inevitably leads to confusion, as well as the misuse or abdication of power.

The Anatomy of Abuse

We can understand abuse of power as a violation of intellectual, emotional or behavioral boundaries (sexuality being included under behavioral boundaries). Before examining specific forms of abuse, let's look at where abusive actions might originate. Some light may be shed if we return to the three strategies for coping with feelings of fear and helplessness.

Adaptive Victimization and Abuse

There are at least three ways to elucidate how employing the adaptive victimization strategy might lead to abusive behavior. A need for revenge and anger are unconscious reactions and can be quite challenging to identify and accept. It is a strategy which is completely focused upon being adaptive and compliant. However, what we resist will naturally persist. Hence, resistance to feeling a desire for revenge and anger find their way out of the depths of denial and are expressed as some form of abuse.

A fear of a loss of merger can also be a source of abuse. When we use merger or enmeshment as a way to protect ourselves, the loss of this option could trigger a perceived lack of safety and an intense need for protection. We may compensate for this loss of merger by abusing power in some way.

The Distancing Strategy and Abuse

It is quite common for those employing the distancing strategy to represent themselves as having no strong emotional position about anything. In order to help themselves distance from the emotions of others they even distance themselves from their own emotions. They can get so good at this that they actually believe they have no emotional life!

Of course, it isn't true. Denied feelings of revenge and anger are bubbling beneath the surface until something is said or done that triggers a volcanic eruption of abuse, such as retaliation or excessive withdrawal. A person who fears losing their ability to distance can also become abusive, throwing themselves into a protective survival pattern.

The Domination Strategy and Abuse

Abusive behavior is less subtle for dominators. Because they are prone to believe that all dynamics can be reduced to either dominating or being dominated, they easily violate the boundaries of others trying to secure a dominating position. Not knowing how to effectively cope with feelings of fear and helplessness results in abuses of power. Dominators are not as likely to deny feelings of revenge and anger, instead they use them to fuel their need to dominate.

Abuses of Power

Abuse is any violation of a person's sexual, physical or emotional boundaries. While there are a myriad of manifestations, there are also a number of common experiences among the perpetrators and victims of abuse. Being able to name these experiences not only offers an opportunity to heighten awareness in regards to abuse of power, but also creates a possible *proper time* for stepping into a more authentic expression of personal power. Most of us are willing to point the finger at someone who is perpetrating abuse, but it is a completely other matter for us to address our own abusive tendencies. Yet we may be embarking upon a significant *proper time* by allowing ourselves to become accountable for being abusive.

Rather than attempt to occupy the high moral ground, it serves us to simply acknowledge that perpetrating abuse is inevitable for all of us. Perpetration may mean that we have not grown out of lingering elements of one of the three survival strategies or that we never received needed instruction and support about personal power. In any case, owning our abusive behavior and what we want to do about it may be an effective way to deepen maturation. Let's examine a number of ways we manifest abuse.

Shame

Shame is an extremely insidious form of mistreatment. Many of us were raised in shame-based families and grew accustomed to shame being an appropriate tool for authority figures to exercise their charge. We think nothing of being whacked by shame from clergy, teachers, coaches, bosses, physicians and even spouses.

Think of shame as an attack upon a person's character. It is aimed at someone's personality, rather than someone's behavior. The goal of shame is to assault essential worth, stripping the person of any sense of having real value. The perpetrator is often attempting to coerce the target into avoiding certain behavior by threatening the severe loss of personal value. Although shame can yield immediate results, a typical reaction is to continue engaging in the behavior covertly and/or to internalize the shame, believing that he or she is fundamentally flawed.

Shaming can be non-verbal. Facial expressions and general body language can easily communicate as well as words, with sentiments like: God, you are a worthless piece of shit! You are an incredible waste of my time and energy! You are the scum of the earth! There's nothing about you that I value! Your mistakes are unforgivable! If we want to address a tendency to be a shaming-type person, then we will need to look at our physical gestures as well as what we are saying.

A local college basketball coach regularly launches verbal and non-verbal tirades of shame at his players. As long as his teams win, resulting in increased revenue for the university, no one will hold him accountable for his behavior. We look the other way when shame is accompanied by success.

Being willing to interrupt a tendency to shame may invoke a significant *proper time* for learning about personal power. It is important to see what we may lose by engaging in shame. Normally, people either begin to avoid us or stop telling us the truth, which hampers our ability to collaborate and build rapport. We also hinder our efforts toward deeper autonomy because our fears and desires for revenge remain unconscious.

Blame

A first cousin of shame is blame. In this case, however, a person's goodness is attacked based upon their behavior and words. Examples of blame might include: "If you weren't so damn insensitive, I wouldn't feel so embarrassed in front of our friends." "Because you're irresponsible, I'll need to go over all of these reports." Or, "it would have been a good party if you hadn't insisted upon telling one ridiculous joke after another."

Blame is typically a substitute for clear expressions of feelings of fear, helplessness and anger. It is corrosive of building trust and creating rapport as well as helping us to avoid our real feelings.

Bullying

Bullying is a form of abusing power where the perpetrator antagonizes, taunts and intimidates. It can be employing our physical stature to impose our will or it can be emotionally-based by threatening to withdraw cooperation, support and attention.

Bullying, like shaming and blaming, allows us to avoid the truth of feeling scared and helpless, while obstructing any genuine need for belonging. The typical responses to bullying are either retaliation or avoidance.

Sarcasm

Sarcasm is an indirect expression of anger, using disparaging and contemptuous remarks aimed at belittling another.

The indirect nature of sarcastic remarks allows them often to go unacknowledged, yet leaves the recipient feeling diminished by the exchange.

It is important to pay attention to our use of sarcasm and make the commitment to be clear about the source of our feelings of anger.

Analyzing

In personal relationships, people typically believe they are entitled to analyze and explain the behavior of the other without asking for permission. However, offering unsolicited analysis of others is a violation of their intellectual boundaries. Deciding who we are may be one of the most personal of all human endeavors and we have the right to decide who will and who will not participate in the process.

Giving feedback where none is wanted is often a reflection of our own feelings of helplessness and anger. We might feel powerless over the choices made by others or we believe we can alter the course of their decisions. Our analysis then reflects our own misplaced anger and is not really offered in the name of clarity, but instead is loaded with ridicule.

Analysis packed with anger has been referred to as "mind-fucking." While not the most elegant term, it is quite descriptive. People use expressions like: "Look how you treat me; no wonder you have no friends." "You sabotage everything you touch, just like your mother." "Your vision is seriously skewed because you're not in touch with your feelings." "If you weren't such a victim wallowing in self-pity, you might be able to appreciate how much I bring to our relationship."

Teaching

Teaching, when unsolicited, is quite often a violation of the intellectual boundaries of others, implying that the recipient is inadequate and will unnecessarily struggle without our esteemed guidance. Similar to analysis, teaching is ordinarily driven by either denied feelings of helplessness and anger. We offer others unsolicited tidbits of information, self-righteously convinced that it is in the recipient's best interest to take our pontifications seriously. It is condescending, diminishing how others have organized their lives around their own beliefs, values and choices, which in turn hampers our ability to live close to ourselves and others.

Deception

Lying by either misrepresenting the facts or omitting valuable information constitutes abusing power through deception. It is common, driven by denied feelings of fear, anger and helplessness, and sometimes a desire for revenge.

Deception violates intellectual boundaries by leaving others either believing misconceptions or partial truths. It violates emotional boundaries because the beliefs created by deception create a set of emotions based upon erroneous information. Behavioral boundaries are violated as deception steals the choices of others. The deceived are making decisions based upon beliefs that are misrepresentations of reality. They very well might make different choices with a more accurate account of what's really going on.

Physical Violence

Physical violence is an obvious encroachment on behavioral boundaries. However, it is important to see it also as a transgression of emotional and intellectual boundaries. When we are physically violated, emotional boundaries suffer as we are besieged with feelings of fear and anxiety, losing our capacity to feel secure and safe. Feelings of shame typically accompany being physically abused. Victims can easily take on the shame of the perpetrator, telling themselves that the abuse would not have taken place if there wasn't something inherently wrong with them. Sometimes victims blame themselves for not having prevented the abuse.

Intellectual boundaries are violated as our beliefs about safety, protection, trust and freedom are called into serious question, replaced by convictions of suspicion, caution, doubt and possibly cynicism.

Predatory Behavior

Predatory behavior is discrete, cunning and manipulative. It is likely the result of denied feelings of helplessness and a desire for revenge. While preying on others is ordinarily an expression of the adaptive domination strategy, the desire for domination is disguised. Predators commonly represent themselves as allies, acting with the most honorable of intentions. However, the image that most easily comes to mind is that of the vampire, a creature striving to dominate by diminishing the life force of their victim.

Predatory activity is the most often denied form of abuse. We normally assign it only to males who are pedophiles, preying on children. However, anyone who claims to have only altruistic motivations, interested only in what benefits others, will be most at risk to engage in predatory conduct.

Healers, teachers and clergy are, sadly, the types of professions in which we often see predators. Perhaps it's the helpful and caring veneer that suits a disingenuous persona.

In his book, *Sex in the Forbidden Zone*, Peter Rutter defines predatory behavior in the helping professions:

> Sexual behavior between a man and a woman who have a professional relationship based on trust, specifically when the man is the woman's doctor, psychotherapist, pastor, lawyer, teacher, or workplace mentor.

Rutter makes it clear that predatory abuses of power are more likely in professions where the purpose is help guided by trust.

> In the forbidden zone, the factors of power, trust, and dependency remove the possibility of a woman freely giving consent to sexual contact.

Abdication of Power

Abdication of power is often seen as benign, as we believe that relinquishing power will support our autonomy and our belonging. However, abdication often has devastating effects upon our own lives and the lives of others.

Abdication of power is an indirect and usually ineffectual way of securing power in an extremely circuitous fashion. We believe that we can gain some form of control over others or over life itself by renouncing our claims to power. We see abdication most often in people who cope by employing an adaptive victimization strategy and by those who are distancers.

One way to look at abdication of power is as an insidious expression of violence to ourselves and to others. This can better be seen by exploring four distinct expressions of abdication.

Disownership of Personal Authority

When we disown personal authority, we are essentially refusing to see ourselves as the primary author of our lives. This particular form of abdication of power is generally manifested by acts of deference and excessive dependence. We literally turn authorship for our lives over to others, asking them to create us. When disownership is intense and pervasive, it is likely we are facing the recurrence of a childhood fear of abandonment, where separation from parents was experienced as the likelihood of dying. Of course, the irony is that we are killing our own creative spirit that would bring life to our beliefs, our values and our choices. Disownership of personal authority is a direct outgrowth of an adaptive victimization strategy.

There is little power available to deepen an understanding of our individuality or our ability to meaningfully connect to others. We cannot strengthen our relationships because our uniqueness is not accessible. We settle into a life that is an extension of others, existing under the illusion that such a move gives us control over not being abandoned.

Relationships can limp along even when one participant disowns any personal authority, leaving their partner essentially alone. An abdicating partner could have been raised in neglect or by very dominating parents, in which case they will be excessively passive waiting for their partners to take responsibility for them. They are very familiar with what it means to be alone in a relationship, leaving them with a high tolerance for solitary life. They may seek a high level of control, if a partner's deference allows, or they may distance themselves as a primary way of coping, leaving them comfortable with the isolated nature of their situation. However, the partner of the abdicating one may sooner or later experience the depths of emptiness and loneliness created by colluding with the abdicating partner.

Confusion and Ignorance

A common way to abdicate power is to live in a state of confusion and ignorance. We simply decide we are off the hook for taking responsibility by deciding we do not possess the skills to develop our relationship to ourselves (autonomy) or our relationships to others (belonging). Of course, life does not grant a pass to those of us claiming ignorance. We will be inevitably faced with innumerable challenges, calamities and crises, leaving us feeling overwhelmed and victimized due to an unwillingness to claim the kind of power that could generate valuable life skills.

Claiming ignorance with no curiosity for the potential of increased awareness is a common form of punishment and revenge. Partners of people who abdicate feel increasingly alone and helpless as they watch their significant others take refuge in their confusion, unable, or more importantly, unwilling to intimately join them.

Addiction

One of the most devastating expressions of abdication is addiction. An addiction will arrest our creative energies, abate our capacity for intimacy, thwart an ability to engage in cogent thought and often extinguish any aptitude to remain personally accountable. An addiction, similar to other forms of abdication, characteristically generates an illusion of power, making it extremely difficult to see the immense loss of power actually occurring.

An active addict can use alcohol, street drugs, pharmaceuticals, or some activity to temporarily anesthetize the emotions. Instead of inadequacy, anxiety, fear or worry, they create a feeling of pseudo confidence and security. Addicts are easily seduced into settling for the illusion of power, leaving them impotent to do anything meaningful for their autonomy and need to belong.

Addicts give us a vivid depiction of what we all do on some level. There are, essentially, only two options when it comes to personal power. We either engage in the work needed in order to engender authentic personal power or we attach to an illusion of power. It may be quite literally impossible for the human psyche to embrace powerlessness for the sake of being powerless. That is, we step into powerlessness because on some level, we believe it to be a potential source of power.

Illusions of power are seductive because they appeal to our desire for a quick and easy path to power. Unfortunately, there is no weekend workshop that will bring us to the core of our personal power. Generating genuine personal power is hard work.

Addiction begets addiction. The partners of addicts commonly become addicted to the addicts in their lives. They can obsess over the addicts' decisions and actions, providing them with ample opportunity to avoid the challenge of attending to the work of their own personal empowerment.

Addicts are often referred to in the research on addiction as chemically dependent victims because of the tendency to live life from a victim's posture. It is an easy move to go from coping by employing the adaptive victimization strategy to falling prey to some addiction. Once comfortable with a victim's approach to life, we can find numerous ways to keep ourselves there.

Refusal to Develop Personal Gifts

I once heard a shaman from a West African tribe describe a practice of his village. As soon as a toddler began walking and exploring the environment, several elders would follow the child about, identifying which gifts the gods had sent to the people by way of this child.

Imagine growing up with the understanding that the people around you believed you were sent to them bearing some prized bounty! We were not by and large encouraged to ask questions about the nature of our gifts, how to develop them or how they might benefit the society. We were not even told we had gifts, and had to assume that they probably didn't exist.

Most of our skills and talents are either used for raising children or generating income. We easily lock into a consumer mentality where our proficiencies are reduced to a means to pay the bills. While we may become adept at putting bread on the table or saving for retirement, we are unable to hold a larger vision that would define our competencies as deserving stewardship and development, as well as our offering to humanity.

When we maintain a connection to our gifts through dedication to a vocation or calling, we are able to strengthen our autonomy by developing what we are good at. Then, we can recognize that our work is an offering made to others, strengthening the impact we have upon our community and enhancing our experience of belonging.

The Challenge

When we use primitive strategies to cope with feeling scared and helpless or we attach ourselves to illusions of power, personal power will elude us and we will be locked in a never ending pattern of abuse and abdication. However, as we recognize these patterns, we also create *proper times* for deepening our understanding of power and how we want to live with it. With this greater maturity comes ever-increasing expressions of curiosity about creative ways of developing authentic personal power.

Abuse and abdication of power are unfortunate, but recognizing these habits could alert us to a *proper time* for learning more about personal power and possibly strengthening our maturation. Cognitive conflict often results when our abusive behavior is in conflict with another value we hold dearly. For example, we might want to generate more cooperation with others and have them feel supported by us; or we would like our children to have a model of non-abusive ways of holding power. If we are able to identify the self-defeating behavior that is thwarting the realization of these other values, then we may very well be at a point where we may realize a more developed relationship with power.

Much as we may be irritated by it, listening to complaints of others can be an effective way to evaluate how we exercise power. We will need to accept ourselves as good people, while allowing our emotional boundaries to be permeable enough to truly hear the discontent of others. The feedback of others may help us to make decisions about power that allow us to live closer to ourselves and others.

By not living closer to our true selves, we have an unfortunate choice to either fight with life or run from it. With our culture's preoccupation with heroic endeavors, it becomes extremely easy to have an overly ego-centric relationship with life. There are endless lures to the authority and primacy of the human will, so we hold tight to the fantasy that if we are clever enough, we can strip life of its insecurity, unpredictability and mystery. Such arrogance can plunge us into an ongoing struggle with life where we swing back and forth between feeling victimized by life and preparing for another battle with it. Unless we are willing to make peace with the idea of life as an impenetrable mystery, we condemn ourselves to a disempowered existence.

Self-loyalty is a significant indication of personal power. When we remain mindful of self-betrayal, allow ourselves to feel scared and helpless, live close to our interior worlds, learn to trust ourselves, employ good boundaries and attempt to right-size ourselves, we make strides toward self-loyalty. Although self-loyalty does go a long way toward strengthening personal empowerment, there are other approaches to creating and sustaining power.

Personal Power and Autonomy

Abdication typically generates strong feelings of helplessness and desperation, which alerts us to our inability to nourish our autonomy. The grip of desperation often tightens as we unknowingly attempt to live our lives by abdicating power. The cries of this existential dilemma can be heard in a variety of lamentations: "My life is not my own." "I don't know who I am anymore." "My work is empty and non-rewarding." "I can't seem to accomplish anything." "Life has little or no meaning for me." "I have no future to look forward to." "Life hasn't been kind to me." Or even, "Life's a bitch and then you die."

We think that abdication is supposed to deliver us power but instead it immobilizes us. A strategy of adaptive victimization originally helped us to cope with feelings of fear and helplessness with the promise of gaining the support and care of authority figures. By distancing, we strive to become so invisible and inaccessible that those with power would find it difficult to harm us further. These are, perhaps, appropriate ways to deal with the defenselessness of childhood, not to creatively engage life as an adult. Each plan gives up power in the name of getting power. The psyche has its own way to overly invest in any tactic that helped us to survive, regardless of whether or not it has outlived its actual usefulness.

When we adopt these strategies into adulthood, we undeniably abdicate our power over and over again, essentially living life from the position of a victim. From such a place, we are unable to summon the power necessary for an autonomous life.

Moving Out of Victim Stories

Living within a victim story means we define some aspect of our life as holding power over us and we define ourselves as helpless to do anything about it, leaving vital parts of ourselves sacrificed in the process. It's similar to how we saw our parents hold authority over us as children. We could protest the injustice of some situation or another, but remained helpless to do anything about it.

As we endeavor to move away from our own victim's story, we need to perceive our lives not as something unfortunate or bad that has been done to us but as an opportunity.

Claiming Authorship of the Story

The very first step toward moving out of a victim's story is to be shamelessly aware of the fact that we have placed ourselves in it. This alone is deeply empowering. There are a variety of stories that we could have chosen as our own and yet, we preferred the story of a victim. Our awareness intensifies when we boldly and openly confront our choices and do not compound our problems by assaulting ourselves with shame. Committing to this level of consciousness can be challenging, but when we protest our victim situation, we are implying that we are deserving of something better.

Letting Go of the Idyllic

Our society pushes a kind of commercialism that appeals to our childish dreams of happy-ever-after. Why argue with these idyllic portrayals of life? After all, culture bombards us with marketing, suggesting we can purchase something that will render life secure and predictable. Accepting the true nature of life can be a tough thing to swallow.

When we recognize life as mysterious, insecure and unpredictable, we shed our victim identities and become courageous adventurers. To have no guarantee we will be alive at the end of the day and still be willing to say "yes" to life anyway is truly a bold act. The very nature of the journey of life is mostly about loss. The challenge is not whether or not we will experience loss, but rather how will we deal with that loss when it comes. When we are willing to see loss not as an undesirable aspect of life, but rather as an essential part of living, we vault ourselves out of a victim's story. Loss becomes a *proper time* for our deepening awareness.

From Happiness to Creativity

What if we were to just let go of our victim stories by replacing our pursuit of happiness with a search for creativity? It is easy to descend into a victim story when pursuing happiness because it is so difficult to acknowledge a proper place for suffering on such a quest. The search for happiness ultimately creates stories that ignore suffering as simply regrettable, which condemns us to a victim's narrative. However, seeking to maintain a creative spirit has the power to point us toward a story about suffering that goes beyond the lamentable.

When we shift our focus from the pursuit of happiness to one seeking creativity, we expand the ways we can support our individual experiences (autonomy) and become suppler in our responses to the vicissitudes of life. No one took the challenge of remaining creative, especially the ability to create meaning in the face of suffering, more than the Viennese psychiatrist Victor Frankl (1905-1997). Frankl's incarceration in a Nazi concentration camp during World War II hurled him into a confrontation with the depths of human brutality. Rather than succumb to being enveloped by victimization, he decided to continue to find meaning, even in the most deplorable of human conditions.

Frankl saw the search for meaning as a discovery, resulting from a determination to live three separate categories of values: experiential values, creative values and attitudinal values. Experiential values place us in relationship to beauty, ethics and the act of loving.

A number of years ago I was hiking with a friend in the mountains of southwestern Colorado. Unaccustomed to the oxygen demands, we would pause, gather our strength and continue the climb. At about 11,000 feet we paused and sat on the ground. As I gazed out across the valley, I was struck with awe at the sight of such overwhelming beauty and I began to softly weep. I suggested to my friend that if he happened to be with me during the last hours of my life that he should ask if I had seen enough beauty. For the first time in my life I realized that to be born of this earth meant to experience as much beauty as possible.

"The beautiful offers us an invitation to order, coherence and unity. When these needs are met, the soul feels at home in the world," writes John O'Donohue in his book *Beauty*. Beauty has the power to draw us out of the chaotic and the confused. Moments that are pregnant with meaning are co-created by what life presents and the quality of vision and imagination we bring to our experience. During those moments high in the mountains of Colorado, I knew my place among the sublime exhibition before me. I recognized my pettiness and I lowered my head in hope that the valley might forgive me and find a way to return me to a sensibility embedded in a gratitude for this wondrous opportunity.

Remaining ethically engaged expands our capacity for discernment. It ignites a desire to understand what we value and how we want to live our values in order to maximize the greatest benefit to ourselves and others.

It is important to distinguish ethics from morality. Morality consists of the pronouncements we make about right and wrong, good and evil. Ethics is the way we explore, create and understand what we value. Ethical considerations might include:

- Who will benefit from this action?
- Will anyone be harmed by this action?

- What am I willing to sacrifice in order to make this action happen?
- Would I prescribe this action to others in similar circumstances?
- What general consequences will likely ensue from this action?
- Are there others with diverse values from my own, and am I aware of how they think about their values?
- Am I in dialogue with those who have different values from me?
- How can I be aware of the fears I have that pull me into morally positioning myself?
- How can I most creatively address these fears?
- What resources exist that might support a creative approach to my fear?
- Am I willing to learn from those who hold different values from me?

Most of us are taught to position ourselves morally rather than remain ethically engaged. Through my Roman Catholic upbringing, I learned it was in my best interest to quickly occupy the high ground of some moral stance. It became obvious there were two groups: the judges and the judged. I was eager to avoid membership in the latter group. I was increasingly invested in being self-righteous, solidifying my identity as a judge, in the hope of successfully leveraging myself against the shaming castigations of others.

It was considerably shortsighted of me to believe I could exploit this kind of thinking without paying a significant price. Typical of self-righteousness, I denied I was using it as a defense, insisting that I was simply attempting to prescribe what was in everyone's best interest. The more willing I was to examine myself and the impact of my moral proclamations upon others, the clearer I became about the consequences. People feared me and avoided me. They didn't feel good about themselves in my presence; and I, in turn, was not being honest about how scared I was to be subjected to moral scrutiny.

In order to loosen my grip on my self-righteousness, I needed to be more receptive to how I was wounded in my Catholic childhood. My attempts to protect myself from further injury had caused me to be a perpetrator of what I had received. I will likely always be prone to being self-righteous as I continue to find it challenging to be passionate about some values position while remaining curious about other perspectives, allowing myself to remain ethically engaged rather than morally positioned.

The following verse from Rumi, a thirteenth century Islamic mystic and poet, helps me remember to remain ethically engaged:

> Out beyond ideas of wrongdoing, and right doing,
> There is a field. I'll meet you there.
> When the soul lies down in that grass,
> The world is too full to talk about.
> Ideas, language, even the phrase each other
> doesn't make any sense.

Frankl believed love was the most profound expression of experiential value. It can be extremely confusing to understand love as a medicine in a culture that excessively romanticizes, eroticizes and idealizes love. With pessimism and cynicism often spinning off from our idealizations, it can be a daunting task even to recognize when love is directly in front of us. And, if we do see it, we may feel too scared or overwhelmed to embrace it.

Giving and receiving love have the power to emancipate us from the confines of victimization and prevent us from being limited by our suffering. Both our power and our sense of worth can be deeply renewed by loving and being loved. However, as soon as we discover that loving can involve being hurt we often find it more appealing to close our hearts. But it is not typically the hurt that seals our hearts, but rather the stories we create about feeling hurt. We employ the excessively *permeable boundaries* of childhood, allowing the actions of others to define us. So when someone does or says something that hurts us, we create the story that we are not lovable or deserving of better treatment.

Most of us don't know how to be hurt. Learning how to be hurt does not mean being impervious to the emotional blows we receive along the way. Immunity would likely close our hearts. Becoming more creative with the stories of our pain gives us resiliency and deepens our capacity to feel hurt. When our stories depict the hurtful actions of others, then they are statements about *their* motivations, beliefs and values. We can feel hurt without betraying our essential value and simply remain good people who feel hurt.

It is common to think that if we are feeling hurt, then somebody in our story is a bad person. Either we are deserving of such treatment or the perpetrator of the hurt is simply a nasty human being. I call these compassionless stories. Notice that if we stopped our moral indictment of someone, self-accusations would likely be the natural consequence.

Sometimes, in order to gain a temporary reprieve from

self-contempt it seems like the best idea is simply to project degradation on to someone else. However, consider letting go of compassionless stories whenever possible, not for altruistic reasons, but rather because it is not in the best interest of your own heart to house that sort of toxic energy.

Again, we do not so much close our hearts because we fear being hurt. Rather it is the devastating stories we create about ourselves. If we can learn to accept the pain and let go of injurious stories, painful interactions may become a *proper time* for learning how to carry our hurt without closing our hearts.

We might think of love as food for the heart. As we shut our hearts, not allowing love to flow freely from and to us, we begin to go hungry and even starve. Some of us actually decide that we really do not need love, especially when we figure out that love is not forthcoming from members of our families. Resistance to love can simply mean we feel out of control because we can't explain the offering as solely a return for something we have given. I refer to this as the love deal. This translates into, "Okay, I've given enough, so you can love me now." And then there are those times when to allow love in would jolt us out of a victim's state, a position we may not be quite ready to surrender.

I have experienced this resistance to love in my own life. It revealed my need to remain loyal to the deprivation of love that I experienced in childhood. Accepting love meant I would have to betray a parent whose love was not readily accessible.

Just four months after I had married for a second time, I declared to my wife that I believed we should end our relationship. Connie challenged me, suggesting that I enter counseling with her either to heal our marriage consciously or else dissolve it. In either case, I was to get some guidance in the process. I agreed.

Almost immediately, our counselor became focused on me and my need to end the marriage. Luckily, he possessed enough expertise to help move me beyond explanations that had no bearing upon my stated need to leave the marriage. At some point, I began to weep uncontrollably, repeating over and over again, "There's no pain here." I could hardly believe what I was saying. The counselor asked Connie to pay particular attention to my utterances.

It became obvious that if I accepted Connie's available love, I would need to betray depriving parents. It also became apparent that my loyalty to my parents had resulted in a definition of love that included a good deal of pain. I didn't experience much pain in Connie's love, so initially I believed it could not be real love. It can take a great deal of hard work to make peace with love, and let go of more primitive ways to love that keep us in a victim's position.

I am inclined to be biased when it comes to understanding the medicine of love, favoring a love story rather than a rational analysis of love's healing power. So I want to tell the story of my daughter Sarah and a woman named Mary Malone.

In 1975, my daughter Sarah was born and before her first birthday she was diagnosed with cerebral palsy and severe mental retardation, which would later be changed to a more rare disability called pachygyria. Irrespective of the change in diagnosis, Sarah had significant fine motor impairment, erratic body movements and she was non-verbal. By Sarah's third birthday, the impact of her disability upon her physical and intellectual development was glaring. Refusing to succumb to a haunting sense of hopelessness, we began to research alternative approaches to Sarah's condition, and soon found a neurological rehabilitation program we thought had the potential to positively impact Sarah's progress.

Patterning, as it is called, consisted of a series of exercises and movements aimed at stimulating lower brain activity. The only problem was that the program had to be done in one-hour intervals, seven hours per day, and six days per week. We calculated that we would need 100 volunteers, two people working with Sarah every hour.

Growing up, my family lived by the mandate that family members did not go outside the family in order to seek help. Such reaching out for help and support itself was considered a sign of weakness. The challenge of assisting Sarah was pushing me toward a larger story of community.

We canvassed the staff and students at the college where I was teaching and ran ads in the local newspaper. Within a short period of time, a hundred volunteers had come forward to participate in Sarah's patterning program. I was learning that letting go of being a victim often meant asking for help. Even more unsettling, it could mean actually getting what I requested! Our small home soon resembled a community center with a constant stream of people moving in and out.

Diagonally across from our home lived the Malone family, a husband and wife with three children, including two teenage boys with a fascination for salvaged automobiles. At any time they might have a collection of a dozen or more junkers, even an old dilapidated bus. When their own property could no longer accommodate their holdings, several of their jalopies would be left parked in front of a neighbor's home. Over time the animosity of the neighbors grew, creating a palpable tension throughout the neighborhood.

When neighbors complained, the Malones would awaken to two or three more of the boy's prized possessions deposited in front of their home. On several occasions the police were called in and explained that their only recourse would be to erect no-parking signs, which meant that neighbors could not park in front of their own homes.

My family and I did our best to avoid any involvement in the neighborhood feud. However, as the unrest grew, we found an increasing number of vehicles left in front of our home, making it more difficult for volunteers to access our property. After several weeks of hearing complaints from volunteers and with great reluctance, we decided to call the Malones and invite them to our home. I had very little faith they would favorably respond to the invitation.

To my surprise, they accepted. The following Sunday afternoon I watched them traverse the street, resembling military officers crossing over into enemy territory for a parley regarding a possible temporary cease-fire. For me, the Malones had lost their identity as neighbors. They were the local terrorists who had waged war on the entire neighborhood with their junk and now my family was a casualty. I did not want to get to know them. I simply wanted them to call off their incursion now advancing towards the front of my home.

I opened the door more out of necessity than a gesture of welcome. Dressed in a brown skirt and paisley blouse, Mary Malone stepped into our kitchen with her chin raised high, her eyes darting from left to right as if she were passing inspection upon our kitchen as an appropriate place for such a summit meeting. Her husband, who stood six feet, five inches tall, followed her into our home giving the appearance of a bodyguard.

"Welcome Mary, I'm glad you could make it," I said, attempting to offer some semblance of conviviality.

"Well, the least we could do was to come over and hear you out," she responded, as her chin rose even higher. I noticed a woman in her forties, looking at least twenty years older.

My wife and I explained our predicament with the volunteers and their parking problems.

"I've never heard anything like this before," she reacted, looking relieved.

"I don't know what you mean," I said.

"I mean you're not telling me what a bad parent I am or demeaning my children," she explained. "This is really different."

"I have no need to insult you or your family," I added, hoping that the disgust I felt would go unnoticed.

"We've been mistreated for years, everything from how we dress to the tires I allow the boys to keep in the living room!" she said.

"I'm sorry to hear that," I replied.

"In any case, I appreciate a man asking directly for what he wants. Ain't that so, Hank?" She banged her fists on the kitchen table. Hank grunted in the affirmative.

We sat in what felt like an extremely long silence. Mary finally stopped nodding her head and said, "As long as you live here, no vehicle of my boys will be parked in front of your property."

She went on to ask us questions about Sarah's disability and the subjects I taught at the local college. When Mary and

Hank left, we were filled with relief. Not only was the problem not exacerbated, but we got what we wanted—free access to our property for volunteers.

Toward the end of the following week, Mary called and asked if she could become a volunteer. We were shocked, but gladly accepted. Mary developed an easy rapport with Sarah as if they had been old friends. As the weeks passed, Mary noted that on occasion, volunteers did not arrive when scheduled. After her hour with Sarah, she would wait to make sure the next volunteers showed up. If someone didn't come, Mary would fill in and do a double session.

Mary suggested that she not only be a regular volunteer in Sarah's program, but since she lived across the street, she should be the permanent fill-in person for volunteers unable to keep their commitment. She quickly became an integral part of our daily life, often sitting in the kitchen with one of us, describing the harshness she faced as a child growing up in an orphanage. I came to understand Mary Malone as a great survivor—with a great heart.

The Malone vehicles soon vanished from the street altogether, as the need for retaliation diminished in the Malone home. Neighbors began to greet Mary's children and stop to chat with her as she made her way back and forth from our home. The love between an embittered orphanage survivor and a disabled child spilled out onto the streets of our neighborhood, removing tensions and restoring a sense of peace and trust.

Mary died shortly after the patterning program ended. Neighbors spoke of the kind woman who had offered so much to our little girl. When town's folk wanted to make a point about what drew a community together, they typically cited Mary

Malone's offering to Sarah as an example of what it means to be a good neighbor. It was said that you couldn't have a better neighbor than Mary Malone.

Mary and Sarah's relationship taught me lessons about the medicine of love. Because of the acceptance they brought to one another, Mary and Sarah were able to benefit from their respective disabilities and create a meaningful relationship. Mary and the neighbors were emancipated from being one another's victim. I, on the other hand, was given a reprieve from being a victim of my own prejudices. I had some strong pre-established beliefs about people who collected junk cars and stored tires in the living room.

Creative Values

Frankl saw participation in the creation of our own lives as affording us an opportunity to engender personal meaning. One way we can understand the idea of creative participation is by focusing upon our gifts, skills and talents. When we are in the position of a victim, we can only see ourselves as passive, as being done in by life. We lose sight of what we bring to our living experience, letting our lives be ruled by fate instead of exercising our own will. When we see ourselves as the predominant player and lose sight of where life is moving us, pushing us, stirring us, we live with too much ego, unable to appreciate the wonder and the vastness of life. Our fate and will do a dance. Sometimes my will is in the lead. At other times, I need to surrender to what is out of my control.

When we grow increasingly comfortable with the terrain of our inner landscape, we can understand how we meet life with our desires, dreams and gifts.

It helps to move beyond our fears of feeling disappointed and instead strive to recognize what we really desire from life. I like to think of life as a mysterious lover who is insulted when I withdraw myself. When we recognize what we want from life, it sets off a creative dynamic driven by longing, desire, satisfaction and disappointment. We can intensify this relationship with life by asking what it is that we are willing to give. We then can boldly cry out at the mystery that is life, "I'm here and I want to receive from you and give to you."

Attitudinal Values

Frankl wrote about three attitudinal values: compassion, a good sense of humor and gratitude. According to him, these values may be the most creative way to approach suffering.

More than any other human experience, suffering has the power to evoke a deep sense of victimization. It easily brings us feelings of helplessness and hopelessness, the foundation of feeling victimized. Even so, I am not suggesting we should avoid feeling helpless and hopeless or pretend it is not being experienced. No, both feelings are essential to the human condition.

It is how we carry our feelings of helplessness and hopelessness that is key to creating meaning during times of pain and agony. Carrying our helplessness with compassion can go a long way toward creating meaning and personal power.

During the first ten years of life with my daughter Sarah, I saw myself as a victim of her disability, struggling daily with feelings of helplessness, which thrust me to the depths of victimization. I had two options: provide direct care for Sarah or work in order to generate funding for her care. I found myself living in a constant crisis of freedom where my choice to pursue

personal interests and support my marriage would be under the
enormous strain of attending to Sarah.

I was lost. I allowed myself the comfort of indulging in
large amounts of Canadian whiskey as I attempted to anesthetize my condition. In a drunken stupor I wandered about the
neighborhood, swearing at God for having condemned me to
such bondage. I continued to protest my servitude for ten years.

One morning shortly after Sarah's tenth birthday, I was
feeding her oatmeal for breakfast when my brokenness hit a low
point. As the oatmeal dribbled out of the side of her mouth onto
the shirt that I just put on her, I heard the horn blowing from
the bus arriving to take Sarah to her special needs program. I
quickened my pace, causing Sarah to cough, projecting oatmeal
everywhere.

I yelled and then started to weep. I had descended into the
depths of helplessness and despair. But, I began to detach from
the horn blowing in the driveway by the weight of my own powerlessness. Gradually, my tears turned to laughter as I reacted to
the absurdity of the both of us being covered in cereal.

Sarah very seldom offered sustained eye contact, but for
some reason, once my laughter subsided, our eyes met with
the gaze of two old friends who had been away from one
another much too long. I quickly became overwhelmed. A
sense of knowing washed over me like water from a water-
fall. I had been convinced that Sarah and I were radically
different people. I was articulate, intelligent, agile and powerful, while Sarah was non-verbal, uncoordinated and vulnerable. In those oatmeal moments I began to find the Sarah
part of myself.

When I finally brought Sarah out to the waiting van, the

driver said, "Good morning Sarah, you're looking as beautiful as ever. I wish I could say as much for your father." The oatmeal was stuck on my shirt and matted to my hair.

"Well, you know, Sarah and I had one of our oatmeal fights," I replied, and for some reason felt much less embarrassed than normal under those conditions.

"Don't tell me Mr. D. Sarah obviously won." The driver and I both chuckled, and I thought about how right she was. Sarah did win and I had benefited immensely from my loss.

I had spent my life until then pretending there was nothing like Sarah in me. I had no compassion for what was weak and sensitive. I had treated my fragility with disdain, not realizing that I was my own victim. At that breakfast, Sarah pointed out that it was time to learn how to create more compassion for her and also for myself so I might make some peace with my humanity.

Hopelessness has its place in the human experience, but in order to prevent it from placing us in the shackles of victimization, we must limit the time in which we live in the future. Whenever I would think of Sarah not being able to date, not creating a significant relationship, not pursuing a vocation and not participating in all those typical coming of age experiences, I would plunge into the depths of hopelessness.

Being Sarah's father taught me to live in the present, not because I thought it was the spiritually appropriate thing to do, but because it was too painful not to. I began to embrace a disciplined focus upon today, doing what was needed to let go of tomorrow. Some days I was better than others at living close to the moment and resisting the temptation to leap into the future.

I began to realize I was learning about suffering and how

we are all destined to suffer, to some degree, all of our lives. When I stepped out of victimization and stopped protesting my suffering, I was able to attribute a deeper meaning to it that extended beyond the idea that it was unfortunate. Regularly confronted by my limits, I saw that suffering can teach humility. I could complain about living with the constraints of having a fully-disabled child at home or I could learn to accept my confines and be the recipient of the learning such acceptance yields. I did both. Suffering often disrupts naiveté, enabling us to access profound lessons about who we are and what life may be about. We can make significant gains towards maturity when we are willing to see our suffering as a *proper time* for curiosity, discovery and accessing support.

Frankl reminds us that gratitude is important. With this in mind, there are essentially three fundamental attitudes we can take toward life.

We can see life as doing us no favors; it's the "life is a bitch and then you die" perspective. Obviously, it's a severe victim's orientation toward life. An example would be telling a lover, "You're always mean to me. I hate being with you and I only stay because the alternative of being alone is more unacceptable."

Another attitude towards life is commonly characterized by indifference and stoicism. It is a neutral message that might sound like this, "You don't move me one way or the other. I'm indifferent to who you are or what you want to give me." This is a long way from being an enthusiastic confirmation of a vital and meaningful relationship.

The third attitude can be described by the Greek notion of *kairos*, translated as the "favorable moment." Believing we are either in a favorable moment or that one is forthcoming is an important message to send to a loved one. It also applies to life itself. It might sound something like this, "I am not naive to the challenges of our relationship, yet I see how much opportunity you bring."

Even as I write these words I have been given a favorable moment, sitting in front of a large picture window. The gift of vision allows me to see the pink buds on the dogwood tree and a robin hoping from limb to limb. I can hear a myriad of birds chirping, Copeland's *Appalachian Spring* is playing in the background and I feel a cool breeze.

The *kairos* attitude enriches our relationship to life. As long as we are alive we face the existential necessity of having some kind of relationship to life, one as a victim, one based upon indifference or one guided by the attitude of *kairos*. Only through death can we escape the responsibility of not creating a relationship to our circumstances. The beginnings of personal power might lie in the awareness that it is a quagmire knowing that we must have a relationship to life, and needing to choose the connection we will create. The *kairos* attitude moves us out of the infantile reaction that we are never given enough. Wouldn't it be great to die believing we both received and gave a lot!

Simplicity can be a great resource in developing receptivity to favorable moments in life. The only favor we can truly acknowledge is the gift of breath we possess in that moment. The *kairos* attitude is not about adopting a positive mental outlook, which has the potential to help us deny the hidden perils and the unpredictability of life. It's about a longing to have an intimate relationship with life where we accept the darkness while championing gratitude as a way to strengthening our connection to the adventure of living.

Transcendent Values

I want to offer a fourth set of values aimed at interrupting victimization and adding to personal empowerment. This approach to de-victimization moves us to an even more profound relationship with life by asking the question: What is life asking of me? A willingness to live with this sort of curiosity lifts us toward a reverence for the gift of life. Living becomes a collaborative encounter, engaging our attention and pulling us away from indifference and cynicism.

Elizabeth, a forty-five-year-old mother of three, came to my office complaining of deep emptiness. She initially characterized the relationship with her husband as one of estrangement and loneliness. She constantly spoke of feeling hopeless and helpless to do anything meaningful about her marriage.

After several sessions, she began to speak about a man she knew. Elizabeth stressed that it was an emotional affair, not sexual, and so there wasn't anything wrong with it. Still, she insisted that it was important to keep it a secret from her husband.

When I asked about her secret love, she described him as married and wanting to remain married. She also described him as relatively detached, unwilling to reveal his true feelings. At that point my attention turned toward the relationship she had with her parents.

"My mom was great," said Elizabeth enthusiastically. "She was always there when we got home from school and was curious about who we were and what we needed."

"And your father, what was that relationship like?"

"Well, my dad wasn't around much and when he was, he was usually busy." She cast her eyes downward and her voice trailed off, almost becoming inaudible.

"It doesn't sound as if your father was very available."

"No, he wasn't, but my older brother was very caring." Elizabeth offered me numerous reasons why her fraternal relationship more than made up for her paternal loss.

"Elizabeth, I hear you received a great deal from your brother and that your father offered very little," I suggested. "I'm wondering what life is asking of you when we look at your experiences with your father, your husband and the other man in your life."

"I never thought about what life was asking of me. What do you think life is asking of me?"

"Well, if it were my story, I might want to notice that emotional deprivation was a common theme in each relationship. Maybe life is asking you to pay attention to the role of deprivation in your life."

"You're saying that following my relationship with my father, men came into my life and gave very little?" she said weeping. "But my brother gave me so much."

"Yes, your brother was very kind to you and it seems that you had hoped that your brother's kindness would redeem the losses you experienced with your father. Life may be asking you to take a closer look at your losses."

"I don't know what to do with them," she said. Her eyes widened and she tilted her head to one side.

"Grieve your losses. You're a woman experiencing death and loss, and life may be asking you to die well."

After some mild confusion and resistance to the idea that

she may be dying, she became receptive to introducing the need to grieve into her story, especially as it pertained to her relationships to men. Elizabeth began to see that the excessive loyalty she felt toward her father needed to expire, that her marriage was dying, that her relationship to the other man called for a death and that her attachment to deprivation needed to end.

She began to explore how victimized she felt by her husband and how her acceptance of deprivation kept her in that position. She continued to connect with her deprivation wound and allowed herself to grieve, which brought her clarity about her losses. She gained the ability to be autonomous and be clear about where she did not belong. She left her husband and broke up with the other man. She returned to school to study art and would regularly remind me what life might be asking of her, even when the response she heard was difficult to heed.

Death of the Inflated Heroic

We love our heroes, from rock stars, to professional athletes, to movie stars. We see their glamorous images and like to identify with them, believing that we too might live a supersized life. The danger is that we become inflated heroes, destined to become victims. These "heroes" attempt to vault themselves beyond the human condition, striving to reach special status. Life has a way of reminding us of our mortality and its accompanying limitations when we attempt to transcend our ordinary natures. The more we allow for the death of our inflated, mythic inclinations and let go of our exaggerated, heroic strivings, the more personal power we produce.

Accepting Limits

The inflated hero or heroine is inclined to either ignore limits or simply deny them. This precarious relationship with limits often leads us into being unnecessarily vulnerable, as we attempt feats outside of our control. The more we invest in excessive heroic posturing, the more confusion we generate about what is and is not in our control.

As we loosen our grip upon the exaggerated heroic, we provoke a curiosity about what actually lies in our control. The more discerning we become about our limits, the more we can begin to mature beyond our heroic inclinations. We are able to find the courage to exercise our will where it is appropriate and suspend willfulness in the face of our limitations.

It can be extremely challenging to let go of what is beyond our power and accept powerlessness. We often include in our definition of love acts that attempt to do for our beloved what we have no control over. This theme is very popular in comedy because it presents ridiculous situations with plenty of drama thrown in as well. When we resist accepting our powerlessness, our lives are inevitably engulfed in drama.

The inflated hero is commonly plagued by hubris. It is not unusual for very kind and caring folks to believe they can change the lives of others with enough benevolence and love. They are often horrified to discover how much of their most compassionate gestures are laced with arrogance and doomed to failure.

Letting go entails a willingness to accept ourselves as powerless. This can be extremely challenging if we postulate our self-worth upon our attempts at heroism. However, the more we undertake to do what is outside of our control, the more we find ourselves stuck with failure and with shame. We then begin the cycle again, seeing our heroic exertions as capable of restoring our personal value.

There are times when we move so far away from the inflated heroic that we fall prey to false modesty, understanding life to be mostly about the will of others as the fulfillment of our destiny. Our own will is sacrificed, draining our desire to meet our destiny.

Our challenge is to remain involved in a deeply creative process where we exercise our best understanding in order to both accept our limits while exercising our wills where appropriate. I like the Italian phrase, *Favorisce il destino grassetto*, which translates to "destiny favors the bold," which reminds us not to sacrifice boldness as we accept our limits.

Reducing Distortions

Releasing our need for excessive heroism gives us a less distorted view of ourselves and life. Okay, so we are no longer able to leap tall buildings with a single bound, but we can claim a more realistic perspective of who we are, making choices compatible with our strengths and weaknesses. From that vantage point, we can begin to know a power that was previously foreign.

The embellished heroic often possesses the burden of seeing life as something to fight with and conquer. Such an adversarial dynamic with life is a struggle that we cannot win.

When the hero in us is defeated, life leaves us feeling hopeless and cynical. We no longer imagine ourselves being the recipients of rich and joyous experiences. Again, we see how the heroic condemns us to victimhood.

In our mind, as the need to live as a hero diminishes, we

can craft an intimate relationship with life, one guided by what we want to receive and by what we want to give. Wonder, curiosity and gratitude take the place of a need to triumph. We can find our place; we can discover where we belong.

Leaving Sisyphus

In Greek mythology, Sisyphus is the king of Ephyra and a notorious scoundrel who regularly engages in a variety of deceitful acts. Finally, as punishment the gods condemn him to an eternity of rolling a boulder up a hill, only to watch it roll down again, forced to begin the task over and over again.

When we are driven by perfectionistic, heroic aspirations, our self-worth must be proven every day. We must either do enough or achieve enough to substantiate our value as human beings. As we step away from this overstated heroic, our personal worth becomes more an expression of who we are, rather that what we achieve.

This distinction is probably best understood in regard to loving a friend. We don't love our friends because of their accomplishments. We love them because of the values and beliefs they hold, because of the love and support they provide and because of the faith they have in us. We love aspects of their essential character. When we are no longer forced to defend the heroic, and allow it to die, we can simply walk away from Sisyphus's boulder, no longer condemned to daily prove that we are good people.

From One to Some

Puffed-up heroes are often driven by a compulsive self-reliance, which prevents them from understanding the role of viable support. They typically understand themselves as able to offer help but have little understanding of the significance of receiving it. This determination to go it alone often leaves them isolated, overwhelmed and victimized by some life challenge, which they simply cannot address alone. It often takes enough pain for inflated heroes to loosen their hold upon a demanding need for independence.

We find liberation from victimization when we become the sort of hero who remains committed to honor his or her humanity, not striving to attain god-like stature. We learn to identify our needs for help, who it is in our life that can actually be helpful and to have the humility to make the request. We can support our dual needs for belonging as well as autonomy as we learn to collaborate and co-create. The act of receiving support is quite often the cornerstone of heroic healing, as we come to understand what constitutes a necessary sacrifice rather than a bombastic display of some alleged gallantry.

A Sacred Reference Point

It can be very difficult to gain clarity about authentic personal power in an extroverted culture. We are constantly directed outside of ourselves for sources of power. We are encouraged to focus our attention upon people, places and things we actually have little control over. There's nothing inherently wrong with wealth, fame, political leverage, the admiration of others, social status or professional success. But, personal empowerment can't be measured by social success.

The sacred reference point for power lies within us. The relationship we are cultivating with ourselves is the only real axis of genuine power. We live close to this axis when we grow compassion for others and ourselves, when we create a conscious and accepting connection with our emotions, when we remain self-examining, when we remain committed to knowing and manifesting our desire, when we continue to clarify our values, when we act with integrity and when we employ effective boundaries.

Sometimes our quest for empowerment requires that we decide whether or not there is something we need to prove. This concept, which I call "arena empowerment," could occur in a myriad of ways. We may need to demonstrate that we are intelligent, can make money, achieve some academic standing, run for political office and win or run a marathon.

There are several keys to engaging in arena empowerment. The first is to be very clear about what needs to be proved. The second is to identify how we will know whether or not the achievement has actually been accomplished. The third is to decide when the mission begins and when it will end. If we are unclear about any of these aspects, we could spend a lifetime attempting to illustrate our value as persons.

Some time back, CBS News profiled Ted Turner, one of the country's most successful entrepreneurs and a man once identified as the nation's largest private landowner. During the interview, Turner acknowledged that his father had been an alcoholic who demanded business success from his son and that at the age of seventy, he was still attempting to demonstrate business mastery to his long-dead father. He went on to explain how uncomfortable it was for him to be alone, haunted by inner demons, how three marriages had dissolved and how he spent most of his life estranged from his five children. This man had long over-stayed his time in the arena. I found myself saddened and angered by a culture's encouragement that such a man be viewed as powerful, and yet unable to have a relationship with himself and those he loves. We love our gladiators, whether they are competing on fields or Wall Street.

We can properly ask ourselves if we have sacrificed a relationship with ourselves for a temporary feeling of potency. When we become confused about the source of authentic personal power, we can simply ask ourselves from where our energies come. Is it outside or inside?

If we look at personal power as the ability to consciously reinforce our needs for autonomy and belonging, in its absence we inevitably become confused and frustrated, leaving us prone to acts of abuse and abdication of power. Personal power is fundamentally an inside job. We must stay focused upon growing some aspect of ourselves.

Now we turn to the role of healing in the maturation process and what it means to step into a *proper time* for our healing and to remain devoted to whom we are meant to be.

6

Time for Healing

Life is trouble. Only in death is there no trouble.

—Nikos Kazantzakis in *Zorba the Greek*

To emerge from the womb and be raised in a family is to move into and around trouble. We are immediately challenged to decide what all this trouble means for us. Life's struggles are inevitable, but we can think of this suffering as our essential wounding. It is an injury that our culture would either prefer we ignore or else purchase some product to ameliorate our pain.

We have created a great gap between healing and maturity. In the effort to present ourselves as credible human beings, flawless and undamaged, we betray the complexity of our characters, relying on society to tell us our appropriate personality. We are left one dimensional, sacrificing the succor that flows from a conscious encounter with life's disturbances.

We may not want to see ourselves as wounded and instead hide behind a well-fashioned veneer, attempting to secure the admiration of others and soothe the tension that stretches between our denial and the injury. So often I've heard people say, "I don't want to talk about the past," which often translates into, "I don't want to talk about my wounds, and if I don't talk about them, I might be able to pretend they don't exist." Yet in some profound way when we wish our wounds into nonexistence, so do we condemn ourselves to an abbreviated life.

The Wound

In an attempt to avoid our own vulnerability, we might create an illusory split between the wounded and the well. We can conveniently position ourselves in the camp of the fit, hoping to avoid any stigma related to being wounded, which might suggest we are damaged goods—and undeserving. Of course, an old adage applies: What we resist will persist. Either we learn to greet the wound or the wound accosts us.

To be born into a family guarantees only two things: we will be gifted and we will be wounded. Most people seem comfortable focusing upon only one of these family dynamics, either the gifts received or the wounds inflicted. More often, the gifts are acknowledged while the injuries are ignored. Family gifts range from genetic predispositions to certain skills and talents, to role modeling that strengthens and, of course, the love and support that guide and nourish us. Irrespective of the trauma you may have received growing up, I can't urge you enough to know and appreciate the gifts you received from your family. I do not suggest valuing these familial gifts as a way to deny your wounds, but rather as a way to become open to a larger story about where you come from, as well as limiting your victim story. What does it mean, exactly, to be "wounded?"

Bumping into Something

One of the etymological roots of the word *wounded* means "to bump into something." From the moment of conception there are many things to bump into. Prenatally, each of us bumps into the biological and psychological circumstances of our mothers. How properly did they eat? Were they exposed to or did they ingest some form of toxic substance? How much stress did they live with during pregnancy? These are questions that might give some clarity to our prenatal wounding.

After we are born there is ample opportunity to bump into the wounds of others. In his book *Why Good People Do Bad Things*, James Hollis suggests that to be wounded is the result of either receiving too much or too little of something.

Bumping Into Too Much or Too Little

Once we emerge from the womb, we either encounter too much of what we need or too little, and then quite often, both forms of bumps occur. We can get too much attention, love or expectation, or too little. If we bump into too much, we can name the wound as emotional abuse, sexual abuse, physical abuse or parentification, in which case a child is expected to act like an adult. Wounds can occur to a child who witnesses a sibling being abused.

If we bump into too little, then the wound is one of abandonment, neglect or deprivation. Bumping into too little is like leaning against a rail that cannot hold our weight, allowing us to fall.

Often, within the same family, we bump into both. Bruce, a forty-five-year-old high school science teacher, was quite willing to tell his account of the emotional and physical abuse impelled upon him by his older brother. It wasn't until I asked how his parents handled his brother's acting-out, that Bruce understood that his parents abdicated their authority and did little or nothing to protect him from his brother's wrath. He began to see that not only was he wounded because of bumping into too much at the hands of his brother, but he was also injured by bumping into too little as represented by his parents' abdicating their responsibility to protect him.

Bumping Into Too Much Defense

The psyche or soul knows how to take care of itself when it comes to being wounded. We bump into too much or too little of something in childhood and quite often, there is no one with whom to share the suffering. We are alone, and yet need to find a way to attend to ourselves with only the limited resources available to us as children. The psyche has a fairly extensive repertoire of defenses it can employ to either protect the original wound or attempt to prevent us from being further wounded. One shelter of our psyche is to attach to the illusion that we can be fully alive while we live risk free.

As we've already seen, victimization, domination and distancing are predominant defenses. Victimization transmits the message, "I am no threat. I'm prepared to sacrifice myself in support of your wishes. Therefore, treat me well." We imagine that we successfully protect ourselves from some wound of abuse or neglect as we hopefully offer others good reason not to harm us. As we bump into this defense again and again, our lives slowly slip away until they are no longer our own. Our lives belong to others.

Domination carries the message, "I'll control you and push you away enough so that you won't re-wound me." As we have seen, domination not only distances us from others but ourselves as well. We become more and more emotionally— and painfully—isolated.

The idea conveyed by distancing is, "I'll remain out of your reach so you cannot re-wound me." This is isolating and usually leads to a deep sense of anonymity. We endure the pain of being invisible to ourselves and to others.

Looking Good

Looking good is another common way of attempting to protect our wounds. We believe that if we project good looks, people will admire us and be charmed by us. Their favorable impressions will protect us. Yet, the more effective we are at looking good, the more people relate only to our alluring veneer and the more isolated we remain. We bump into emptiness, loneliness and a riveting sense of being cut off. Of course, the ultimate danger is that we come to believe that *this* is all there is to us. Life loses its meaning; we neither feel known nor loved.

Judith, a forty-year-old housewife, came to her first appointment offering an account of her days filled with despair and hopelessness. She explained how she often considered crashing her vehicle into the large boulder sitting along the sharp turn in the road near her home. Despite this, Judith had a deep commitment to the beautiful life: beautiful home, car, husband and beautiful body. It took her an hour to prepare for a trip to the local convenience store, gathering the proper plumage that included makeup, jewelry and attire she felt was fitting for such an outing. Judith was as she appeared. She accepted that the constitution of her identity was the result of a myriad of accolades elicited by her meticulous presentations.

Judith was lost in her daily exhibitions. Her defense was aimed at protecting a wound of neglect created by a mother overwhelmed by her care for six other children and a father absorbed by his work. She struggled to protect the child she once was, who believed she was deprived because she was undeserving of attention and care. A defense that once offered her some semblance of feeling good about her self had evolved. Now she walled herself off from others and from herself. She was hurting herself deeply, continuously bumping into her attachment to an attractive appearance.

It was arduous work for Judith to confront her childhood belief that she should create as little disturbance as possible in order to support a mother who felt continuously overwhelmed. Creating a favorable impression helped her acquire some of the attention she longed for. Once she was able to loosen her grip on her need to look good, she addressed the losses of having bumped into neglect in her childhood.

Addiction

Addiction is a powerful defense as it not only numbs the pain of an earlier wound, but can also create euphoric illusions of contentment and grandiosity. An addiction is an intensely habitual relationship with a substance, a person or some experience that increasingly calls us away from ourselves—our emotions, our ability for critical thinking and creative decision-making. Addicts live separated from their wounds and separated from themselves. It is not surprising that addiction is commonly accompanied by denial. Who in their right mind would be willing to let go of such a salve and drop into the suffering of an open wound?

It is not until we bump into the addiction again and again that we might be willing to surrender to its pain and its power.

There is a double-sided challenge with addiction. On the one hand it is important to directly address the addiction without asking many analytical questions about its cause. However, recovering addicts are often quite willing to identify their addiction as the only wound, never treating it as a defense of another injury. They never develop the story of their original wounding.

Shame

Shame is another powerful form of protection. It shields us against personal accountability and personal change. Shame is quite insidious and can be effectively employed without being named or understood. It often travels by an alias, "low self-esteem."

Mitch was a fifty-two-year-old man who had relocated from Detroit. A plumber by trade, Mitch made it clear in our first few sessions that he had been actively pursuing psychotherapy and had experience with a variety of different personal growth endeavors. As we progressed, Mitch identified ways he wanted to enlarge his life, but he would constantly pull up short and say, "If I consider going there, I would be completely overwhelmed in shame," as his chin raised and his voice deepened with an uncanny sense of satisfaction.

Indeed, Mitch ended all of his stories with some reference to shame, which had become a dear ally in his attempt to protect some core wound. He seemed insulated from this until I finally suggested that the narrative of his wound might be larger than shame. Mitch slowly loosened his grip on shame and cautiously allowed himself to move closer to the trauma and fear he experienced at the age of ten when his mother died. Mitch gradually added to his wound story the need to limit his life experience; this shame helped him not to betray his dead mother by living too much. Arguing against life placed him closer to the mother who died.

Anxiety and Depression

Anxiety and depression are widespread forms of protection and bumping into them can be extremely damaging even while we use them to defend against some other wounding. Unfortunately, they are often identified as the essential wound, with pharmaceutical companies offering a variety of medicinal antidotes.

Depression offers an effectual numbing of pain and often a lethargy that excuses us from taking full responsibility for our lives. Reactive depression, a response to a specific stressful event, can protect us from feeling swamped by intense grief due to trauma or loss. On the other hand, intra-psychic depression is a way of refusing to live life with some part of us sitting in abeyance waiting to be claimed. A narrative of depression needs to include an account of a fear of facing our lives. By its nature, depression has an affiliation with death. We may have a fear of experiencing more loss if we live more fully and more empowered.

Our story can be further developed by several key questions: Where and how did I learn to fear life? What is it about life that frightens me? What is it about life that angers me? What do I resist accepting about life? Am I willing to continue to make peace with life and if I do, how can I go about the peace-making process? Who in me needs to be reclaimed in order for me to live life on life's terms?

Anxiety agitates and arouses energy, vibrating us away from the suffering associated with our wounding. Anxious worrying carries an illusion of control as we obsess over some anticipated crisis in the name of making sure that we are neither shocked nor surprised. We prefer to worry rather than feel powerless over some anticipated event. Excessive anxiety can be a way of avoiding anger and rage.

Anxiety can be seen as an effort to come into alignment with life by attempting to quell our fear of death, magnifying our concerns, and reminding ourselves we are fully alive, vibrantly vigilant. We can ask similar questions about our death fear: Where and how did I learn to fear death? What is it about death that frightens me? What angers me about the inevitability of my death? How can I more fully accept my anger? How can I continue to make peace with death?

Anxiety can also be the psyche's way of getting our attention. It may announce the presence of some wounded part of us that is seeking acceptance and integration. Hence, anxiety may be a significant *proper time* for reclaiming parts of us we need in order to mature.

Functioning creatively with anxiety and depression calls for a willingness to visit the original wound. Our receptivity is strengthened as we build the narrative of our depression and anxiety and allow the story of our wounding to unfold.

Intellectualization

We can significantly hurt ourselves by becoming excessively top heavy. Translating our experiences into cerebral musing, we might believe we can avoid the heartbreak and belly ache that inevitably occurs if we allow ourselves to be touched by the story of our emotions. We can trick ourselves into believing we can avoid our original wounding or any further wounding by translating our experience into a network of interconnecting concepts.

However, the very opposite is true. We can hurt ourselves by inflating our lives with excessive air, forcing us further and further from the fire of our desire and the water of our emotions.

We might say that we dry up when we push ourselves to the edges of our experience, moving further and further away from the river of life. We lose the capacity for involvement, to be touched and able to embrace our physical existence that allows us to live with a sensual fullness. We take up residence in some marginalized position, taking solace in the maintenance of our public posture. Our hope is to gain distance from our wound as we gain distance from life. We seek the sanctuary of knowing life and maybe knowing ourselves without having to live life or be ourselves. Like other defenses, intellectualization can hurt us deeply.

Idealization

Wouldn't it be wonderful to create a world where there is no bumping, where the goodness of life is as close as a couple of clicks of the ruby slippers or the ruby cerebellum? That is what idealization does. Rushing toward the ideal is a refusal to live life on life's terms. We say to life, "I just know that it all can be better than what you're presenting to me."

Reality for idealizers can be experienced as mostly unfortunate. We can organize our lives by attempting to avoid life and all of its bumps. We give ourselves permission to refrain from conflict, commitment, integrity, accountability and many other aspects of real life as we immerse ourselves into a longing for purified states of being. With the belief that we can escape the reality of the wound, we can ruminate upon how things could be. Idealization tends to spur self-righteousness and a life unlived.

Denial

We all engage in denial on some level. We protect ourselves by simply disavowing any suggestion of our wound. We can pretend that any emotion, attitude or shortcoming doesn't exist and can be easily renounced. We slip into the delusion that as long as we don't acknowledge the wound, the wound doesn't exist. Of course, similar to any injury, the more it is ignored, the greater is the eventual upheaval.

Dissociation

Dissociation commonly accompanies denial and allows us to separate our sensual body from our emotions. It is aimed at insulating us from painful emotion. In her book *Trauma and Recovery*, Judith Herman reminds us that dissociation, like any defense, can become as challenging to deal with as the actual, original wound. "The extensive recourse to dissociative defenses may end up aggravating the abused child's dysphoric emotional state, for the dissociative process sometimes goes too far. Instead of procuring a protective feeling of detachment, it may lead to a sense of complete disconnection from others and disintegration of the self."

We have seen some of the ways the psyche marshals its defenses in an attempt to protect itself against further wounding. Unless some life situation or individual informs us that it may be a *proper time* to examine our defenses, it is likely we will remain oblivious to how we guard ourselves. We can easily live our entire lives paying an exorbitant price for our protection.

Resistance

Instead of examining our defenses, the typical response is resistance. One etymological root of the word *resistance* is "to pause, stand still and fight back." What could be more appropriate when someone challenges our defenses, but to pause, stand still or fight back?

We are wired so as to prevent any further wounding. Even if we do not possess any real understanding of our initial injury, we are ready to engage in flight—pausing and standing still—or to fight when someone tampers with our defenses.

The greater the act of bumping into abuse or neglect, the greater the trauma and need to entrench ourselves in our defense system. Judith Herman refers to violations that go beyond the psyche's ability to support autonomy and a need to belong as chronic trauma. Under these conditions an elaborate set of defenses is erected in an attempt to prevent further injury. Herman explains:

> These three major forms of adaptation—the elaboration of disassociative defenses, the development of a fragmented identity, and the pathological regulation of emotional states—permit the child to survive in an environment of chronic abuse…Her desperate longing for nurturance and care makes it difficult to establish safe and appropriate boundaries with others. Her tendency to denigrate herself and to idealize those to whom she becomes attached further clouds her judgment. Her empathic attunement to the wishes of others and her automatic, often unconscious habits of obedience also make her vulnerable to anyone in a position of power or authority. Her disassociative defensive style makes it

difficult for her to form conscious and accurate assess-
ments of danger. And her wish to relive the dangerous
situation and make it come out right may lead her into
reenactments of the abuse.

Any healing that might happen occurs when we slowly
and methodically dismantle primitive defenses and replace
them with creative safeguards, providing security as well as a
chance to live fully. We must be active in the healing process,
even when a healer, tampering with our defenses, causes us to
pause, stand still and fight back.

One way we can cope with our resistance is to employ the
"risk manager," a central aspect of Cliff Barry's psycho-dramat-
ic model called *Shadow Work*. The risk manager is the part of
ourselves that acts as a protector and defender, alerting us to
danger or potential harm. When we make exchanges with our
risk manager, we will be focusing on the protection provided
by our risk manager, generating some appreciation for the support provided and offering a discerning assessment of the risk
in question. Dialogues with the risk manager can be very helpful toward clarifying our defenses and being more intentional
about which risks we are willing to take.

Much of what it means to heal involves responding to the
proper time to evaluate the nature of our defenses, appreciating
how they took care of us in the past, acknowledging the price
we may be paying for employing them currently and exploring
our resistance to loosening our grip on defenses that have outlived their usefulness. As consciousness of old defenses rises,
opportunities to employ more creative forms of protection take
their place.

Here, we can see the payoff of learning about employing

effective boundaries. Knowledge of good boundaries prepares us for the *proper time* for further deepening. As we strengthen our use of semi-permeable boundaries, we can risk letting go of old defenses that limited our vision, constricted our capacity to give and receive love, diminished personal empowerment and likely even abated our ability to love ourselves.

Constructive boundaries provide security while allowing us to think and act expansively. We become willing to take risks that old defenses would have likely prevented. We exercise greater curiosity, daring to venture down paths previously labeled taboo. We become allies to our own evolution, scared but not paralyzed by the vicissitudes of life.

In their exuberance to protect, old defenses inevitably confuse *feeling* vulnerable with *being* vulnerable. Good boundaries offer an opportunity to discriminate between the two. We can capitalize on the *proper time* to understand being vulnerable as the experience of an actual threat to our physical or emotional well-being. A truck bearing down on us as we cross a street is being physically vulnerable. Hearing a significant other declare an intention to leave us is being emotionally vulnerable.

Telling a friend we are angry may be an example of feeling vulnerable or hearing someone hold us accountable for breaking an agreement may be another such situation. When we are being vulnerable there is an actual loss and when we feel vulnerable, there is no tangible loss but rather feelings of fear and helplessness.

Confusing the experience of feeling vulnerable with being vulnerable easily ignites the need for excessive employment of defenses and tenacious resistance. When we believe all incidents of vulnerability involve some actual threat or violation, we likely remain hyper-alert and vigilant, unwilling to become curious, exploratory and open to new possibilities.

It takes some earnest personal psychological work to become more discerning regarding these two different expressions of vulnerability. It is only too easy to define an ordeal that has the potential to hurt our pride as holding the power to leave us vulnerable. However, if we examined the situation more closely, we probably wouldn't see hurt pride as constituting a legitimate tangible loss. The more we allow ourselves to respond to *proper times* for understanding our emotional lives (i.e. what we are feeling and why, the difference between a feeling and a thought and how to be responsible for our feelings), the easier it is to discern between *being* vulnerable and *feeling* vulnerable. Again, one of the payoffs for such discernment is we do not need to be overly defended, when we can see we are simply feeling vulnerable with no threat to our safety or impending loss.

Feeling Vulnerable

It will be extremely difficult to maximize *proper times* to learn about freedom, power, love, wellness, intimacy, introspection and other lessons contributing to our expansiveness if we are unwilling to learn how to feel vulnerable. Typically, primitive defenses have beliefs attached to them that offer meaning and stability. Expansiveness happens as we allow ourselves to separate from these beliefs, leaving us feeling vulnerable.

To advance our ability to feel vulnerable, it is particularly helpful to get support from people who are also learning how to feel vulnerable. They can acknowledge the task at hand, remind us we are not alone and encourage us to

separate from old constricting beliefs. Then, if we can act
with integrity, our choices are integrated with our beliefs and
values. Our actions reflect what we truly believe. There is
solace in feeling vulnerable when we know that some risk
we are taking reflects a commitment to retain integrity. Here
again, we see the critical role of good boundaries. They help
us from either being unnecessarily assailed by others or falling prey to a need for approval, either of which could easily
derail our attempts to live with integrity.

It is misleading to suggest that feeling vulnerable doesn't involve some level of tension and discomfort. It is inevitably a gamble
to let go of the familiar and venture into unknown territory. There
are risks of failure, feeling disappointed, getting lost and being
overwhelmed. Healing requires vulnerability. We let go of old defenses, heading toward a rendezvous with our original wounding
in order to access the medicine suitable for our suffering.

The capacity to address suffering is, for most men, a very
illusive undertaking. The cultural mandate goes something like
this, "Real men are not wounded and if you are, get over it!"

The result is that men are unable to own their early injuries, address their defenses and move beyond the companion
psychological contractions. Society condemns men to suffer in
silence. However, the typical American male lives without com-
plaint, and instead passes on a legacy of anguish and denial.

It is important for young men to find older men with
courage, who have rebelled against the cultural sanction to
deny their wounds and live without the appropriate medicine.
Let these men offer a map which describes what it means to
descend into the terrain of the wound. The following is a poem
written by one such elder:

The Words of the Lesson

O ye men, hear me now...
These are the words of the lesson.
I am a man. I am a wounded man.
Oh God... I am a deeply wounded man.

And in my fear, my pain and my fatigue, I have covered
my wounds with a blanket of lies and illusions...
For I would feel them no more...
For I would look upon them not again.

And these are the words of the lesson.
I am a man. And when I would reach out to men,
When I would walk among them and give them my love,
And take their loving for me...
My wounds rise up between me and them and turn me
back against myself...
For I am he who torments me.

I am a man. And when I reach out to that powerful
(woman) lover,
That the two of us might come together and go to that
place where no one goes alone, my wounds rise up between me and (her) the other and turn me back against
myself...
For I am he who torments me.
No more! God damn your eyes, no more.

And these are the words of the lesson.
I shall rip the blanket of lies and illusions and pull it back!
I shall go down into the darkness and fight for my right to
decide!
I shall fight for my right to live!

And I shall puncture a hole in that blanket of lies and
illusions.
And I shall take me a soft hand and go down into the

shadow among my wounds,

and I will rub the salve of compassion and understanding
into those old wounds, that they might have a moment to
heal, that they might have a moment to close...
And surely I will do this...
For I am he who cares for me.

And these are the words of the lesson.
I am a man. And I shall own my wounds and all the power
therein,
And I shall reach out to men and walk among them.
I shall give them my loving and take their loving for me...
And surely I will do this...
For I am he who cares for me.

And I am a man. And I shall take up my wounds and all
the power therein,
And I shall make a safe place for my children to tarry.
I will hear them speak of dreams and loving, that they
might have but a few safe moments, before they go out
alone...
And surely I will do this...
For I am he who cares for me.

And I am a man. And I shall take up my wounds and all
the power therein,
And I shall reach out to that powerful (woman) lover,
And I shall share with (her) the other, my wounds
And I shall give (her) the other to drink deeply of all the
power and passion therein, and I shall hear (her) the
other's wounds and I shall take those for mine own; we
shall come together and with our power, we will go where
no one goes alone, the two of us...
And surely I will do this...
For I am he who cares for me.

And these are the words of the lesson.
I am a man. I am a wounded man.
Oh God, I am a deeply wounded man.
I own my wounds and all the power therein belongs to me,
to do as I wish, to do my bidding.
And the world shall yet be moved, and men's lives shall yet
be touched, by the power of my loving, the power of my
wounds.
And surely I will do this…
For I am he who cares for me.

—Spoken in the oral tradition,
by New Warrior, Elder Bruce Wolf Boehiem

The Medicine

The Greek translation for the word *pathology* is "a suffering of the soul." We can ask, "What is the medicine necessary for a suffering soul?"

As C.J. Jung says in *Memories, Dreams, Reflections*:

Clinical diagnoses are important, since they give the doctor a certain orientation; but they do not help the patient. The crucial thing is the story. For it alone shows the human background and the human suffering, and only at that point can the doctor's therapy begin to operate.

From the Latin, the word *medicine* translates into "to embellish" and so, one way we can understand healing as taking place when we embellish the narrative of our wounds. As Jung explains, the story reveals the human background and the human suffering; and as they are amplified and elaborated, opportunity for healing takes place. Both the content and perspective of the story begin to shift.

We can start to understand how our defense obstructs a fuller understanding and offering of compassion for our injury. Deconstructing our defense allows for the possibility of loss and grief accompanying our wounds. Loss is an inevitable aspect of bumping into too much or too little.

The embellishment of the story can then include themes of what we need now and what was absent in our lives. We can identify what must be learned, developing a benevolent, inner psychological parent to replace our actual parents. The skills of this internal parent will include the ability to employ effective boundaries, and offer encouragement, nurturance and discipline.

Finally, the narrative of our injury will be adequately embellished to include the gift of the wound. This becomes a critical consideration in the story of the wound to see the affliction as not simply unfortunate, casting us into the unyielding grip of victimhood.

As we shall see, we can include a depiction of the wound as contributing to the building of a unique character.

I would suggest there are three medicinal elixirs that can greatly increase the creative energies of embellishing the narrative of our afflictions. When each elixir is poured into the vessel of psychotherapy (Greek translation: "nursing the soul"), and slowly mixed together, they are transformed into a healing potion.

The First Elixir

Healers are potentially a very valuable resource for mentoring a *proper time* for learning and healing. Hence, the presence of an authentic healer constitutes the first elixir. It is often easy to be seduced by charm and charisma, both of which have nothing to do with healing. It behooves us to get clear about the nature of the genuine healer.

One characteristic of authentic healers is that they see the power to heal as lying within the person who seeks the healing. This can be extremely powerful for those seeking to tend to their wounds, since they get the opportunity to concentrate healing forces within themselves. The task of the healer is to help people discover the medicine carried within. It can be humbling for healers to acknowledge they do not possess cosmic, therapeutic powers, but rather an aptitude for guiding people toward their own healing.

Healers must balance between two polarities of acceptance and confrontation. On the one hand, acceptance of our wounds is critical so we might anchor our strength to create and heal within ourselves. Excessive acceptance morphs into an act of complicity whereby the healer helps keep us immobilized within the status quo of our wound. And so confrontation allows the healer to actively participate in our evolution, avoiding tendencies to support inertia. However, a disproportionate confrontation on behalf of the healer suggests that the one seeking healing must adhere to the healer's schedule, disregarding the student's readiness and adeptness to move forward. With the rapport of the healing relationship, the healer needs to be prepared to push as well as honor the pace of the person being healed.

A second quality of authentic healers is they understand that the mastery of the healing process comes from their willingness to have a conscious, creative relationship with their

own wounds, which involves a process of continuous healing
and learning. They are willing to infuse the narrative of their
wound with compassion. They have learned how to let go of a
narrow and restricted story of their suffering that helped move
them out of a victim's position. They weave themes having more
heart, more soul and more vision, and open new perspectives
of suffering, humanity and life. The narratives of their wounds
take on a power, leading them beyond the limits of their own
personalities, offering luminosity to a fuller vision of the human condition and kindling sparks of wisdom. C.J. Jung suggested, "At the bottom of the soul, we find humanity."

The wounded healer understands suffering as not simply
unfortunate and in need of eradication, but rather as a major call
to self-examination and an opportunity to address some fractured
way of relating to the self. This attitude can be a significant offering to those seeking healing; or without it, they are likely condemned to an adversarial relationship with their own wounds.

In his book *Original Self*, Thomas Moore suggests that our
wounds offer us an opportunity to move closer to the basic stuff
of the soul:

> Our neuroses are the raw material out of which an inter-
> esting personality may be crafted. They are sometimes
> dangerous and debilitating but nonetheless valuable.
> They are the basic stuff of the soul in need of lifelong
> refinement. Working this annoying and embarrassing
> material for a lifetime is realistic work compared with
> the search for psychological hygiene—ridding our-
> selves of failure and confusion.

The genuine healer is not interested in psychological hy-
giene, but rather a realistic work that reveals the challenges,

legacies and longings of the soul. Such healers are not insensitive to someone's need for a respite from suffering, nor are they naïve about our capacity to transform and mature during our *proper times*. They appreciate that we have not evolved, but rather remain evolvers, either resisting or surrendering to the desire to become who we are meant to be.

The Second Elixir

The second elixir is composed of the relationship between the healer and those seeking healing. The relationship is the container where the healing and learning will take place. The healer must be invested in knowing the student. The Greek and Hebrew word for *knowing someone* also means "to have sexual relations with." We can understand sexual relations as a metaphor, suggesting that the healer desires to know the student.

If the relationship is imbued with eros, the student will experience a level of being chosen rather than an object being studied. Ancient alchemists believed that fire was the only ingredient needed in order to transform two elements into a compound. And so it is with a therapeutic relationship, transformation is made possible by the presence of fire or desire. The key is to have adequate boundaries that keep the work focused on the learning and healing edges of the student, rather than accommodate the healer's personal agenda.

If the rapport can be infused with trust then their collaborative efforts will likely be creative and generative. Trust is deepened when each believes he or she will be the recipient of the other's truth and compassion.

The healing relationship is a mentoring relationship, and

as such it requires that the mentor accept the mentee as he or she is, while holding a vision of who the mentee is meant to be. The healer needs to be perpetually self-correcting, holding compassion for a student when he is unable to do it for himself and when the student is strong enough, calling him to who he is meant to become. If the healer extends an inadequate degree of acceptance, the student is unable to affirm who he is and often becomes increasingly resistant to the healing process. If the healer offers too much acceptance, he may leave the student bewildered, secure in who he presently is but without clear expectations of who he will become and no firm understanding of where to direct his curiosity and exploration.

The healing relationship is infused with power when a healer commits to letting go of the heroic aspirations of rescuing and saving. Under the umbrella of such a pledge, a healer communicates that the power to heal truly lies within the student.

Truth-telling and good boundaries preserve the integrity of the healing relationship. Both mentor and mentee need to be committed to telling the truth, especially as it pertains to their relationship. Both individuals can make a periodic assessment of their relationship with the following questions: Do I feel supported here? Are we committed to the same purpose? Does the student genuinely want my help? Are we clear about what we want from one another? Is either of us angry at the other? Is our relationship remaining creative? Is our relationship deepening?

Besides supporting integrity, good boundaries provide clarity and identity to the healing relationship. The length of meetings, expectations of the mentee, remuneration expected by the mentor for services rendered, identification of unacceptable behaviors, and the extent and scope of interactions outside of scheduled meetings must all be determined.

The Third Elixir

The primary ingredient of the third elixir is the student's ability to learn, to create a conscious and compassionate relationship with his or her wounds. When the first two elixirs are in place, the medicine of this third elixir is more easily attained.

A healing relationship to our wounds depends upon a willingness to take back control of the emotions that accompany our defenses. If we are numb and dissociated, we need to learn how to track emotional energy in our bodies while creating safety. If we have overcompensated by amplifying one emotion in order to avoid another, we need to learn to calm ourselves down.

It is common for a family to designate at least one particular emotion as taboo, thus communicating that it is unacceptable to express that emotion or even shameful to do so. The more control and acceptance guide our relationship to our emotions, the more ready we are to craft the narrative of our wounds.

Naming the wound is a critical step toward weaving its story. Remember, being wounded meant bumping into something. We either bumped into too much or too little attention, expectation or love. If we received too much of one or more of these energies, the wound can be named an emotional, physical and/or a sexual abuse wound. Sometimes such abuse can be called a parentification wound when we are expected to leave childhood and act beyond our years. If we received too little love or attention then the narrative becomes about a wound of abandonment, neglect or deprivation.

Once the wound is named, we can begin to compose its narrative. There are a number of questions that bring meaning and depth to the story: How was I hurt in the story? Who hurt me? How do I feel about the person who hurt me? What relatives before me were hurt in a similar manner? What losses have I suffered in the story and am I ready to grieve those losses? What will it take for me to move out of a victim role in the story? Because of this wound, have I perpetrated hurt upon someone? What is this wound asking of me? What part of me in the story needs to be welcomed?

Probably the most compelling curiosity in the story is: What part of me do I need to welcome back into my identity? We typically survive the abuse or neglect of childhood by walling off the most injured parts of ourselves. The quality of care offered the soul will greatly depend upon the fervor of the welcome.

Jennifer, a forty-year-old single woman, entered her first session with me despondent and angry at herself for the way she handled her relationships with men.

"I'm a damn wimp! I let men dominate me, hurt me and forget about me! I can't believe I allow myself to be such a victim," she exclaimed with an exuberance aimed at making sure I understood the severity of her situation.

Her palpable anger was directed at herself. She understood that her wound had something to do with being a victim. I invited her to describe the nuances of her "wimp" story. She detailed her deference to the wishes of men, which seemed to project from her decision to comply in the wake of an older sister who acted out during childhood. Her story grew to include her mother who remained in a constant gridlock with her sibling and also with her confused and overwhelmed father.

For Jennifer, it was important not to be a screamer like her sister and mother. She began to understand that the theme of deprivation ran deep in her story with her preoccupied mother and floundering father. Neither offered the family direction and stability.

We focused upon the response of "Oh, okay," which she often said when a man broke a date or some agreement. I asked her if she knew the person who was constantly dealing with the lack of accountability of others by saying, "Oh, okay." With eyes cast down, her breathing becoming shallow, she said, "It's the ugly, fat ten-year-old."

It did not take long for Jennifer to figure out that the narrative of her deprivation wound needed a perpetrator, someone responsible for the deprivation. The question that would enrich Jennifer's story was, "How did the fat, ugly ten-year-old become responsible for her deprivation?"

Jennifer began to understand that the response of "Oh, okay" was the ten-year-old's way of surviving and loving her family through compliance. Her mother had no reserves left after dealing with her sister, and her father appeared disoriented. She concluded that the neglect she experienced directed any anger towards herself for being fat and ugly and undeserving of parental love and attention.

The narrative of her wound became a love story, a story of adaptation and survival, and a tale of self-induced victimization. Resistant at first, Jennifer gradually identified her ten-year-old as the one in need of welcoming and began to redirect her anger at her family members. She realized that she had the same expectation of men that she had held of her father, that they would be helpless and irresponsible.

Jennifer acquired a fresh sensibility that brought several new themes and a new direction to her wound narrative. The focus of her relationship to men became secondary as the fractured rapport between her adult self and her ten-year-old self became paramount. Jennifer's self-empowerment deepened as she grasped more fully who she was protecting and why. She saw that her deprivation wound was asking for the externalization of her anger and compassion for a ten-year-old girl.

As the ingredients of all three elixirs mingle, we participate in our own healing. We can never be completely healed. Instead the goal is to be fully active in the healing process as a realistic life's work. We can say that as the narrative of the wound is embellished, or amplified and beautified, relief is possible.

These stories of our suffering begin to take on a sublime motif and luminosity when they reflect the wonder and mystery of the human condition. What was originally characterized as misfortune begins to recede into the back pages of the story. Our narratives become seamlessly linked to loyalty, love, compassion, legacies and the inherent insecurity of life itself. The more depth and breadth we bring to our wound stories, the more able we are to see the gift of the wound.

The Wound's Gift

In a culture where to be wounded means anything but being a whole and complex person, it can be extremely difficult to see the gift the wound gives us. However, every wound bears some gift, and to become aware of the offering and its contribution to our lives vaults us out of victimization and strengthens our healing. From such a shift of view, our injury neither defines us as damaged goods nor does it call for some psychic repair. Rather, the robustness and rigor of our wound narratives allow us to carry the wound with more resiliency, revealing a strengthening of character.

Even at the age of seventy-eight and retired, Thomas remained active in business and politics. My client, Virgina, invited him to a session so that they might use the time to explore their relationship. Thomas immediately struck me as soft-spoken and hard of hearing, with eyes that sparkled and a manner that appeared eager to please.

We spent a few sessions focused upon his family's reaction to his relationship to Virginia. His adult children believed that their father's relationship with Virginia was inappropriate given the death of their mother three years earlier. They seemed to believe that their father should still be in mourning.

It became apparent to me that Thomas had not intentionally attended to any meaningful healing in his seventy-eight years. I began to ask about his life, its challenges and its blessings.

"I haven't talked much about the past. How far back should I go?" he asked, appearing somewhat embarrassed about the correct protocol of the setting.

"Well, let's start with your childhood," I suggested, thinking I would hear some of the more typical childhood agendas.

"I grew up in East Haven. I liked the neighborhood. Life was pretty much okay until the summer of 1939."

I noticed that his speech increasingly resonated from his throat. "I'd like to hear about that summer," I said.

"You know, both of my parents drank quite a bit. I would often find one of them passed out on the kitchen floor in the morning. Once I found my dad passed out on the front steps of the apartment. That was kind of embarrassing. You know what I mean?"

"Sure, I get just how embarrassing that would be, especially for a kid. Thomas, have you ever told this story before?" I asked. I wondered just how much and how long he had been inhibiting himself.

"Well, I did tell Virginia some bits and pieces. It's a story I've tried hard to forget." Thomas' jaw tightened and the boyish glow on his cheeks drained.

"I'm sure it's not an easy story to tell," I added, wanting him to gather some ease as he stepped into his story. "Take your time. There will be time later to cover whatever you don't address this evening."

"In a lot of ways, I'm very lucky."

I reassured him. "It sounds like life granted you a periodic reprieve from its challenges."

"You could say that. Things started to go downhill in June that summer. My father went on a drinking binge and we never saw him again."

"That's it, he never showed up?"

"Not until forty-five years later. He contacted me when I was fifty-five. He came to live with me. He was practically broke and homeless, and had leukemia. He died a year later. I guess he came back to die with me."

"What was that year like for you?"

"It was okay. He said he was sorry for having left me and my mother. I was glad he spent his final days with me."

"What about the rest of the summer of 1939? What was life like for you and your mother after your father left?"

"My mother told me that my father was probably not coming back. She would emphatically explain that our lives would be better without him. She said that it only meant that she would be working more and I would be spending more time alone, which was okay because I was old enough to handle it. She came home later and later, often after I had gone to bed. I knew it was hard on her to be working so much."

"I don't hear that she was able to provide you with any real parenting," I suggested, curious whether or not he could acknowledge that aspect of his story.

"No, she had her hands full, probably more than I realized. One morning in late August, I awoke and discovered she had not come home yet. I sat on the front step of the apartment all morning, well actually, all day."

I could imagine that the same confused look that Thomas now had on his face was likely there sixty-eight years ago while sitting on that step waiting for his mother.

"Did she come back before the end of the day?" I asked.

"Not exactly, I made a sandwich and went back to the steps of the apartment. I started to worry about her. We didn't have any family nearby and after my parents started drinking more, friends stopped coming around. I didn't know who to call for help. I decided to get a pillow and stay right there on the step for the night. I tried to stay awake but I fell asleep. The next morning the landlord woke me." His voice modulated back and forth from the tenor of a ten-year-old to that of a seventy-eight-year-old man.

"Did the landlord have any news about your mother?"

I found myself wishing for some positive outcome to his tale.

"No, he didn't know anything about my mom and asked

me what I intended to do. I wasn't sure what he meant. I just
wanted to be there when my mom came home, in case she
needed me. So I told him that I planned to stay right on that
step until she came home."

As he spoke, I noticed Virginia gently weeping, which
only momentarily distracted me from my own tears.

"How long did you wait for her on the step?"

"One more night; the landlord showed up early the next
morning. He told me that there was as shack out back with a
cart in it and that I could stay there. He knew my mom wasn't
coming back. But I wasn't ready to accept that."

The sound of false hope still echoed from his words. "Your
mother never returned," I offered, still wishing for a different
story line.

"My mother never returned," he repeated, dropping his
head in shame, suggesting that somehow he must not have been
worth the effort of returning.

"Thomas," I pointed out, "you've been blaming yourself
for your mother's abandonment."

"Who do you blame when you're ten? Certainly not your
mom," he assured me.

"How long did you stay in the shack?"

"About a year. I started back to school in the fall. That
was hard. The kids teased me because my clothes didn't fit. But
worse than that, they made fun of my mother. I found out that
she was the town hooker. Boy, that was a hard one to swallow!"
His shame was now conspicuous.

"That must have been extremely difficult for you to hear."

"Yeah, initially I thought they made it up just to harass
me. I told the landlord and he confirmed the rumors as true. I

wasn't sure what the town hooker was but I was convinced that it wasn't a good thing. When I finally discovered what it meant, I think it broke my heart."

"I imagine it would have. How did you eat and make it through the winter?"

"I ate dinner with the landlord and his wife. She was good to me. I didn't eat breakfast much and took leftovers from dinner for lunch. The landlord told a cop friend about my situation. The policeman came to visit me and introduced me to this guy who I later found out was in the Mob. This fellow got me a job at a neighboring amusement park. I really liked working there."

"You sound like you're still grateful for the assistance some of the adults were offering you," I suggested, clearly hearing how thankful he was.

"Oh yes! People were great to me! I mean I wasn't close to any of them; but the landlord, his wife, the cop and the guy from the Mob all didn't want anything bad to happen to me."

"Through the years, did you ever hear from your mother?"

"Yes. Years later I tracked her down, living in a retirement community in Florida for members of the Mob. When she left East Haven she went to Las Vegas and became a call girl. I didn't realize that the Mob took care of their people by supplying them with a retirement community. She lived there with a male companion."

"Did you get a chance talk with her?"

"Yes, I visited her in Florida. It was like two acquaintances whose paths briefly intersected years ago. We exchanged incidental information and I was glad when the visit was over."

"Thomas, that's a hell of a story and I appreciate your willingness to share it with me."

"Well, thanks for listening," he responded, without a note of anything artificial in his expression of appreciation.

Thomas and I had no difficulty identifying who needed to be extended a welcome. We were regularly joined by a sensitive, loving ten-year-old boy with a narrative of his abandonment. After living one year in the shack, he moved in with an aunt and uncle living some fifty miles way. He described them as being kind to him and after graduation from high school, he enlisted in the Navy. Following his discharge, he was married, had two daughters and started several successful businesses.

At first glance, it would be easy to decide that Thomas's wounding was simply deeply regrettable, that he had been a severe victim of destiny. And certainly, there is trauma in Thomas's story, especially his intense commitment to be adaptive in the hope of warding off any possible abandonment by a loved one. He increasingly appreciated the depth of his self-betrayal. However, his story also exemplifies the power of the wound to bear gifts.

Thomas lived with an uncanny sense of simplicity, without a presumptuous bone in his body. He carried a profound spirit of gratitude for all that life gave and continued to give, which was complimented by an abiding faith in the human condition. I kept expecting to hear some cynicism or bitterness expressed because of the trauma of his abandonment. At first, I was suspicious about his tremendous optimism and the zeal behind his buoyancy. He was a complicated man, excessively sweet but also deeply authentic. Even when he slowly removed his rose-colored glasses and accessed his anger and disgust, it did not replace his attitude of reassurance.

At ten years old, he had been betrayed, abandoned and basically stripped of the world as he knew it. We could say that life hurled him mercilessly into what the Hindu religion refers to as the highest level of spiritual development, that of the mendicant or beggar. On this path, all or most of one's worldly possessions are given up with an ensuing emptiness, making room in Thomas's case for a heartening perseverance and determination, as well as a profound measure of humility.

From the depths of his losses, he received the little that was given thankfully. Had the wound taught him about appreciation? Had his loss of control over his destiny helped him to live closer to the moment? Did the wound help him to avoid being excessively self-absorbed? Had his injury helped him to avoid the superfluous and live closer to what really mattered?

Thomas's story is to some degree unique, yet it captures the gifts common to all wounds. Wounds of abuse and violation often yield offerings of tenacity, fortitude, toughness, assertiveness, boldness, stoutheartedness, steadfastness and conviction. Wounds of neglect and deprivation often provide patience, self-reliance, tolerance, acceptance, understanding, empathy, compassion, responsiveness and dedication. The key is to find both the curses and the blessings in our own wounds.

It is important to remain vigilantly honest about how we relate to our wounds. The tendency is either to drift off into denial in order to avoid seeing ourselves as less than human due to our injury or make too big a deal about being wounded. It is critical to know where we are on the continuum between denial and aggrandizement. Moving away from denial, we create greater acceptance of our particular injury and a willingness to develop its story. Moving away from aggrandizement, we let go of a tendency to be a victim and see our wound as simply a necessary way to fully participate in the human condition. It may be as we understand our wound as both real and necessary, we discover its power to initiate us into deeper levels of character.

Wounding and Healing as Initiatory

It is common in many indigenous cultures for the initiate to experience some physical wounding as part of the initiation process. For example, legend has it that those female warriors, known as Amazons, underwent an initiation whereby the initiate was expected to remove a breast with a dagger. We don't have to lose body parts in order to experience a significant initiation. We can see these rites as a metaphor for our life experiences, specifically our wounding. Viewing our injuries as an initiation affords us the opportunity to avoid seeing ourselves as victims and hopefully prevent us from seeing life as an evil perpetrator.

We can view an initiation as happening in three stages: separation, trial and resolution. The word *initiation* means "something is starting or beginning," but as with all beginnings, something is also dying. This death occurs in the first, or separation, stage of an initiation.

Separation

Our wounding occurs in this first stage. Our injuries suggest some kind of loss, whereby we are losing a relationship, a belief, a thing or experience we deem valuable. For example, in the case of a broken heart, we may be separating from a person or a set of beliefs about relationship, as well as moving away from feelings of security and contentment to feelings of fear and grief. We may be also moving away from a circle of friends who supported our relationship. A wounding like a broken heart can involve numerous separations leading to a major initiation.

There are several characteristics to the separation stage that are important to note. The first is shock and disbelief that such a separation is actually taking place. The second is considerable fear. We wonder if we can live without whom or what we are separating from. What will replace the feelings of loss? How can we face the uncertainty of the future?

Separation leaves us feeling lost. As the wounding moves us away from either familiar people or beliefs, we experience ourselves as adrift, no longer clear about who we are or where we are going. Typically, a situation that offered stability and security has been forfeited.

In the separation there is usually a significant loss of faith. We easily see what is dying but find it almost impossible to summon enough faith to hold a vision of what will be born in its stead. It can be useful to name our experience as a crisis of faith as it tends to diminish the feeling of being overwhelmed.

One root in Greek of the word *crisis* means "to separate." We can say that any significant separation hurls us into a crisis that echoes our emergence from the womb. The French obstetrician Frederick Laboyer suggests that in birth, the fetus is experiencing more death than life, as it is leaving the safest place it will ever know. Similar to the fetus being pushed into the world, our separation feels like it announces our demise with no hope of new life.

It is common for a separation from old beliefs and values to significantly alter our perceptions of the world as well as where we belong. Spouses wake one morning not knowing who their partners really are and wondering what they are doing in bed with them.

I recently heard a fifty-two-year-old man report the following: "I was making my usual morning stop at Dunkin Donuts for coffee. As I stood five deep in line waiting to be served, the young man in front of me turned and said, 'You know, this Dunkin Donuts has two doors. Most only have one.' In that instant I didn't know where I was or what I was doing there. It was like I was a complete stranger and my surroundings transformed into a foreign land, where I knew neither the language nor the customs."

Clearly, a dramatic shift in beliefs and values occurred for this man. As the contours of his interior landscape reconfigured themselves, he was entering what Joseph Campbell called a special world. For most of us, the idea that we are headed for a special world seems absolutely absurd. We are more likely to seek comfort from someone who is eager to save us from our upheaval by suggesting that our wounding was simply an aberration and we would do ourselves a great service by putting it all behind us and getting on with life. Or we might turn to alcohol, drugs or pharmaceuticals, all aimed at anesthetizing the fear and tension produced by the separation. We can say that those choices typically indicate a resistance to allowing the initiation to work its power.

The Trial

Whenever we are being tested, we are likely to succumb to some of the temptations mentioned above. The trial is largely about the challenge of accepting our wounding and whether or not we are willing to carry our injury with compassion and mindfulness.

During the trial we will encounter enemies, forces dedicated to thwarting our attempts at reconciling with our wounds. Some of these adversaries will be people who are eager for us to disown our wounds in order for them to remain more easily in denial of their own injuries. However, the more worrisome nemesis dwells within. Fear, shame, pride and vanity will present us with very attractive arguments for abandoning the journey and returning to the common world of denial and delusion. Internal voices call us away from what is disorienting and uncomfortable, even when the journey is about healing, deepening and becoming who we are meant to be.

In the land of healing, we must follow a set of rules in order to make our way in the special world. Some of these rules might include:

- Stop blaming others.
- Take responsibility for your own life.
- Learn to feel, identify and voice your emotions.
- Be clear about what you want and ask for it.
- Come to know what is in your control and seek it.
- Be aware that your freedom and power will not be given to you; they must be taken.

You get right with yourself when you live with integrity and when your choices reflect what you truly believe and value.

A mentor is often particularly valuable in helping to distinguish the rules of the ordinary world with those of the special world. Besides new rules and the voices aimed at sabotaging our progress, there are puzzles and quandaries to be solved: Where is the appropriate medicine for the wound? Where can I access the help I need in order to bring a measure of healing to my wound? Am I willing to do whatever it takes to understand this wound and what it is asking of me? Who can effectively mentor me through this initiation? What is dying in me? What in me is asking for a fresh chance to live?

It is nearly impossible to navigate the waters of the trial stage without a mentor. However, it can be very seductive to encounter a mentor who is willing to steer us away from the demons that accompany any wound. These demons reflect all the fears we carry. We remain susceptible to any suggestion to avoid what's uncomfortable, allowing ourselves to be lured away from our deepest cuts. We may become bewitched by an image of how we want to see ourselves instead of a depiction of our ordinary, broken humanity, which fails to flatter a hungry ego.

Trials are aimed at teaching and strengthening, but quite often they incite fear, sending us running from parts of ourselves we don't dare welcome. They prepare us for the ultimate ordeal of our initiation, where we must confront our greatest fears. When we face this trial with clarity and courage, we create favorable circumstances for entering the third stage of the initiation, the resolution and return. We can come back to ourselves with more understanding and acceptance of who we are, allowing us to heal and make peace with ourselves and with life.

Resolution and Return

Finally, we can begin to inoculate the wound with needed medicine. When we are pushed to feel, think and act in different ways, and we allow these character-forging forces to continue to knead our psyches, we will receive the healing benefits of having made the journey. If we had turned back and not endured the ordeal, we would not have received the gifts inherent in the resolution and the blessings bestowed upon us when visiting the special world. In facing our wounds, we emerged with more understanding, peace, acceptance, and power.

The quest for healing is analogous to many traditional initiation rites that culminated with a vision quest. This final challenge involves the initiate being told to go off alone to a mountain top, desert or deep forest in order to face the ordeal of seeking a vision of their life's purpose. In the traditions of Native American tribes like the Lakota, the vision quest is preceded by a period of fasting in order to focus on the spiritual rather than the physical being. Then the initiate goes into the wilderness with only a supply of water and remains there for up to four days. During this time, he gets in touch with his soul and seeks spiritual guidance, hoping for visions that will direct him in the next stages of his life. Initiates participating in a vision quest are often instructed not to return until they have resolved their ordeal and gained clarity regarding their purpose. And so it is with many of us, we don't make it back to our authentic selves; instead we wander aimlessly with provisional personalities aimed at helping us survive.

Facing our fears and core wounds is a heroic endeavor, not one based upon fame and notoriety, but rather one aimed at deepening integrity. The resolution of our conflicted values, beliefs and intentions ultimately allows us to experience a greater recognition of who we are, and allows us to let go of the illusions we carry, and to accept that life is deeply mysterious and insecure. We pretend less, welcoming the parts of ourselves previously deemed inappropriate or unacceptable. We have found an authentic place to wait, ready to embark upon yet another initiation.

Relationships as Initiations

Robert and Deloris faced what I sometimes call a nuptial initiation, where the marriage becomes the container of the initiation. In their sixties and semi-retired, they had been married for thirty eight years and had four adult children and three grandchildren. Seven months before their first appointment with me, Deloris had found a note in their vehicle addressed to Robert, clearly from a lover. During those seven months they went in and out of denial regarding the nature of the betrayal and the implications for their marriage, until it became obvious to Deloris that she needed help.

"I don't know where to begin. We've had our ups and downs but I always trusted Robert. I never thought it would come to this. What would make a man, age sixty five, stray from his marriage?" exclaimed Deloris, her shock and disbelief still visible on her face.

"What do you understand about this relationship your husband had?" I asked, believing it important for Deloris to demystify the betrayal.

"Nothing! I know nothing! We're here because he won't talk to me about it!" Delores caught herself and lowered her voice, but not before her anger and frustration echoed through the office.

I made several attempts to solicit an account of the affair from Robert, but that only yielded a narrative about what it was like for him to serve as a consultant to the small manufacturing company where he had met the woman. He did not want to reveal anything about this relationship.

"Robert," I said, "every time I ask you about the affair, you give your job description and the challenges. The two of you are not going to be able to heal this betrayal unless Deloris understands the nature of the violation. She won't be able to let go of what she doesn't know." I hoped he might see that his grip upon anonymity was serving no one.

"Well, I don't want to hurt Deloris any more than I already have."

"So, you think that describing the affair will only hurt Deloris and wouldn't help her, and it might even make you feel guiltier."

"Yeah, that's probably right," he responded, but appeared more ready to tell his story.

Robert had stepped into the separation stage of their initiation when he chose to deceive Deloris and violate their commitment to a monogamous relationship. He was also separating from his own value of honesty with his wife, and thus violating his integrity. For Deloris, the separation stage began when she read the note. Deloris was separating from her capacity to trust her husband and separating from her belief she would always be the recipient of Robert's loyalty. They were both experiencing the death of their marriage as they knew it and were feeling scared and lost, with little or no faith that something vital could be created from the ashes.

As they sat before me, they had entered into the trial stage of their initiation. Was I the mentor, they wondered, who could guide them through the ensuing challenges? They were facing the most extraordinary conundrums of their life together, and were concerned that my guidance might not procure the needed help. For now, however, they were willing to take the risk.

Deloris's trial focused on her confusion. What exactly would she do with the violation of trust, the deception and the betrayal? Robert's trial coalesced around how to be accountable for what he did, while at the same time minimizing Deloris's pain and saving his marriage.

Robert began to talk about an adventurer who lived in him, who he shamed as an impractical dreamer. He spoke of having come through prostate cancer surgery a year earlier and of his fear of death. Clearly, he wasn't at all sure if his life was one well lived.

The enemies in Robert's life began to show themselves: his constant attacks upon his adventurous spirit, his avoidance of his fear of death and his tendency to blame Deloris for his own limitations. He denied his resentment toward Deloris's need to live close to her family early in their marriage.

Robert appeared more comfortable talking about his affair by understanding what motivated him. He began to see that his need for adventure guided him into another woman's arms, proving that he remained vitally alive. After some time, he was also willing to see the affair as a passive aggressive attempt to punish Deloris for supposedly holding him back from a full life.

Deloris's enemies also became more apparent.

"I don't know what's wrong with me!" she pointed out, exasperated by how disappointed she was in herself. "Why don't I leave him? I always thought if this kind of thing happened, I would leave!"

We spoke more about her frustration and in the course of the discussion she referred to herself as a "wimp" repeatedly. She went on to describe her tears and depression as "wimpy." Deloris's number one nemesis during her trial was her refusal to grant herself permission to grieve the death of her marriage as she knew it and the dream that her husband's loyalty would be a mainstay. The enemy loomed larger as she fortified her resistance to grieve by shaming any expression of loss.

Deloris and Robert had a nonverbal agreement that also served as an enemy. They had established that they would not speak about any issue that they believed might upset or make the other uncomfortable. Now they were preparing for a change in the rules affording them a greater exchange of truth, especially as it pertained to emotions aroused by the behavior of the other. This meant consciousness needed to be raised about the nature of semi-permeable boundaries. They were both learning how their "no-talk" rule had produced emotional anonymity and isolation.

Dynamics in the relationship were changing (dying) as the trials they faced caused them to confront what they had co-created over the years that no longer served them. Their willingness to endure the turbulence and challenges of the trial prepared them to face their ordeal.

Deloris continued to complain about her sadness and depression, but insisted that these emotional pests had outlived their welcome.

"I've really had it!" she explained. "I'm tired of crying and feeling depressed! I want to move on!" She demanded that her emotional life attain a harmonious homeostasis.

"I hear your impatience," I said. "It can be helpful to address a current wound of betrayal by attending to an old betrayal dragged to the surface by the recent duplicity. Can you imagine an old betrayal that may be attempting to get your attention?" I hoped she might be ready for a very new perspective of her life.

Her face was expressionless. "I don't remember any."

"Well, I guess I'm wondering if your family of origin treated your emotions in a manner similar to the way you do—un-welcoming and preferring they go away."

"Yes, my family saw emotions as childish and inappropriate even if you were a child," she responded. Her attitude suggested that that was the proper way for a family to deal with its members' emotions.

"Your siblings and your cousins teased and demeaned you and your mother mercilessly!" blurted Robert indignantly.

"My siblings were very unkind to my mother, and I guess my cousins have not treated me very well," she said, lowering her voice and looking like a child who had just violated a no-snitching taboo.

"So Deloris, I'm getting the picture of a family that harassed you and did not permit the expression of any emotion," I said. "I also get the image of a very sensitive teenager who survived being betrayed by her family by deciding she's tough enough to handle the abuse, with no need to have her emotions received and supported."

Deloris quietly wept, hearing an account of her family that must have rattled the shackles of her denial.

Deloris was now at the core of her ordeal, facing how she had been betrayed by her family and how she conspired against herself by shaming her emotions and pretending she was not in possession of an extremely generous heart. Deloris gradually let go of the injunction against her own emotional life, allowing herself to grieve her losses, and enter resolution, the third stage of her initiation. Over time, she returned to herself and her marriage with more suppleness and grace.

Robert's ordeal surfaced as he faced a paternal legacy that he carried for many years. His father had betrayed his own dream of owning a schooner, which he imagined renting to vacationers for weekly excursions in the Caribbean. He had blamed his wife for his own duplicity, becoming increasingly bitter and resentful before an early death from a heart attack.

Robert had become a stranger to his anger. Tucked away in the caverns of his psyche was a rage at his father for having been disloyal to his dreams, at his mother for not helping his father liberate himself, and at Deloris for doing to him what his mother did to his father. He began to understand that his sensitive, meek demeanor functioned as a veneer for the acrimony burning deep within him. He gradually accepted responsibility for walking away from his desire and blaming Deloris for his self-neglect.

Robert stepped into the resolution stage of his initiation when he became more accountable for betraying his wife by offering a concrete account of his affair accompanied by amends. Unlike his father, he acted on his desire for boat ownership, purchased a boat and began running daily excursions to local lighthouses from May through October.

The initiation of Robert and Deloris reflects what it means to allow a wounding to move us away from victimization and further deepen and connect to ourselves and those we love. The process is an invitation to sustain a dynamically creative relationship with life where our wounding can indicate what aspects of ourselves need to die and what needs to live, allowing us to mature.

The Many Faces of Healing

There are many faces of healing. Each depicts a unique encounter with the wound; each reveals a particular way of carrying the injury. It may be that beyond the contours of the brow and the lines of the cheeks, there is a depth in the eyes exposing one's personal rendezvous with the wound. The look often tells of an energy that has been transmuted. We know that we do not become healed, but rather participate in healing. With this knowledge comes an understanding that our wounding is not a unique experience; it is an inevitable part of being human.

The eyes may signal an ever-deepening integrity; our actions may resonate more closely with what we value, what we believe and what we desire.

We might see a countenance that indicates an ongoing devotion to remain self-examining. Rather than a heavy, driving, analytical introspection, we see eagerness and a curiosity to know ourselves and to live closer to what we know as a budding friendship.

Finally, the face of healing often reveals an increased comfort and joy with the adventure of living. There is an acceptance that we can't get life right. A lightness replaces the rancor caused by tenacious attempts to perforate the impenetrable mysteries of life.

We have been examining what it means to confront and accept our wounds, rather than deny the wound and let it define us. We saw that entering into a conscious and compassionate relationship with our soul's injuries allows us to deepen and mature. We explored how creating a relationship with our wounds allows us to develop character. Now we turn to the most dynamic of all *proper times*, the path of emotional intimacy.

7

Forged by Intimacy

The image of the "happy marriage" causes great harm.
—Adolf Guggenbuhl-Craig

Philip, a biology professor, was approaching his birthday and curious about how he might honor an important milestone.

"I want to create a meaningful way to acknowledge my fiftieth birthday. I was thinking about a monastic trek in Tibet. What do you think about that?"

"It sounds like a great idea," I said. "But if you're looking for an experience that will bring you to your depths and open opportunities for new growth, try falling in love." I watched Philip come to the edge of his seat in what I suspect was disbelief.

Committing to create an emotionally intimate relationship with another human being may offer more *proper times* for deepening and learning than any other human endeavor. With our culture offering idyllic, romantic images of relationships, we can hardly face the formidable challenges inherent in any serious attempt to generate emotional intimacy. Hence, we enter relationships naïve and ill-equipped to deal with the demands and difficulties of intimacy. It's a setup for profound disillusionment, which I spell this way to denote the opportunity for letting go of illusions.

We might say that all awakening involves some departure from tightly held illusions accompanied by feelings of disappointment. There are probably only three fundamental reactions to feeling disillusioned about a relationship. The first is to blame the other, suggesting that we simply have the wrong person. The second is to blame ourselves, deciding that there must be something inherently wrong with us. The third response is to attack relationships in general, determining that they are not fulfilling or worth our investment.

I want to suggest that all three reactions run the risk of sabotaging our chances to experience profound opportunity for fulfillment. A commitment to emotional intimacy will call us to ourselves like no other undertaking.

Emotional Intimacy

After some level of liberation from the quixotic influences of Hallmark greeting cards and Hollywood's enchanting representations of romance, we may be left with abject confusion about the nature of emotional intimacy. Unfortunately, there are not that many opportunities to learn. We might stay confused, disillusioned or desperate enough to find our way to couples counseling; and if that counselor has been devoted to understanding emotional intimacy, some wisdom may be possible.

Hopefully, it will become clear that emotional intimacy is ultimately an impenetrable mystery, making it an exceptional environment for maturation. It offers us endless chances to learn about ourselves, as well as the nuances and dynamics of creating something vital with another. Sometimes poetry and art may tell us more about emotional intimacy than any attempt at rational exposition. This poem by Ellen Bass is a good example:

Gate C22

At gate C22 in the Portland airport
a man in a broad-band leather hat kissed
a woman arriving from Orange County.
They kissed and kissed and kissed. Long after
the other passengers clicked the handles of their carry-ons
and wheeled briskly toward short-term parking,
the couple stood there, arms wrapped around each other
like she'd just staggered off the boat at Ellis Island,
like she'd been released from ICU, snapped
out of a coma, survived bone cancer, made it down
from Annapurna in only the clothes she was wearing.
Neither of them was young. His beard was gray.
She carried a few extra pounds you could imagine
Her saying she had to lose. But they kissed lavish
Kisses like the ocean in the early morning,
the way it gathers and swells, sucking
each rock under, swallowing it
again, and again. We were all watching—
passengers waiting for the delayed flight
to San Jose, the stewardesses, the pilots,
the aproned woman icing Cinnabons, the man selling
sunglasses. We couldn't look away. We could
taste the kisses crushed in our mouths.
But the best part was his face. When he drew back
and looked at her, his smile soft with wonder, almost
as though he were a mother still open from giving birth,
as your mother must have looked at you, no matter
what happened after—if she beat you or left you or

you're lonely now—you once lay there, the vernix
not yet wiped off, and someone gazed at you
as you were the first sunrise seen from the Earth.
The whole wing of the airport hushed,
all of us trying to slip into that woman's middle-age body.
her plaid Bermuda shorts, sleeveless blouse, glasses,
little gold hoop earrings, tilting our heads up.

Although the poem is filled with sensual delight, there is
an undercurrent of connection offered in this airport greeting
that goes far beyond the physical exchanges between two people. We implicitly understand that something significant was
built before this meeting at Gate C22, and it is this something
that we will attempt to offer as a luminous portrait.

What It Isn't

Let's dispel several myths about emotional intimacy before shedding more light upon its true nature.

It Isn't Natural. The first myth is that emotional intimacy
takes place naturally as we fall in love and get to know one another. Emotional intimacy is not natural. It doesn't happen because people care about one another or spend time together; it
must be learned. We must become skilled at identifying how we
obstruct it from developing and what we need to do in order to
cultivate it.

It's Not Sex. When I use the word intimacy in a conversation, people inevitably interpret what I'm saying as pertaining to
a sexual act. It is common to describe two people as intimate to
mean that they have a sexual relationship. However, friends, relatives and even spouses can be intimate without having any kind
of sexual rapport. And, two people could be sexual partners without any element of emotional intimacy. Of course, it is possible,

and in many cases preferable to be both sexually and emotionally intimate, but the presence of one does not ensure the other.

Fusion. This is a common replacement for emotional intimacy. Fusion usually occurs when one or both partners decide to betray their individuality by taking on the beliefs, values and desires of their companion. Fusion is an attempt to pretend there is genuine intimacy by diminishing the presence of diversity and conflict. If we gave fusion a voice, it might sound like the following: "Isn't it great that we have so much in common and we never fight? Isn't it wonderful to be one?"

When couples are fused they employ excessively permeable boundaries where at least one member of the relationship uses compliance as a way to generate an emotional connection. The complying partner attempts to safeguard the success of the relationship by meeting the other's expectations and limiting the possibility of being abandoned. This injures the relationship in several ways. The complying partner's individuality can become seriously stinted, and can even lead to a genuine crisis of identity. Trying to live with someone else's expectations often makes us feel inadequate, angry and prone to passive aggressive behavior. Partners who are the recipient of the other's compliance often feel alone, burdened by responsibility and angry. Fused relationships are commonly riddled with resentment and deep feelings of isolation. Both partners are left wondering what went wrong.

Excessive Separateness

Partners who engage in excessive separateness often pretend that they are in an emotionally intimate relationship since each party's individuality is well-accommodated.

Employing non-permeable boundaries, they defend their separate identities, hoping to protect themselves from the expectations of the other. Individuals pursue their separate interests, vocational callings and sometimes even their own households. If both partners buy into the separateness, they may look at what they have created as very positive, since there is limited opportunity for conflict and interference from the other. However, similar to fusion, excessive separateness is a breeding ground for isolation. Partners don't really know one another and engage in little that resembles collaboration leading to a rich sense of belonging.

Intimate Events

Intimate events are often confused with emotionally intimate relationships. An intimate event is frequently some meaningful self-disclosure that goes beyond an everyday account of a recent experience. Two people connect with an exchange that includes encouragement and acknowledgment. What's missing is commitment, where they develop their autonomy *and* deepen their belonging to each other. That is, they won't see that the relationship can offer opportunities to develop their maturity either individually or collectively. It is also likely that they will not view each other as valuable allies during times of crisis.

Love

Love, much like sex, does not guarantee emotional intimacy. People can love one another, choose to be fused, excessively separate or share in an occasional intimate event. Love can be feeling that doesn't necessarily have implications about how people relate to one another. It would be quite odd to think of people who are emotionally intimate not loving each other, but perfectly reasonable for people who love each other to not be emotionally intimate.

What Is It?

Emotional intimacy must be learned. We must develop a proficiency to attend to our needs for autonomy and belonging while someone with whom we are in a relationship with is also attempting to meet his or her needs for autonomy and belonging. We can say that emotional intimacy is what may be created when two separate (autonomous) and unique individuals choose and commit to unite. They choose each other as the place to develop their autonomy and their capacity to belong. This choosing is not a one-shot deal either; the choice will have to be made over and over again.

There is something deeply endearing and invigorating about making this choice consciously and with intention. There is a closer connection both to ourselves and to another when we say, "It is with you that I choose to grow whatever in me is asking for development."

The choosing can become a true act of courage. After all, we face rejection or possibly the end of what we cherish. Emotional intimacy is strengthened when we don't remain in a relationship by default, but rather due to a conscious decision.

Working with couples for decades has revealed an important perspective about the end of relationships: *People do not usually end a relationship because of the behavior or character of their partners, but rather because of the tension created when the time has come for a deeper learning. Something unlived within is seeking the light of day.*

A Cornucopia of Proper Times

Much may be revealed about emotional intimacy if we take a look at the bounty of *proper times* that naturally accompany a relationship where two people are committed to building something meaningful and enduring. Such a commitment is likely the most intense opportunity for maturation that can be found in the human condition. Hence, in his book *Passionate Marriage*, David Schnarch refers to a committed relationship as a people-making machine.

The dilemma is that the commitment is a setup, a kind of cosmic joke. Making such a commitment automatically places us in a bewildering labyrinth of attitudes, expectations and desires that prod and shove us down paths where we will be inevitably hurt and lost. And when we lose our way, we are in a *proper time* to either employ primitive forms of guidance, or allow our disorientation to teach us more developed ways to take care of ourselves and our relationships. At the very least, it's messy, and understanding the nature of the mess should reveal more about the complexion and character of emotional intimacy.

Four Overwhelming Forces

In every relationship where the partners are committed to creating emotional intimacy, there are four forces at work that overwhelm everything else: our need for autonomy, our need to belong, our partner's need for autonomy and our partner's need to belong. Generating emotional intimacy greatly depends upon our ability to support and balance these energies.

Emotional intimacy is not a state to attain. It is a willingness to remain vigilant since a need for autonomy can pull a relationship into excessive separation and a need for belonging can easily move us into fusion. Think of it like being at sea, where sailing requires regular responses to the prevailing winds and currents in order to keep the vessel on course.

We simply will not be able to get these four forces perfectly aligned. At best, we can remain open and curious, resourcefully responding to challenges that enlarge our capacity to attend to our own needs while remaining an ally for our partner.

It is important to recognize and acknowledge that women and men approach these challenges quite differently.

Women, in general, have learned the skills required to maintain their needs to belong and also to offering support for a partner's need for autonomy. Women are not encouraged to learn how to back their need for autonomy. While men are acculturated to cultivate their own autonomy, they remain confused about their need to belong, and often are not quite sure how to support a partner's need for autonomy. Typically, men see a woman's need for belonging as a female thing, and will accommodate it as long as it doesn't threaten the male's investment in autonomy.

Supporting Autonomy

A committed relationship is a rich opportunity to develop our sense of autonomy. In a fused relationship, we often expect our partner to know what we want and to make it happen. But when we learn to maintain an awareness of what we desire while remaining accountable for meeting that desire, this increased consciousness and responsibility allows us to mature. This is especially true for women who are often encouraged to focus on the needs and desires of others, while neglecting their own.

One way to sustain our own autonomy in a relationship is not to expect our partner to love us because we don't want to learn to do it for ourselves. Quite often we enter a relationship disheartened by our inability to maintain a consistent and reliable self-love, so we ask our partner to do it for us. When we don't take responsibility for our own self-love, we set our partner up for failure, since the person can never provide the level of love that can only come from ourselves. The more we accept the responsibility to love ourselves, the more we set the stage for emotional intimacy to grow, limiting blame and expectations of the impossible.

A third approach to buttressing our autonomy is the use of semi-permeable boundaries. This is especially important as we genuinely respond to our partner's expectations and requests, saying "yes" only when we mean it. We move away from a propensity to please to more authentic declarations of what's acceptable and what isn't.

We back and assist our partner's need for autonomy by offering encouragement for the same three strategies: offering clarity about what they want, doing what it takes to maintain a deeply abiding self-love and employing effective semi-permeable boundaries. However, supporting our partner's need for autonomy can be quite threatening.

We wonder if we'll discover just how different we are from one another. Will our partner's preferences and interests turn us off? Will a growing independence cause our partner to lose interest in us? Backing our partner's autonomy is an act of courage since all these considerations really are possible. However, offering support for another person's autonomy can lead to deep emotional intimacy, not simply because of the risks but also because such an offering can reflect a loving interest in a partner's well-being.

We can move beyond considerations of protecting what's comfortable and familiar to a larger vision of what contributes to the flourishing of the other's individuality. We can make offerings of time, energy, money and acceptance as ways to minister to our partner's autonomy.

Supporting Belonging

What do we really want from our partner? The truthful answer increases our sense of belonging and might lead to a deeper connection. I have mentioned how difficult this can be for many men, who have learned to use sex as the only way to satisfy their need to belong. It might be helpful to take a holistic perspective to the issue of belonging in a committed relationship.

We can formulate behavioral, emotional, intellectual and spiritual dimensions to belonging. The behavioral aspect might include the recreational activities that you enjoy with your partner. Or home-related projects. What kind of adventures do you relish with your partner? What satisfies you sexually? How do you like being sensually touched? What other types of touch do you find nurturing?

The emotional segment might involve identifying when you need emotional encouragement from your partner: Can you ask for acknowledgment of your feelings from your partner? When you have experienced a loss, can you ask for attention? Can you expect your anger to be listened to?

The intellectual portion could include: What types of intellectual conversations do you want to have with your partner?

Do you enjoy attending cultural events together? How about classes or seminars? What books do you want to share?

A spiritual dimension might involve: Is there a spiritual practice or ritual that feeds your spirits? Is there a pilgrimage or adventure that would vitalize your spirits? Do you want to pray or meditate together?

Clearly, some understanding of ourselves is a prerequisite to knowing what enriches a connection to our partner. In that way, a committed, intimate relationship also becomes a crucial *proper time* for nurturing self-examination. Self-awareness contributes to the expanded emotional intimacy and, in turn, more emotional intimacy calls for more self-awareness.

When we back our partner's needs for belonging, we risk some loss to our own autonomy. Will we be consumed by our partner's need for affection and connection, unable to sustain the life of our independence? Will we face our partner's disapproval as we express resistance to cooperate with some aspect of belonging?

Supporting our partner while remaining an exponent for our own autonomy calls for the courage to be a separate and unique individual. We risk our partner's accusations that we are self-centered and unwilling to create real partnership. Standing for our autonomy can be perceived as a threat to our partner's need to feel connected.

Establishing our need for belonging risks being perceived as demanding or needy. It takes courage, but is a prerequisite for creating authentic emotional intimacy.

Determining a clear personal definition of belonging can be especially challenging for men who are taught that belonging should remain a female initiative. Therefore, men must step outside of societal renderings of manhood in order to access the meaning of belonging that dwells in the hearts of men.

We should not take lightly the impact this cultural injunction has upon men. They will often allow a marriage to disintegrate and family to fracture before accepting a challenge to their persona as *real men*. Men are expected to be ignorant about what renders them a deep sense of belonging, except for their participation on teams and military service.

Our word for *courage* comes from the French word for "heart." Until men are willing to stand up to culture's common formulations of manhood, they will remain seriously handicapped in their attempts to walk a path with a heart. Learning how to bring their own expressions of belonging to a relationship creates a significant opportunity for the maturing of men.

Learning About Boundaries

There is no better container for learning about boundaries than in a committed intimate relationship. Let's say one partner in a relationship—typically a man, but quite often a woman— employs non-permeable boundaries in an attempt to secure more space needed for autonomy to thrive. But the lack of permeability can diminish the flow of affection, warmth, sex and collaboration.

The second partner responds by pushing for excessively permeable boundaries as a way to attain a much needed desire for belonging and as a way to compensate for the inability to penetrate the partner's boundary. Inevitably, the second partner's call for greater permeability threatens the first partner's need for autonomy. A provocative dance ensues with each partner's differing boundary entrenching them in their separate causes.

When this struggle for differing levels of permeability goes on with one partner championing non-permeable boundaries and the other supporting very permeable boundaries, the three primitive coping strategies often kick in.

Adaptation is dependent upon permeable boundaries and so the partner advocating for those boundaries may become excessively adaptive.

Distancing calls for non-permeable boundaries, with the partner who desires those boundaries beginning to distance. A partner may utilize domination as an attempt to control and define the status of boundaries in a relationship.

Domination appears to utilize a curious combination of boundaries, as dominators strive for their partners to respond with excessively permeable boundaries, allowing them to be more easily influenced. However, dominators themselves employ non-permeable boundaries in an attempt to limit the amount of influence their partners can exercise over them.

Adaptation is ordinarily a way to support belonging. Distancing is aimed at providing autonomy, while domination is typically used to influence our partners to accept our needs for autonomy and belonging, while ignoring their own. As pointed out earlier, these are primitive strategies aimed at coping and surviving. They neither possess the artistry nor the efficacy to bring about the richness of emotional intimacy. Couples are locked into the use of excessively permeable boundaries (adaptation), non-permeable boundaries (distancing), and a combination of excessively permeable boundaries and non-permeable ones (domination).

A relationship can easily be taken hostage by one or more of these survival strategies, hurling a couple into a struggle for autonomy and belonging, often resulting in a crisis. Amy and Peter are such a couple.

"It's never enough...all he does is complain," declared Amy. "I'm either with the children too much, at work too much or with my friends too much. I can't take it any more!"

"So, Amy, how do you ordinarily respond to Peter's complaints?" I asked, hoping to see what kind of boundaries she employed.

"I really have had it! I don't encourage his complaining. I back off and refuse to participate." She clearly felt very comfortable distancing whenever Peter expressed his annoyances.

"I get a picture of you coping by backing up and away."

"That's right. I'm tired of dealing with it."

"Peter, how do you handle it when Amy backs up?" I asked.

"I try to keep the conversation going," he suggested, soliciting my support for his constructive efforts. "I mean, couples need to communicate."

"Sure, couples need to communicate," I said. "But I'm wondering how effective your pursuit of Amy has been."

"Well, not very effective," he said. "She shuts down and there's not much I can do." He implied that although his efforts were the right thing to do, he simply could not overcome her obstinacy. I had hoped that Peter would see that Amy's retreat from the conflict was an attempt to do something for herself, as opposed to doing something to him.

Amy and Peter were locked into a struggle for autonomy and belonging respectively. The more non-permeable Amy's boundaries were, the more Peter advocated for excessively permeable ones and vice versa. They could not see that each of their needs was valuable to the relationship, and they had no understanding of semi-permeable boundaries.

I encouraged Amy and Peter to see the present status of their relationship as offering them a *proper time* for learning how to merge their needs for autonomy and belonging with semi-permeable boundaries.

It was relatively easy for both of them to see how Amy's non-permeable boundaries sustained her need for autonomy, diminishing the likelihood that she would take on Peter's desires and beliefs. She began to see how her boundaries became less and less porous every time Peter complained, not only preventing her from supporting Peter's need for belonging but also her own.

It was more difficult for Peter to see that his more permeable boundaries were not really helping his cause for more belonging. With some work, he saw that he wasn't simply calling Amy to be closer to him, but also was holding her responsible for him feeling desirable and lovable. Learning about this level of self-awareness was no small undertaking for Peter, but once he did he and Amy were both ready to discover the power of building a relationship with semi-permeable boundaries.

I reminded them that an emotionally intimate relationship was possible when two unique individuals committed to unite. I suggested that the definition calls for both of them to remain responsible for their own self-esteem, while advocating for the other's autonomy and deepening their connection to one another. They began to grasp how overly pervious boundaries led to fusion while non-porous ones generated alienation. Neither Amy nor Peter wanted to sacrifice their autonomy, and they very much wanted to feel closer to one another. Their relationship had become a *proper time* for discovering more personal power by learning how to support their own and the other's need for autonomy and belonging.

Amy and Peter began to appreciate the power of semi-permeable boundaries, allowing themselves to be touched by each other. We talked about the most relevant application of semi-permeable boundaries being those places where fundamental conflicts surfaced in their relationship. They could see that the more their relationship served as a rich breeding ground for both autonomy and belonging, the more they would face the challenge of integrating different desires, beliefs and values.

Differing Desires

Once the honeymoon phase of a relationship is over, which is the stage where a couple simply celebrates their common yearning to belong to one another, they begin to experience how different the desires of two people can actually be. With some guidance, a relationship leavened with varied aspirations can be a significant *proper time* for learning about ourselves and creating emotional intimacy.

Following the disillusionment that couples inevitably experience when they discover they have less in common than they initially believed, fear ensues. There is a concern that if we clearly represent what we want, our partner will experience our yearnings as a burden. But when we aren't clear about what we want, our needs will not be met and we may feel neglected and resentful. Sometimes we fear that our competing desires may indicate a lack of compatibility.

Divergent desires can be a valuable expression of each person's attention to his or her own autonomy. Unless we consciously accept our fears, it will become almost impossible to experience the richness created by our differences, nor will we be able to develop the kind of internal support needed to champion two unique expressions of autonomy.

A mature relationship becomes a container for the awareness and expression of fear, as well as the knowledge about how to live creatively with it. We will likely need to find new pockets of courage within ourselves that we did not know existed. We need to learn how to allow our differences to feed a relationship.

First, it is important for us to hold the belief that two people can simultaneously get their needs met. This is not very simple, since so many of us were raised with the attitude that when people have competing needs, someone wins and somebody loses. Secondly, whenever possible, your partner should not be the only person who can meet your needs. You should be able to meet your needs alone or with the help of friends if your partner chooses not to participate. Remain an ally to your partner. Offer encouragement or helpful action and after the fact, evaluate your effectiveness in meeting his or her needs directly or indirectly. Indirect support is expressed through encouragement and well-wishing although we are not directly involved. However, before we are even open to these possibilities, we likely will need to deal with one of the three primitive strategies that inevitably surface as a way to cope with fear.

The Fourth Alternative

Nothing quite so threatens our pursuit of autonomy and belonging in a committed relationship more than confronting our diverse needs. As a result, a propensity to adapt, dominate or distance can be quickly activated. Once engaged, these strategies make it nearly impossible to strengthen autonomy (adaptation), or meet needs for belonging, frustrated by distancing and domination. The result is that no real experience of emotional intimacy can take place, leaving couples feeling hopeless, alienated and desperate. Rather than continuously falling prey to psychological maneuvers that suffocate our efforts to relate to those we love, we can commit to developing choices to bring us closer to our partner and to ourselves.

There are four elements of the alternative aimed at taking us beyond the limits of the three primary defenses we normally use. These steps are not about saving a relationship or a marriage. They simply offer us an opportunity to honor our own uniqueness and also our partner's while still remaining connected. They identify action that can be taken in order to more deeply respond to diversity.

Step 1 – Commit to remaining conscious of which strategy (adaptation, domination or distancing) is being used and be willing to learn how to interrupt it and replace it.

When we choose to remain conscious about how we use these defenses, several challenges ensue. After all, our psyche has been employing them unconsciously, like the reaction of a blinking eye to a bright light. We might say our psyche is wary of protecting itself without the usual defenses. We need to learn to calm ourselves, reassured that new forms of support are being developed.

Hours or even days later, we may not notice any change. This is not about a lack of effort or intelligence. We have psychological structures in place aimed at keeping the process automatic and unconscious. We can gradually learn to replace primitive defenses with more sophisticated ways of safeguarding ourselves.

Step 2 – Acknowledge feelings of fear and helplessness while not shaming ourselves or blaming our partner.

Being mindful separates us from the defense, arousing feelings of vulnerability, fear and helplessness. It can be extremely challenging to stand in the presence of our partner expressing ideas and desires that we usually will not attempt without the assistance of our old protection.

Contrary to some popular attitudes of adulthood, maturity is to some degree a measure of how aware we are of our fear rather than just blindly allowing that fear to dictate our behavior. With more awareness of our fears, the more creative and compassionate we can hope to become.

We will probably need to learn to calm ourselves when we become anxious. We can stop fantasizing about the catastrophe that awaits and remind ourselves that we are only feeling vulnerable and we are not actually vulnerable. We can have feelings of fear and still be quite safe. For example, tapping key acupuncture points directly above and beneath the eye in what is known as the Emotional Freedom Technique (EFT) can reduce stress, and is just one example of a very useful tool to calm yourself and more effectively process a traumatic incident.

It's always easy to blame our partner for creating a situation that is causing us to be afraid. Those who are accustomed to using domination and influence are especially prone to blaming others for any uncomfortable feelings they are experiencing. Their intent is to provoke enough guilt to cause their partners to reconsider their stance. Of course, blamers become victims of the blamed, as they hold the others responsible for validation of their own feelings. Eliminating blame and making peace with our feelings of fear and helplessness can deepen our capacity for personal empowerment and responsibility.

Step 3 – Ask for reassurance since diversity can easily remind us of our existential solitude. When afraid of losing our partner we can: ask for reassurance, confirm our own lovability, access same gender support and work on accepting our inevitable aloneness.

My wife has taught me much about asking for reassurance. Once in a while, she calls me from work, explaining that she feels insecure in our relationship, and asks me for encouragement. I usually offer her some simple words denoting my devotion. She thanks me and moves on with her day.

Connie's effortless way of soliciting support has shown me that I am often ashamed of my need to be reassured. Receiving reassurance from a loved one should help quell the vibrations of our insecurities. When it doesn't, we are likely to feel unlovable, making it difficult to accept that our partner actually does love us. However, when we fear losing our partner, we have an opportunity to renew our commitment to define ourselves as deserving of love.

When relationships are in crisis and times are rough, we may be getting very little assurance from our partner and struggling to feel good about ourselves. This may be a moment for both men and women to turn to their respective genders for support. Same-gender support can be very difficult for men, since they are conditioned to either get support from women or else remain emotionally isolated. It can be an extremely important *proper time* for men to learn about accessing other men for emotional support. Shedding the emotional dependency upon women nudges men away from a tendency to maternalize women and points them in the direction of manhood.

Step 4 – When we are afraid of losing ourselves, we need to employ semi-permeable boundaries that support autonomy while promoting engagement with partners.

If adaptation has been our method, we become frightened by the possibility of losing ourselves. This is especially true when our partner has been clear about definitions of belonging. Adapting partners often limit themselves to either complying or distancing and then, when scared enough, choose distancing. Men often find themselves in this role. Culturally, men are only given permission to define the sexual expressions of their need to belong, not the emotional. However, it would be particularly misleading to suggest that it is only men who feel their autonomy threatened in committed relationships.

Regardless of gender, when a partner experiences the distancing behavior of his or her significant other, a frequent response is to intensify efforts toward convincing the distancer that he or she is acting inappropriately. A destructive web begins to be woven. Dominators become more vocal and distancers increasingly distance, determined not to lose themselves.

Brad and Terry had been together for six years when they came to my office reporting such an emotional quagmire. Before long, Terry launched into an intricate analysis of Brad's intimacy-evading tactics. She had some academic training which made her an even more threatening adversary for Brad who would cope by indulging in ever-increasing dimensions of physical and emotional distancing.

Terry was quite receptive to my suggestions that her attempts at influencing Brad were not empowering her. After a number of sessions, she was able to identify why she was so desperate to engage with Brad. "I guess I am still waiting to be chosen by him," she explained. "I get scared when he continuously decides to engage in activities that don't include me."

"I hear your fear. You seem to know that you can't talk him into choosing you," I pointed out. "Even if he responded favorably to your arguments, he would simply be complying with your solicitations and not actually choosing you."

"Yes, I know now that I can't tell him how to be connected to me; he has to figure it out on his own. I just get scared that he won't know how he wants to belong to our relationship."

"Although you're scared," I said, "you seem more accepting of how out of control you are with Brad's construction of how he wants to be connected to you."

"I've never known such helplessness," Terry confessed, visibly shaken by her loss of control over Brad.

"Brad, how are you supporting yourself, your autonomy, in the relationship?" I asked.

"Well, since Terry has backed off attempting to influence me, I feel more comfortable. Although the other night she started yelling at me. She said that I probably will never get clear about how I want to be connected to her."

"How did you take care of yourself when she started yelling?" I asked. I wanted to encourage him to see himself as less of Terry's victim.

"I explained I had not had time to give it much thought," he replied. He clearly hoped that I would agree the matter called for extensive reflections.

"Explaining yourself is probably not the most powerful way to support your individuality or autonomy," I said. "We talked about the use of semi-permeable boundaries, which allow you to be yourself while remaining engaged with Terry."

"I probably need to go over this boundary thing again."

I suggested to Brad that when you're employing a semi-permeable boundary you don't need to distance as a way of providing yourself with a boundary. Terry's words would define her alone and not him. I cautioned him that he might then hear some unmet need of hers, or maybe even her fear.

"I guess my biggest challenge is to remember that I'm okay when she's upset or angry at me," Brad said.

"That's right. It's your responsibility to affirm yourself in the presence of Terry's anger while remaining open to what she needs. If she can't articulate the need, table the conversation until she can talk about it clearly. If she can express what she needs, then you need to be clear with her about whether or not you're willing to offer her what she's requesting."

Brad understood that supporting his autonomy was toughest when Terry was angry at him. He could see that his inclination to distance was reflective of his need for a boundary. Although challenging for him to understand, he began to appreciate how much power he gave to Terry to define him when she was angry.

It helped Brad to hear what a concrete application of a semi-permeable boundary sounded like. We talked about acknowledging Terry's frustration and anger, as well as asking her what she needed as ways to support each of their autonomy while maintaining engagement with her. When Brad began to feel comfortable supporting his autonomy without distancing, he felt increasingly secure enough to define how he wanted to meet his belonging needs with Terry. His definition included walks on the beach, candlelit dinners that he prepared, massage exchanges, playing tennis and cribbage with her, and vacations together. As Brad initiated these activities with Terry, the more she felt chosen by him.

We have been looking at the role of differing needs which inevitably arise in a committed relationship. We now turn to the challenge—and invitation—of dealing with competing values.

Values Diversity

When our values are different from each other, we have stepped into a superb *proper time* for learning how to relate to others and ourselves. The pre-Socratic philosopher Heraclitus suggested, "It is what opposes that helps and from different tones comes the fairest tone." An assortment of values in a relationship has the power to hurl us headlong into a "fight or flight" pattern, or into new levels of emotional maturity. The same demons we saw aroused with a diversity of needs are magnified tenfold in the face of contrasting values. We typically find ourselves bracing for either a serious threat to our autonomy or to our connection with our partner. Why do we find disparate values so alarming and dangerous?

Values naturally reflect core beliefs and personal ideals. Any threat to them on a civil or international level often leads to revolution or war. When we experience our values as being at risk in a committed relationship, the existing rapport may be in serious jeopardy. It is easy to view competing values as a serious hazard to our needs for autonomy and belonging.

Imagine how extremely difficult it would be to support our autonomy or receive support from our partner when our values differ.

Often, couples are even unaware that some difference of values has surfaced and are too busy defending against the idea.

Child-rearing, politics and religion are all rich mines for values disputes. When these differences arise, there are several approaches that can help us creatively support autonomy and the need to belong.

Deepening an Understanding of Our Own Values

In the midst of conflict over values, we quite often feel threatened by the clarity and strength of conviction held by our partner. In such a situation we might fall prey to adopting our partner's values since our own are poorly formulated. Rather than adapting as a way to support our need for belonging or distancing in order to keep a grip on our autonomy, it can help to devote time and energy toward clarifying our own values. This exploration might be best accomplished with some assistance from a therapist, life coach or values clarification workshop because it can be quite confusing, since we've been impacted by the values of family, church and school.

Once we feel more secure with our own values, we might feel more comfortable with the values of our partner, allowing us to be less frightened about losing ourselves and those we love.

We may even find ourselves becoming an ally to our partners' pursuit of their own values. It requires that we take our partner's values as seriously as our own.

Becoming a Source of Support

There is much to be gained when our partner views us as a source of support for their values. If our partners are taking their own values seriously, and living with integrity, then that will be reflected in the choices and decisions they make. Inevitably, they will perceive the encouragement and assistance we offer as a significant gift. In the presence of such a blessing, belonging is strengthened. Our partners experience the relationship as a place where their autonomy will be honored.

I experienced such a deepening of rapport in my own marriage. My wife Connie brings a great deal of attention and care to our home, in contrast to my efforts at maintaining a minimal amount of order with little concern for the aesthetics of our domicile. I found it difficult to grasp why anyone would want to expend that much energy toward embellishing a domestic environment. In my judgment she would have been better off exercising that kind of effort in some other direction. Essentially, I was of the opinion that she should adopt more of my values.

One day as I was coming upstairs from the basement, I paused to notice Connie tending to a "Christmas cactus" in the living room. Her movements were sensuous and nurturing, indicative of a mother offering care to a small child who took a bad fall. A late afternoon light streamed through the window, illuminating the scene like theater lights focused in order to bring attention to a particular action.

I was mesmerized by the scene, witnessing for the first time the care she brought to the ambiance of our home. As I stood in the stairway, my understanding of her values expanded, allowing me to become more supportive of her need to bring order and beauty to our home.

Before we can offer support to our partner's values, we may need to become more aware of how values are used or how they bring meaning and fulfillment. However, such understanding may come only after we have become more comfortable with our own values and confront any fear we may have as a result of the divergence.

Modeling

Rather than try to influence and persuade, demonstrating the credibility of our values may be a more effective way to communicate. The intention behind modeling is to heighten an understanding of how another actually lives his or her values. It can be beneficial to witness the concrete manifestation of the values we seek to better understand.

Modeling is best applied as a kind of visual aid rather than an attempt to influence or as a source of competition. Modeling is not about proving who has the best values, but instead offers us an opportunity to understand another's values as they are lived. We get to witness how our partners' values might concretely serve them.

My friend Peter believes firmly in accepting and honoring the diversity of sexual orientation. He found himself in the middle of the men's locker at the local gym, listening to some loud gay bashing. He thought about either walking away or lecturing the assembled. Instead, he turned to Joe, the main instigator and said, "For Christ's sake, Joe, you've been yelling 'don't tell and don't ask' since you started school and nobody knows what the hell you're talking about." The men all laughed and the offensive comments came to an abrupt end. Fortunately, Joe was willing to laugh at himself. Peter reported feeling glad about being able to interrupt Joe's behavior without putting him down in some way.

The more lucid our understanding is of one another's values, the more likely that we'll know what we are accepting or rejecting. And with some level of acceptance comes a willingness to learn from one another's values.

Becoming More Accepting

The more secure we feel with our own values, the more accepting we can become of our partner's. To a great degree, gaining security with our own values depends upon a willingness and an ability to move away from values we adopted simply because they made us feel safer or more secure in a time of fear. When we are insecure about our values, we tend to become dogmatic, rigidly rejecting beliefs that do not completely line up with ours. Devotion to a set of values, however, is characterized by an eagerness to be curious about their sustainability and applicability to changing times. We are more concerned about our ability to infuse our decisions with compassion and tolerance, rather than insisting that our values reflect some high order of thinking best left to some higher power.

Under most circumstances, our partner's diverse values should not interfere with our decisions to live our values. Even people with differing religious beliefs can pursue their own religious convictions without obstructing a partner's religious pursuits. Even in child-rearing, where reconciling competing values may take more work for couples to support each other, there is an opportunity to learn something from one another.

Learning from Our Partner

Once a level of acceptance of our partner's values is in place, it can become a *proper time* for learning. Maturing is often about acquiring the willingness to leave a comfort zone and be open to learning from a partner who carries very different values. My own marriage continues to offer me numerous opportunities to venture cautiously out from the sanctuary of my own values.

Several years ago, a landscaper we hired was treating our lawn. He told me that he was responsible for thirty different lawns, and twenty-eight of them were doing marvelously. He emphasized that the twenty-eight well-performing lawns were not only treated by him but also that he took care of mowing them and that our's was one of the two not flourishing. The suggestion was that my mowing was not meeting his expectations. He pushed me to let him do the mowing over the next month. I reluctantly agreed and went into the house angry about the exchange.

"Paul, you look distressed. What's up?" asked Connie, noticing the fallout I carried from the conversation with the landscaper.

"That guy has a lot of nerve!"

"What did he say?"

"He doesn't like the way I cut the lawn. He wants to do it in order to see if it makes a difference," I explained, eager to express how incredulous I was at his suggestion and in the hope that Connie would empathize with me.

"Did you agree to have him do the mowing?"

"Yes, I did, but I don't like the idea of hired help mowing my lawn."

"Well, I actually don't recall a family member of ours ever mowing the lawn," said Connie, with eyes tilted upward in search of an illusive image of some unusual incident where a member of her family might be mowing the lawn.

"What? My grandfather died cutting his lawn!" I exclaimed. "The men in my family always mowed their own lawns!" I was in a state of disbelief about the values that guided Connie's family when it came to lawn care.

This conversation reminded me that Connie came from an upper-class white Southern family, while I had been raised in a very blue-collar Northern family. The value of hard work was the bedrock of our family's values and belief system. Along with it came a sprinkling of stereotyping expressed in the belief that we lower-middle class folks were somehow better people because of our devotion to hard work.

I certainly knew that Connie did not shy away from hard work; this offered me a chance to confront my class bias. Then, there was the issue of entitlement. Connie believed that she was entitled to quality service for a reasonable fee. While my belief suggested that I likely would not receive quality service and upon closer examination, it was clear that the belief was founded upon a lack of entitlement. I simply did not carry the sense of entitlement that characterized Connie.

There I was, at fifty-four, looking for the first time at a value stemming from my socio-economic background. I did not believe I deserved a quality service and therefore I was better off performing the task myself. Thankfully, I was willing to learn about entitlement. I haven't mowed the lawn since and I have even begun to feel good about it, evidenced by my willingness to sell my lawn mowers some six years later.

Attending to a Wound

Tim and Joan, both in their second marriage, felt stuck in a quagmire of values diversity. Joan had been a school psychologist for twenty years and enjoyed her work. Tim worked periodically as a handyman, primarily for relatives and friends, while Joan had taken up a second job tutoring in order to augment their income.

"I must admit that I feel deeply resentful of Tim not pulling his weight. The financial burden of the family is mine alone!" declared Joan.

"I do my fair share," said Tim. "Besides working a variety of carpentry jobs, I maintain the home, do the grocery shopping and most of the cooking. You don't value what I do!" Tim defended his understanding that Joan was defining him as a freeloader.

Joan continued to build her case. "I appreciate what you do, but it still basically leaves me responsible to pay the bills and plan for our retirement."

At that point I intervened, asking Tim if he ever saw himself in a career or pursuing a vocation.

"Well, not really," he responded, becoming sullen. Tim placed both hands over his face and gently sobbed.

"Tell me about your sadness," I prompted, attempting to welcome the pain that Tim was experiencing.

"I just can't imagine anyone in the world seeing me as possessing valued skills or talents," he said. "I mean, who would think that I actually have something to offer?" He strained to catch his breath between every word and gasp.

I pointed out to both Tim and Joan that what appeared to be a serious difference in values was at the core—strong, primal feelings of self-loathing—leaving Tim believing there was no place in the world where his skills would be appreciated. I suggested that they stop discussing the value of Tim making more of a financial contribution to the family. But, rather, that Tim step into the story of his self-contempt and how it blocked him from valuing himself. Sometimes, before a meaningful values diversity conversation can take place, an early childhood wound must be attended to.

Can There Be Too Much Diversity?

I am often asked if there is such a thing as too much diversity of values in a relationship. Before responding, it may be useful to instead ask if there is such a thing as too much homogeneity or alikeness of values in a relationship.

The experience of having common values can be very seductive. It appears to diminish tension, expand harmony and create the illusion that there is less reason to abandon the relationship. However, the tranquility can be short-lived. When the values held by two people are extremely alike, it is likely that someone's autonomy is being sacrificed. And with the loss of autonomy comes diminished experiences of belonging.

Unlike a commonality of values, differences are seldom seductive. Quite the contrary, they are usually seen as repulsive to us, bringing tension and ensuing effort. Yet, there is opportunity to deepen and expand as we move from what's comfortable and familiar to what makes us uneasy and strange, pointing us toward our psychological frontier where conflict can prompt our development. However, unless a couple is willing to engage in some serious learning, significant degrees of disagreement will generate separation and distance with little or no fulfillment.

Rebecca, a thirty-eight-year-old physical therapist, was concerned about her seeming incompatibility with her partner Mike and came to see me. It soon became obvious that the extent of their differences was such that they weren't interested in learning from each other's values and could only practice tolerance and forbearance.

Their values concerning religion, politics, child-rearing and education were radically different. Each could see the other's compassion and at first that was enough to bring them to-gether. Rebecca had realized that they were not interested in learning much from each other. Their communication became organized around innocuous topics aimed at avoiding argu-ments, in which they were always trying to persuade the other rather than accept.

There does appear to be a point where there is simply too much divergence of values. When two people are pursuing dif-ferent life purposes, they will be unlikely to choose one another. They are on separate paths with little opportunity to expand their connection to each other. If they truly wish to experience emotional intimacy, then it may be a *proper time* to learn about letting go and allowing themselves to discover the richness of belonging in a relationship where there is a greater compatibil-ity of values and purpose.

Rebecca spent several years being tolerant and being toler-ated. She came to learn how she had little or no understanding of what it meant to receive deep emotional support. In her fam-ily of origin, her older brother was prone to acting out, creating an exceptionally stressful situation for her parents. Her gift of love to her parents was a deep abiding capacity to adapt, refus-ing to contribute to an already difficult environment.

Like so many adapting children, Rebecca made sure she would not burden her parents with her needs, so she simply eliminated them. This dynamic placed her into a posture of giving as she related to others, with a crippled capacity to re-ceive genuine support. As she confronted the dissonance in her relationship, she slowly identified what she might want for herself and gradually unearthed the entitlement to expand her ability to receive.

Rebecca separated from Mike. Regularly she reminded me that he was a good guy. It was important to her to remind herself that her departure from the relationship was not a statement about Mike being less than a good person. She knew how to protect those she loved. Now was a proper time for her to learn to safeguard her own emotional investments by learning how to receive more.

Emotional Generosity

Being receptive to the learning presented to us during *proper times* allows us to nurture a capacity for emotional generosity. An ancient meaning of the word *generous* is "to gift." There is much power in seeing a relationship as a place to give much and to receive much. Such a perspective defines each person in the relationship as a gift to the other.

We are being emotionally generous when we declare we want to get a lot and give a lot. It is a gift to communicate to another that we choose them for emotional support (i.e., to be encouraged, heard, understood, loved, nurtured, respected and believed in). In order to ask for such things, we must be aware of what we want and possess enough sense of self to feel comfortable needing others. When we bring our needs to our partner, we communicate that we choose that person as a source of emotional support.

Curiosity is another expression of emotional generosity. When we are curious about our partner, we offer an immense gift. We are clearly telling him or her that we remain invested and we won't take his or her evolving self for granted. Rather, we are interested in who the person is becoming, the struggles and victories of his or her personal journey.

A third characteristic of emotional generosity is empathy. The word is derived from the German *einfuhlung,* meaning "to feel into." By exercising empathy we extend a welcome to our partners' emotional lives. We communicate that we will not analyze, advise or attempt to change the emotional states of our partner. Instead, we will do our best to identify with, understand, relate to and simply accept our partner's emotional life. This process does not necessarily involve compassion or sympathy, but rather a joining into our partner's emotions. Through empathy we communicate: You are not alone. I am with you on this emotional journey.

A final characteristic of emotional generosity is self-disclosure. Rather than retreating into the invisibility that accompanies anonymity, we give a voice to our dreams, our regrets, our desires and our loves. We expose ourselves, risking possible ridicule and rejection. This gift to our partners is a clarity about whom they are choosing. Our partner is able to make a more informed decision because we have done our best to demystify ourselves.

A relationship is infused with new life when we accept that we need to choose one another over and over again for the duration of the relationship.

A commitment to create an emotionally intimate relationship offers us an intense call to maturation. The substitutes that are often interpreted as authentic emotional intimacy—sex, fusion, excessive separateness, intimate events and feelings of love—show us that creating emotional intimacy is not natural; it must be learned. When we say that something must be learned, it is synonymous with saying we must *commit* to learning. Such a dedication to create emotional intimacy will be an invitation into adulthood.

8
Wind and Breath

Being religious means asking passionately the question of the meaning of our existence and being willing to receive answers, even if the answers hurt. —*Paul Tillich*

I t's all too easy to sidestep questions of spiritual maturity and avoid the tension that inevitably accompanies painful questions like, "Who are we, really?" and "Who are we meant to be?"

Three Faces of Spiritual Immaturity

Many of us were taught as children to surrender our spirits to the care of an institutional religion, and often this leaves us still hungry. Others may not have been shown how to care authentically for our souls, ignoring questions of a maturing spirit.

At best, these experiences may have left us spiritually wanting and at worst, cynical about the possibility of finding a satisfying spiritual path. We may have survived exhortations of fire and brimstone as well as reminders of our sinful natures, but our spiritual longings continued to howl for attention. If our families and churches neither modeled nor realistically taught us how to attend to our spiritual appetites then we will likely succumb to a famine of the spirit.

When faced with spiritual bareness, we are left with basically three immature, undeveloped responses to our deprivation. The first is a gripping indifference. We pretend our spiritual starvation is an illusion. Metaphysical disinterest is a way to succumb to the fear of facing the immensity of life, shying away from a call to the sacred. Inattention to our inner lives will cause estrangement from larger questions. It is difficult to wonder about our purpose when we are preoccupied with running errands, scores of ballgames and living with an abiding loyalty to television sitcoms. Our apathy has us drifting away from a search for personal meaning, community and a need for forgiveness. However, our unfulfilled spiritual needs continue to beckon and this often leads to an expression of immaturity that might best be called idolatry.

Idolatry materializes when we are attempting to avoid hard truths, pretending that we are genuinely meeting our spiritual hunger; instead, we are settling for fast food. Some examples of idolatry might include falling in love, professional achievements and social status. While these events may enrich other parts of our lives, they likely will not fulfill the spiritual prowess we often ascribe to them. The third is the choice to attach ourselves to some form of literalism where we surrender the development of our own spiritual truths and adopt some conventional expression of religion or spirituality.

One goal of literalism is to diminish or actually eliminate the struggle of seeking the truth. The literalist hopes that by some belief held or action performed, the quest is over; truth has been found. The more this attachment is driven by fear, the more rigid the literalist's grip is upon some alleged truth. The price of such inflexibility is that we can no longer hear mystery whispering its secrets to us.

Spiritual Food

What are expressions of idolatry and literalism attempting to provide? Jungian analyst James Hollis suggests that our spiritual sustenance may be seen as our needs for transcendence, meaning and community. I would add redemption as a fourth means of spiritual nourishment. The word *transcendence* from the Latin means "to go beyond" and from the Greek, "over and above." We can ask: To go beyond what or above what? How does it serve our spiritual lives to go beyond or above? What happens to us when we go beyond?

We often view transcendence as simply an escape from the existential predicaments that plague the human condition. We hope to surpass our financial situation by winning the lottery, escape our loneliness by meeting new friends, leave behind our self-loathing by meeting our soul mates or rise above our pettiness by somehow moving into a more purified personality. In each of these cases, we are attempting to escape some unfavorable situation through transcendence or by moving beyond what we deem unacceptable. However, transcendence as a form of escape may not be spiritually nutritious, but rather be like trying to satisfy hunger by eating cotton candy.

When transcendence is coupled with *kenosis,* the Greek word for "emptying," we may find ourselves moving much closer to spiritual fulfillment. For example, let's imagine wishing to transcend our experience of narcissism. Rather than simply judging our self-centeredness and wishing to move beyond it, we could be willing to acknowledge our ignorance about empathy, and empty ourselves of any pretense and illusion that we actually know about being empathic. Transcendence moving in tandem with emptying allows us to rise above and be receptacles for deeper learning and development.

Emptying allows us to be touched and deepened by creating fresh surroundings. We not only consent to let go of the old, but also develop new understandings of who we have been. Seeing ourselves at the center of the universe, with excessive self-focus, yields only an illusion of control. This fictitious power helps us to cope with a chaotic environment. Such a perspective would have helped to buffer us from the inevitable trauma of a chaotic and hurtful environment.

To bring meaning to our lives is essentially to be able to name our lives. When we have borrowed that name, the meaning of our lives does not belong to us. It is an imitation, lacking in originality and authenticity. Often the names of our lives are defined by some event or role. We are known as the one who went to the concert, the one who attended a party, the one who works at such and such a job or the one who graduated from such and such a school, etc.

When the naming is authentic, gratifying and bountiful, it reflects our values. However, desires and beliefs must be clarified before our naming can be characterized as uniquely our own. This kind of naming will sound like: The one who chose to strengthen personal empowerment, the one who is willing to learn to be more generous, the one who took a spiritual life seriously, the one who develops a capacity to receive love, or the one who practices silence in order to listen more effectively.

For many of us isolation infests everywhere we live and work. We can easily become accustomed to an alienated life, with no viable vision of authentic community. We pretend that we are experiencing genuine contact. We walk past people on the street, separated, even in our proximity. Working in our cubicles, we hear the voices of co-workers down the hall. This allows us an illusion of genuine involvement.

I often ask my clients: Who knows you? More often than not, people report feeling known by one person or none. It is a peculiar expression of belonging when we spend time with others and yet we are not known by them. Engagement is reduced to the exchange of innocuous information. A positive interaction is often simply described as no one leaving an encounter disgruntled. We don't expect to be especially helpful to one another, or committed to mutual support, nor do we expect to know one another more deeply.

There are many expressions of idolatry. One of the most popular instances is the masses of casino-goers.

In a 2008 lecture, Jungian analyst James Hollis noted that the number of people pilgrimaging to American casinos far exceeds those traveling to traditional holy sites such as the Vatican, Mecca, The Temple at Khajuraho (Hindu), Lumbini (birthplace of the Buddha) and the Church of the Holy Sepulchre and the Western Wall in Jerusalem combined.

Driven by the search for the deeply spiritual experiences of transcendence, connection, meaning and redemption, throngs are swarming to casinos seeking fulfillment. Scott Peck captures the idolatry of casino life in his book *People of the Lie*:

> Having recently visited Las Vagas, my own latest vision of hell is that it is an endless slot machine emporium, far removed from the variety of night and day, monotonously noisy with the repetitive clamor of meaningless

jackpots, jammed with dull-eyed people spasmodically yet regularly yanking machines for all eternity. Indeed, the tasteless glitter of Las Vagas is a pretense designed to hide all that terrible dreariness.

Our hope is that our casino visits will help us move beyond the mediocrity and emptiness of everyday life. We become emotionally involved with the distraction provided by a myriad of external stimuli: lights, sounds, entertainment. That environment is meant to invigorate our senses, propelling us out of the ordinary, eclipsing the commonplace and exposing us to what seems to be a preeminent experience of reality. However, similar to all promises of transcendence, the church of the casino can't be trusted, and at times leaves us stripped of our life savings and all those things we have worked hard for.

Of course, a gambling establishment also falls quite short of providing us with a connection or a sense of community as well as any deepening and enduring meaning. Connection is defined as the transactions between patrons, waitresses and dealers, and banter among players. Instead of authentic involvement, there are simple perfunctory exchanges signifying little or nothing. Even so, we find it easy to be seduced by the clamor and animation which, combined with the large crowds, suggests to us that something truly engaging is, in fact, happening.

The pursuit of meaning is reduced to a possibility of being a winner at the tables, ignoring the fact that gaming is simply a form of income for the casino. Redemption or forgiveness is offered as free drinks and food. Kind and attentive treatment by attendants presents a temporary reprieve from self-accusations and guilt.

A third immature pursuit of the spiritual life is often seen in a kind of literalism, which does not denote a particular sect or denomination but an attitude. The hope inherent in this attitude is to diminish the mystery of our spiritual paths by attributing truth to some literal interpretation of a particular text or by adhering to the decrees of a religious leader. We can plainly see that such focus is characteristic of intolerance with life's insecurity. Hollis concludes that there is a literalist in all of us, since it may not be possible to fully make peace with the deep insecurity of our life's journey.

The great appeal to aligning ourselves with literal religious dogma is often shame-driven. This is especially true if we were raised in a family where our essential goodness was regularly assaulted. When we carry core shame, we lack the strength and entitlement to claim our own goodness. It becomes easy to cling to recipes and formulas that offer temporary relief and the illusion that we can escape the grip of shame by acting in complete accord with some alleged higher authority. This is akin to children defining their goodness by whether or not their behavior is compatible with parental expectations.

Literalism is not really equipped to help us move into an experience of the transcendent or deepen the meaning of our lives with authentic community and genuine redemption, since the authority for this lies outside of ourselves. But, as long as we do not accept the responsibility and power to create our own spiritual lives, we are avoiding growing up spiritually. We are adapting and complying with someone else's vision, which eliminates the opportunity to walk a genuine spiritual path.

For richer and more meaningful spiritual and religious lives, we may need to step away from what seperates us from ourselves and to life and create a new vision, one that sustains our awakening. As C.G. Jung wrote in *Mysterium Conionctionis*, "The ultimate fate of every dogma is that it gradually becomes soulless. Life wants to create new forms, and therefore, when a dogma loses its vitality, it must perforce activate the archetype that has always helped man to express the mystery of the soul."

Jung reminds us that spirit thrives on movement and change; and unless we are willing to sacrifice rigid attachments to literalism, we will not be able to meet our evolving needs. Such a sacrifice calls for courage and a willingness to be moved and touched by a spiritual vision that feeds our souls and enlivens our hearts. We can say that spiritual maturity is finding the energy, at the *proper time*, to infuse old dogma with new meanings, meanings meant to expand, enliven and deepen a capacity for compassion.

We have been exploring three underdeveloped forms of spirituality: indifference, idolatry and literalism. We now turn to what a *proper time* for the expansion and deepening of our spirits might look like.

From the Latin word *religio*, C.G. Jung says the following about religion: "By 'religion', then I mean a kind of attitude that takes careful and conscious account of certain numinous feelings, ideas and events and reflects upon them."

In his book *The Soul's Religion*, Thomas Moore describes religion as "a constructive means for being open to the influence of mystery." We can say that a mature religious path might encourage us to take careful and conscious account of a relationship to the mystery of life and the mystery of the self.

In its most immature nature, religion is caught up with the task of designating its own members as exemplary, while castigating non-believers as reprobate and sinful. This good-guy/

bad-guy attitude is nearer to what children do in playgrounds and gangs do on street corners.

As mentioned, we can accept the challenge of valuing and prioritizing at a higher developmental level by focusing less on morality and more on ethics. Morality is simply declarations of what we value, while ethics is a devotional commitment to remain curious about the relevancy and applicability of certain values. When driven by fear, morality can become a set of proclamations aimed at being divisive rather than healing and inclusive. Ethics keeps us questioning, provoking a deeper understanding of what we deem important rather than succumbing to a kind of moral lassitude.

If we are to move beyond spiritual indifference or devotion to our Casino Temple or to a literalism that precludes us from experiencing life at a deeper level, then we will need to take our relationship to life seriously.

Betrothed to Life

In Hebrew, Latin and Greek, an early meaning of the word *spirit* was "wind" and "breath." Wind offers us images of movement, power, air and the ethereal. Spirit easily makes peace with change and wants to find a way to lean into what is in flux. Wind moves easily through and around objects and possesses the potential to generate energy when needed and, as a storm, generating destruction. In order to have a creative relationship with life, we will need to learn how to cope effectively with its storms while not allowing ourselves to be victims of the inevitable tempest. Then again, it may be the gentle breezes of compassion and love that are difficult for us to take in.

The air itself can show us how to shed light through reflection. The ethereal might point us in an upward direction where spirit is eager to elucidate claims to virtue and justice.

We can also understand the maturing spirit as a fullness of breath. We might consider the words *inspire* and *inspiration* as taking life in as well as the word *expire*, which is an outward breath, a letting go of life. Spiritual maturation may be seen as learning how to take in an experience and then how to let it go, allowing the moment to pass. Moreover, our relationship with life begins with ourselves. The self-examining life is dependent upon welcoming what we discover about ourselves.

One definition of our spiritual lives might be the willingness to take our relationship to life seriously, or as Jung pointed out, "a careful and conscious account of certain numinous feelings." Our spirituality reflects a devotion to remain curious and in wonderment about how to take life in, how to let go of life and how to weather life's winds, both the strong current and the gentle breeze.

The three expressions of immature spirituality (indifference, idolatry, and literalism) do not allow for a full breath, as it were, nor do they foster discernment about when to take life in and when to let it go. They fail as aids to help us be clearer about what we see when we are self-examining and how to hold what we actually do see with compassion. It is a path of indifference, numbing us and limiting our vision and openness.

Idolatry offers false promises of vitality and renewal, while leaving us with ephemeral feelings of excitement and temporary distractions from the inevitable realities of life. An attachment to dogma can bring rigor mortis to a spirit hungering to move rhythmically with the tides of change. We are guided down a spiritual path like child following an over-protective parent, sacrificing our curiosity and wonder, and striving to remain obedient to someone else's vision.

It is appropriate to reassure children that family and friends will do their best to provide safety and a feeling of security, even though we may know that the typical family will likely fall short when it comes to offering such sanctuary. However, during adolescence it is proper to initiate young people into the understanding of life as mysterious, insecure and unpredictable. If we neglect such initiation, we place the maturing spirit in serious jeopardy.

The Novice Mystic

Many of us, including me, are novice mystics. We live in a culture that forgot to tell us that our life experience constitutes, as James Hollis points out, an ongoing adventure into four profound expressions of mystery: God or the Transcendent Other, nature, other people and the self. In order to infuse our lives with the spiritual energy of transcendence, meaning, connection and redemption, we will need to take seriously our relationship to all four manifestations of mystery (i.e., essentially, to become mystics).

A mystic has traditionally been understood as a person who is devoted to creating unity with the divine, leading to a personal relationship with God. We can expand our understanding of a mystic to include anyone committed to developing a deep, personal relationship with one or more expressions of mystery. Such a commitment arouses the vitality of our spirits and allows us to move beyond parochial visions of God, nature, our relationships to others and to the self.

How do we go about creating a personal relationship to a

particular manifestation of mystery? How do we become mystics? Courage and curiosity are basic ingredients of the life of a mystic. We will need to find the capacity for wondering beyond what is generally acceptable, allowing our hearts to lead the way and haaving the courage to stand alone, if necessary, in what we cherish and believe.

Many religious mystics faced adversity as they allowed themselves to be guided by inspiration and intuition. A number of Christian mystics were the recipients of this kind of intolerance—even from their fellow Christians. For example, Benedictine mystic Augustine Baker (1575-1641) was forbidden under Holy Obedience to teach the nuns at Cambria the practices of contemplative prayer. Spanish mystic John of the Cross (1542-1591) was kidnapped and imprisoned by his own religious order. The visions of Franciscan Tertiary and mystic Angela of Foligno (1248-1309) were declared to be of the devil. German theologian and mystic Meister Eckhart (1260-1327) was considered a heretic as was the Flemish mystic Jan Van Ruysbroeck (1293-1381). Other faiths have similar histories. In the Islamic tradition, for example, Al Hallaj of Basra (858-922) was martyred in Iraq for his Sufi beliefs.

In his book *Inventing God*, Nicholas Mosley writes: "People are likely to be Moslems or Christians more from a need to belong to a group that would provide emotional reassurance in a difficult world, rather than as a result of a personal search for truth and meaning."

Mosley suggests that it is in our relationship with God that we run the highest risk of infantilism by allowing ourselves merely to remain childishly obedient to some theology or code of belief. It may be that we are settling for religious affiliation in an attempt to diminish the aloneness of a personal spiritual path or to reduce the tension inherent in any search for truth and meaning.

Our relationship with God can involve an immense *proper time* to allow inspiration and intuition to shape and guide our relationship to the mystery of the Transcendent Other. In doing so, we can allow our God relationship to be dictated by a source outside of ourselves. The act of praying may be a way to invite the divine. And as Kierkegaard pointed out, "Prayer speaks more about he who prays."

Prayer, as an act of beseechment, confirms our place in the universe, not as children begging for parental consideration, but rather as adventurers on a perilous journey. Our petitions especially reflect a mature sensibility when they either express gratitude or they ask for the strength to make a more fitting offering to life.

Just as inspiration, contemplative prayer and intuition guide the mystic's relationship with God, our relationship to the mystery of nature can be guided by science, art, poetry and imagination. Some mystics of nature might include Francis of Assisi, Thoreau, and Einstein.

Our understanding of the mystery of others can be guided by science, intuition, imagination, empathy, reflection and art. However, only through a devoted relationship with ourselves will we be able to step closer to others with creativity, compassion and truth. When we refuse to go within ourselves, we will certainly not dare to meaningfully engage others.

The mystery of the self can be a valuable starting point for the novice mystic. The Anglican mystic Julian of Norwich suggested, "We cannot know God until we know our own soul." Indeed, it is the mystery we live closest to. And as we shall see later in this chapter, we can create a personal philosophy that offers us ways to create a meaningful relationship to the different expressions of mystery. We can explore the self through introspection, dreams, analysis, psychotherapy, meditation and a myriad of retreats, trainings and workshops. For me, some of the most profound mystics of the self include Freud, Jung and Kierkegaard.

It is quite easy to take up residence in one of the areas of mystery (God, nature, others and self) and sooth the natural angst that arises when facing the boundlessness of mystery. We may become literalists, clinging to a set of principles that help us create the illusion that we have penetrated the depths of mystery and insulate us from the unknown. Rigid, religious devotees may exhibit no curiosity about nature. Social activists committed to ecological sensitivity might be immune to a relationship to God, self and others. And those pursuing personal growth may be disinterested in their relationship to God and nature. By remaining loyal to the mystical tradition, however, we will tend to follow our hearts no matter what mysterious portal we step through. Maintaining marvel and inquisitiveness in one area will likely leave us open to other renderings of mystery. We see this in an excerpt from *Sayings of Our Lord,* an early Greek papyrus discovered and edited by Bernard P. Grenfell and Arthur S. Hunt:

> Jesus saith,
> Ye ask, who are those that draw us to the kingdom if the Kingdom is in Heaven?
> …the fowls of the air and all beasts that are under the earth or upon the
> earth and fishes of the sea, these are they which draw you and the kingdom of Heaven is within you
> and whosoever shall know himself shall find it.

Strive therefore to know yourselves and ye shall be aware
that ye are the sons of the Almighty Father; and ye shall
know
that ye are in the city of God and ye are the city.

We see a similar theme in Luke 17:20-21:

The kingdom of God is not arriving in a way you can
see directly. Nor will people be able to say, "That's it!" Or
"There it is." The thing is, the kingdom of God is within
you.

In Sufism, a mystical tradition in Islamic thought, the
mystery of God is readily merged with the mystery of the self as
depicted in the following passage from Rumi:

I am filled with you.
Skin, blood, brain, and soul.
There's no room for lack of trust, or trust.
Nothing in this existence but that existence.

In *The Gift*, the Sufi poet Hafiz also echoes this marriage
between the mystery of God and the mystery of the Self:

The earth has disappeared beneath my feet,
Illusion fled all my ecstasy.
Now like a radiant sky creature
God keeps opening,
God keeps opening
Inside of
Me.

It is important for the beginning mystic to appreciate the
challenge of being receptive to how intensely life is lived in the
presence of what is hidden and numinous. We have the opportunity to take back our spiritual lives by accepting the nearness of

the unknown and the power of our hearts to relate to that mystery. This knowledge of the heart allows us to shed juvenile versions of spirituality and embrace a much larger story of spirit.

It may be helpful to the apprentice, as it has been for me, to merge the mystery of God, nature and others into the mystery of life. A mystical pilgrimage can begin by simply asking, "How do I create a deeply personal and meaningful relationship with life?"

Initiated by Life

Many of us continue to cling to the childhood belief that we understand life and can provide ourselves with protection from disappointment, hurt, betrayal and even death. This places us in an estranged relationship with life. It is similar to refusing to accept a lover for whom he or she really is. Instead, we define this person to meet our own needs, not letting ourselves be touched by his or her uniqueness. We comfort ourselves with the illusion of togetherness, denying the inevitable conflict and challenges.

For an authentic relationship with life I suggest characterizing life as a *thou* rather than an *it*. After all, we only have two options, either to personalize or depersonalize life.

If we are willing to personalize life, we call upon more of ourselves as we choose to live fully and truthfully. As we saw in the last chapter, any committed relationship calls upon more of our autonomy and individuality to be awakened and invested in the relationship. When we personalize our relationship to life, we create a valuable *proper time* to access and allow for all we are meant to be. We have the opportunity to arouse more of our emotions, our imaginations, intuitions, instincts and reflections in a committed relationship where we pursue the truth about life and about ourselves.

This deeply personal arousal is captured in Soren Kierkegaard's understanding of truth: "An objective uncertainty held fast in an appropriation-process of the most passionate inwardness is the truth, the highest truth attainable for an existing individual." Of course, the challenge will be to hold some belief with a passionate inwardness. Once we understand that life will not shed its mystery, we can see that all of our beliefs must be condemned to constant uncertainty. Our spirits breathe fully because we hold fast to dreams, longings and hungers that receive and cradle what we believe. Then our deepest understandings bear the marks of our own essential uniqueness and in this state we decide we belong to life and life belongs to us.

On our mysterious and insecure journey, we can begin to strengthen our relationship to life by asking some relevant questions: What is my purpose on such a journey? What am I asking of life? What is life asking of me?

Being betrothed to life suggests a willingness to enter into a deeply intimate relationship with the mysterious and unpredictable, and to commit to a rapport laced with hidden and incomprehensible perils. In our betrothal, we promise to both give and receive abundantly. The ensuing commitment is to live the questions: Am I giving enough or too much? Am I getting enough or too much?

Nothing betrays these promises more than retreating into a victim's posture, which routinely defines life as an evil perpetrator. Life may at times be harsh and even cruel, but as we have seen in our exploration of power, it does not serve us to simply define our life experience as unfortunate. Besides, our betrothed may become cantankerous and ornery when characterized as venomous.

Generosity and Gratitude

We can support our desires for transcendence, connection, meaning and redemption by choosing to be generous and grateful. To expect generosity from ourselves is simply to define ourselves as one who has much to offer.

Allowing gratitude to flow freely through us, we also define ourselves as willing and deserving to be recipients of life's gifts. It is a blessing and infectious to see our beloved as bestowing good things in our direction. We should characterize life as a gracious benefactor and challenge our spirits to find gifts in our most arduous experiences. This is not meant to be a call to naïveté and excessive idealism, but rather to arouse our most creative energies while permitting ourselves to accept whatever dark emotions may be present. Remember, we can acknowledge the unfortunate and even the tragic without taking up permanent residency in victimhood.

As in any good love affair, we will inevitably feel betrayed by life, which can be a important *proper time* for deepening our spiritual existence. Life's betrayals cast us into an existential predicament where we must decide how to respond to life's duplicity. We are forever making unconscious deals with life. We might think: *I'll study hard and succeed academically. My academic success will bring about a lucrative and fulfilling job. I'll work hard and be duly rewarded. I'll be kind and supportive in my relationships and no one will hurt me. I'll faithfully attend to my religious practice and my family will be safe and healthy.*

The first thing to notice is that such deals will likely not make life any less unpredictable and insecure. Nevertheless, we ceaselessly keep trying to generate the feelings of well-being. Minimizing such pacts and making peace with life's mystery, instead of defining it in accordance with the demands of our egos, may be a significant way to depict spiritual maturity.

One perspective, which does not attempt to strip life of its mystery and unpredictability, is to commit ourselves to what's being taught, no matter how cruel or compassionate the teaching. The only exception is when the instruction involves loss, in which case we likely will need to grieve first.

We can choose to remain devoted to learning about the human condition, especially how that condition lives in us. Such devotion allows us to breathe fully, continuing to welcome life, rather than turn against her as an unfaithful lover who deserves condemnation.

The Hasidic mystic Martin Buber (1878-1965) advocated for nurturing a devotion to our humanity: "A person cannot approach the divine by reaching beyond the human. To become human, is what this individual person, has been created for."

We can say that we become more fully human as we learn to expand our relationship to life. As in any committed relationship, this deepening capacity is reflective of a greater aptitude for compassion, truth, and creativity. The mature spirit can be characterized by an unbridled boldness, a refusal to shrink and withdraw from the challenge to move intimately close to life. It can be helpful to see our spiritual journey as an ongoing initiation into the mystery of life and the mystery of our own personhood.

Life Offers Initiation

Just as we were able to view committed relationships as a significant container for initiations into deeper levels of maturity, so we can see life more than capable of initiating us. And, of course, unlike our partners, life is not terribly concerned about our resistance or, for that matter, what we wish for ourselves. In fact, the spirit of life may show up as a storm, without consideration for our welfare.

We might think of fate or the will of life as either greeting us warmly or banging into us. The word *fate* comes from Latin meaning "to be spoken of by the divine." Fate is composed of all those forces that create who we are and lie outside of our control such as genes, legacies and our own past choices. The vicissitudes of life reflected by natural events and the choices of others also contribute to our fate.

Goethe suggested, "At the moment of commitment, the universe conspires to assist you." However, the assistance may not be pleasant and we do not contribute meaningfully to our destinies by seeing ourselves as victims of fate. Nor is it helpful to infuse magic into our relationship to fate by declaring that some law of attraction will bring our positive intentions in perfect harmony with our destiny.

The task is to be honest about how we experience the impact fate has upon our lives without evoking victimization or magic. We can remain creative by asking: What else is here besides something unpleasant? What is my fate asking of me? Is there learning that needs my attention? What kind of support do I need in order to avoid defining myself as a victim of this situation?

It is seductive to believe that our wills or intentions alone guide our destinies. This idea encompasses a kind of adolescent narcissism whereby we neatly exclude all extraneous forces in the universe, aside from the predilections of our own egos. Life is reduced to the role of restaurant waiter whose job it is to simply serve our wishes. Another popular alternative, which also reflects spiritual immaturity, is thinking that fate determines all. This strips our will of any potency, often leaving us feeling deeply victimized.

Each of these beliefs strips the creative tension necessary in any vital and evolving relationship with life, leaving our experiences unable to develop who we are. We can recapture the creative forces of a genuine relationship with life by seeing our destiny as the natural outcome of our wills dancing with the will of life, or fate.

It is a courageous and bold act to dance with one who is mysterious and unpredictable with the intention of stepping into a courtship and eventually creating an intimate relationship. We know that such a romance will inevitably yield suffering, growth and death.

We can see that the same four elements present in any committed relationship also apply to our bond with life. There is our need for autonomy and belonging, and then there are the ways life seems to pursue those same goals. We may find our autonomy developed by an experience of loss, in which events remove people, places and things from our lives. These events may include a divorce, the death of a loved one, the loss of a job, geographical relocation, catastrophic illness and weather disasters.

Life events can also trigger the development of our sense of belonging, as we find ourselves presented with new people, places and things, irrespective of our intention. Examples, big and small, might include a new co-worker, new neighbors, an unexpected inheritance, a call from an old friend, a stray cat on our doorstep, and the birth of a baby in the family. Whether favorable or not, life brings something to us, removing from or adding and pushing toward the frontier of ourselves. Just as we previously explored the stages of initiation pertaining to a relationship, we can track life initiating us.

Separation

Let's consider Clint Eastwood's film, *Gran Torino*, with Eastwood playing the character of Walter Kowalski, a man whose fate presents him an experience of belonging along with a connection that is deeply unwanted. Walter is a cynical and embittered Korean War veteran who scoffs at any belief or attitude that is not totally compatible with his own. His bigotry knows no limits, and his degrading comments cover a broad racial spectrum.

The film opens with the funeral of Walter's wife. We see him experiencing a profound separation, both from his beloved spouse and his own identity, making him even more contemptuous. He is dying as a husband, with all the appropriate ritual and routines of a marriage ending. We get the impression that his wife's death has only added to the hardness and acrimony of his life. Having experienced a significant separation, Walter is ready to step into the trial of his initiation.

The Trial

Walter is portrayed as essentially vexed by his Southeast Asian neighbors, members of the Hmong people. It is suggested that his clear and strong racial bias is probably a remnant of his combat experiences in Korea.

When the will of life, or fate, enters into Walter's life, he strongly resists.

A mêlée involving the extended Hmong family spreads onto Walter's lawn, and he intervenes in order to remove the intruders from his property. Inadvertently, he rescues the neighbors' son, Thao, from the harassment of his cousins. The neighbors view Walter's actions as heroic; and they bring offerings of flowers, plants and food as expressions of gratitude, all of which he vehemently rebuffs. He does not want to belong to life the way life is choosing to be connected to him.

The trial of the initiation intensifies as his Hmong neighbors continue to build their connection and rapport with him, irrespective of his contempt-laden response to their overtures. Typically in a trial the hero or heroine is faced with the will of life (fate) either removing parts of his or her life or, in Walter's case, adding unwelcome elements.

Walter crosses a significant threshold when driving home; he encounters the neighbor's daughter being bullied by three males. He decides to intervene and gives Sue a ride home. During the drive he discovers an appreciation for her spirit and brightness. Soon after she invites him to a family picnic, enticing him with mention of good food and beer. Walter opens his cooler, noticing that his stash of brews has been depleted and accepts the invitation.

He finds himself enjoying the food and drink at the picnic as well as the pampering he's receiving from the women in the family. He begins mentoring Thao in the ways of macho scripts for manhood. Even though many of the male prescriptions are superfluous and not germane to any meaningful expression of manliness, their rapport deepens, solidifying a level of belonging that has been absent in Walter's life.

When Sue returns home beaten and raped, Walter faces the ultimate ordeal of his trial. He must decide how to protect these people whom he's come to love without allowing Thao to replicate the kind of violence that has haunted Walter since his Korean War days.

The transformation of his trial involves the death of isolation, bitterness and cynicism, and the birth of connection, devotion and renewed faith. Life wills a sense of belonging into his life that ardently works on his soul, opening him to others and to himself.

The Return

The return for Walter is tragic as well as redemptive. Tricking Thao and locking him in the basement to prevent him from seeking retribution, Walter then goes to the apartment of the gang responsible for the rape. He appears at their residence and the gang members promptly aim their weapons in his direction. With a cigarette in one hand, Walter casually asks for a light. Their guns remain aimed at him when he says, "Never mind, I have a light." He reaches into his breast pocket, provoking a flurry of gunshots. He dies on the ground, his body riddled with bullet holes and his cigarette lighter in his right hand.

We are told earlier in the film that the trauma of his war experience was not about something he did, but rather about something he did not do. Walter finds a way to redeem his past, save the people he has grown to love, and not perpetuate the violence in his life. Police round up the gang members and succeed in prosecuting them in part due to the willingness of witnesses to come forward, apparently a reflection of Walter's devotion to his neighbors.

Although the return has a tragic theme, like all returns, more life is created. His neighbors can live in peace. Thao inherits Walter's Gran Torino as well as gains a renewed sense of confidence. A climate of intimidation and threat are transformed into amity and goodwill.

We can see fate, or the will of life, as calling us into a significant relationship when life either takes something away or presents us with something new. With either the introduction or extraction of some experience, we are called to make new choices as well as to surrender to the influence of fate. When our wills begin to interact with our fate, our destiny to some degree is the result of how much consciousness we bring to the interface of these two forces.

Fate's Assistance May Not Be Obvious

Linda, a forty-five-year-old high school history teacher, came from a family where any form of boundary was forbidden. As a result, she found it difficult to assert her will and say "no" to others. In our sessions, she was beginning to learn about the qualities and functions of good boundaries as well as to recognize how her weak boundaries allowed people to take from her without much resistance. She began to see that this loss of personal possessions could happen on many levels; and, following a series of unusual events, she was eager to learn how her will and fate might live together more creatively.

"There have been some strange things happening in my life recently. I'm starting to think it's more than just coincidence," Linda explained, leaning forward. She looked like she needed answers.

"Tell me what's been happening." She did not seem like she was prone to excessive drama.

"Well, several weeks ago I could not find this brooch of mine," she began, "and I'm not in the habit of misplacing my things. I began to think that someone may have stolen it. We don't lock the house and one of our neighbors comes in freely."

"You never lock your house?" I wondered about her attachment to such a lack of boundary, both physically and psychologically.

"Almost never. I know it's a bad boundary, but even if we did lock the house, our neighbor has a key. Don't worry, we're going to change the locks soon." She reassured me that she knew about good boundaries. "Well, last week we took a trip to New York City," she continued. "While I was in the middle of a crowd a guy stole my purse off of my shoulder." She shook her head. "I know. I probably shouldn't have been carrying it so carelessly."

"Obviously, thievery has decided to enter your life," I said.

"It seems that way. And, then, when I got home from New York, the broach was back and a necklace was gone."

"Life seems to be taking from you what it will and returning what it deems fit."

"Yes, that's the story of my life. I've allowed people to take whatever they've wanted from me, ever since I was a little girl. I used to hope that if I was responsible enough, taking care of everyone's needs, then maybe the abuse and hostility in our family would end. Truth is, I've lived a stolen life. My life belongs to everyone but me!" Tears rolled down Linda's cheek offering testimony to her collusion with a life of pilfering.

I sat quietly, letting her weep. I knew she felt she didn't have the right to tears. After all someone might be uncomfortable with her sobbing. She had allowed even her grief to be stolen.

"What shall I do?" she asked, feeling more composed and ready to explore.

"Fight for your life."

"Fight for my life?" she repeated. Her facial muscles became more relaxed and her voice carried a sense of conviction. She realized how she was losing herself to the expectations and needs of others. In order to turn the tide, she would have to take control and assert her own will.

Over several more sessions, Linda became devoted to asking what fate was calling her to. Every now and then she would repeat the phrase, "Fight for my life!"

She was grateful for the thieves that had come into her life, since the loss of tangible possessions served as a metaphor for her stolen life. Linda was able to follow that lead into deeper regions of the self and to become a spiritual warrior. She employed more effective boundaries that allowed her to give more authentically and to receive the love that had been trying to reach her. However, fate's call to us may be more potent than a series of unfortunate incidents. It may be a tempest howling through our lives as an arduous crisis.

9

Calls to Spirit

Knowledge of life is one thing; effective occupation of a place
in life, with its dynamic currents passing through your being
is another. —William James

O ften life begins to illicit a strong and dramatic invitation to the unknown self by way of a spiritual crisis.
The more conscious and resourceful we are with a spiritual crisis, the more we can utilize this *proper time* for expanding our
spirit. Every personal crisis offers opportunity for transcendence,
meaning, community and redemption. In the midst of each crisis, we can rise above old values, beliefs and choices, giving birth
to new attitudes.

Since menacing voices will inevitably warn against the
path ahead and implore our return to the familiar, mentoring
from those who have come through these ordeals can be extremely beneficial.

The turbulent winds of these crises may throw us back
upon ourselves, bewildered and eventually succumbing to the
grip of cynicism. It can be only too easy to believe that taking
sanctuary in familiar ways is preferable to facing new trials, no
matter how vital their meaning.

Let's delve into four specific spiritual crises and how we

might open to the invitations and possibilities offered by each. They are *crisis of faith, crisis of freedom, crisis of power,* and *crisis of meaning.*

An original meaning of the word *crisis* suggests a "turning point, a critical moment or a dividing line." When we enter a spiritual crisis, we approach a threshold where we must decide to go on or turn back. We have the choice to see life as beckoning us to a *proper time* for insight. Typically, the choice is either to allow something to die or to refuse to let go. In a way, we can say that in a spiritual crisis we are going to decide how much breath we will choose to live with, how much life we will welcome. Such a decision is permeated with tension, fear and trepidation.

In a crisis, the beliefs, loyalties and values that offer our lives a sense of well-being and security are called into question. We can deny these questions, retreating from a critical moment in the crisis as well as any other considerations that may disrupt our world. This immature posture does not allow us to wonder what might be going on at the dividing line nor entertain questions like: Am I running from something? How do I feel about this new vision? What frightens me the most about this new way of looking at life? What story have I created about this threshold? What resources will I need if I decide to cross this dividing line? What price will I pay if I cross this threshold and what price will I pay if I don't cross it?

We all make use of denial, particularly when we are faced with the importance of a spiritual crisis. The key is to become more effective at examining the nature of a particular threshold and who we are as we approach it. Naming our crisis can be a critical way of entering into a stronger relationship with the ordeal and being more receptive to what it might offer. It requires courage to face the doubt, grief, anger, and fear invoked by a spiritual crisis. I want to caution against pathologizing a spiritual crisis by defining ourselves as crazy or mentally deficient simply because we allow these powerful emotions to impact us.

Crisis of Faith

Doubt is what energizes and gives rise to a crisis of faith. An immature faith does not allow for doubt. It relies upon a rigidity of belief in order to subdue the tension evoked by wonder and curiosity. Faith wrapped in denial and dogma will be unable to lead us to where our longing may be calling us. By throwing off this cloak of denial, we can see faith as an act of acceptance and loyalty to certain beliefs and ultimately a personal world view that may change as we move into the unfamiliar. We might test the value of our loyalty to certain values by asking ourselves how these beliefs serve us.

We remain faithful or loyal to a belief because it might offer us reassurance, a feeling of security, hope, diminished anxiety or some other form of comfort. It is naïve to view our attachments to certain beliefs as simply an intellectual exercise, with no connection to our emotional lives. Taking a position, seeing how that position serves us and being willing to entertain doubt calls for emotional courage and creativity. It is a willingness to be open to new perspectives and to have an evolving relationship with life.

In order to maintain a kinship with the mystery of life, we need to continue to invite ambiguity as an essential ingredient to our convictions. When we experience more ambiguity than we are accustomed, we are likely at the doorstep of a crisis of faith. The gift of the crisis is that it can evoke the courage to embrace mystery. A crisis suggests we that we not only no longer know where we stand, but that we might be willing to endure our doubt, rather than be inoculated by beliefs we cannot truly call our own. However, not knowing where to stand creates great tension and is often accompanied by shame.

Held in the grip of this tension, we likely descend into an identity crisis. We have plainly lost our way, each path seemingly leading further into the wilderness, with no sign of our ability to make it to somewhere we can call home.

In a culture committed to an inflated-ego orientation toward life in which we are expected to know where we are going, being lost in this manner can seem like a taboo. Hence, when we are lost, we are supposed to pretend we're not lost. This sabotages our advance. After all, the strong do not get lost or generate feelings of shame. It's better to be immune to real doubt. Unfortunately, this often is perceived by others as confidence and maturity, rather than a compensation for a deep sense of insecurity. We may feel alone wearing the worn threads of a persona that only divides us from the person we truly are.

Maturation does not mean that we are conveniently insulated from uncertainty, having arrived at some cerebral resting place. Instead, we can see doubt as possibly alerting us to the arrival of a *proper time* for letting go of beliefs that no longer serve us. Doubt can be perceived as the gateway between who we were and who we are called to be. Doubt is the labor of our souls. What is being born is a new heart and a new mind. If we can learn to bear the tension and darkness associated with doubt, we can move beyond cynicism into the restorative energies of wonder and awe.

A crisis of faith can teach us as much about how to carry our beliefs as it does what to believe. Here again, we encounter the value of semi-permeable boundaries. Such boundaries are strong enough to allow us to position ourselves while porous enough to allow for doubt and curiosity. It may make it less likely that we will succumb to the shame stimulated by the cultural mandate to shed all ambiguity and remain steadfast and certain.

We have been indoctrinated to believe we should hold the right beliefs or the proper beliefs, and it can cause great hesitancy and fear to move away from the popular convictions of family and friends. A crisis of faith may be beckoning us to move closer to ourselves and quite possibly further from others. The threat of unbearable aloneness seems eminent, adding to the tension. What if the people I love don't believe what I do? What if I can't generate a consensus in order to confirm my views? What if my conclusions prove to be a fool's folly?

We all find ways to cope with the threat of aloneness. As I already mentioned, one strategy is to simply deny our doubt, maintaining an inauthentic relationship with our current beliefs. Another tactic is to compromise. We hold fast to old beliefs hoping to gain some sanctuary from the ridicule and disdain of our contemporaries and wandering only a short way from reigning ideologies. We attempt to remain loyal to both ourselves and the prevailing social constructs. It is empowering to acknowledge such compromise with integrity, owning our fears and concerns.

A third way of attempting to deal with the conundrum of moving closer to our own vision without jeopardizing our bonds to others is to simply refuse to admit that we are alone by recruiting others to our vision. I have employed this strategy by maintaining a passion to seek my own perspectives and assuming that my friends must have the same views. Again and again I have discovered a clash of belief between me and a friend, and blame them for misleading me. The truth is that I simply projected my own convictions to others, hoping to subdue the tension of my evolving aloneness. I now strive to ask my friends who they are, reminding myself of the differences between us.

A crisis of faith is a *proper time* to welcome our aloneness and discover what it means to be true to ourselves. We saw earlier how any meaningful act of belonging to others calls for an authentic connection to ourselves. Others can only make a sincere offering of acceptance and invitation if we ourselves show up in a genuine way, rather than masquerading as someone we believe others might find more acceptable.

As we shall explore later in this chapter, an ancient meaning of the word *sacred* is "to sacrifice." A crisis of faith is a sacred experience where we are asked to sacrifice the comfort and security of some old belief that no longer deserves our loyalty. We can begin to respect one who is willing to let go of old beliefs, step onto an unknown path, be lost and surrender to the unglamorous undertaking of moving closer to the person we were meant to be.

When we let go of some belief, or refinement of principle, or maybe discover a completely new insight, we step into the sacredness of our own mystery. A crisis of faith announces that we are alive. Our doubts usher in new curiosities and wonderments aimed at revealing some unknown part of the self. We are humbled to greet the stranger who dwells at the frontier of our souls. Such a welcome may be a way of participating in the mystery of our own divinity.

Crisis of Freedom

This spiritual crisis reveals itself as a concern about choices. Perhaps it's a nagging feeling about a lack of choice or a worry about making the wrong choice. In some cases, the core of the crisis is a feeling of being overwhelmed by too many choices.

Sometimes, the issue may not be that we don't have enough choices, but rather we don't have an alternative that we can truly identify with and call our own.

Some two decades ago, after years of defining myself as a pacifist, I began to see the hypocrisy in my position. I discussed this with my mentor and explained that my identity seemed fraudulent since I did not even know how to fight. Much to my chagrin, he agreed. I interviewed a number of senseis, masters of martial arts: aikido, karate and kung fu. I studied kung fu for three years, each week more able to confirm my choice to be non-combative. I learned that the genuineness of a choice often comes from the actual existence of the opposite alternative, such that true choice is possible.

We can ask ourselves several questions that help to reveal the authenticity in our choices: Do I need to acquire some understanding or skill? Is there some experience needed? Do I need someone's blessings?

Powerful forces can reduce the quantity of our choices. The first is ignorance, the second is our own present values, and third is the will of life, or fate. Let's look at how ignorance can propel us toward a crisis of freedom.

From the time of my earliest work with couples, I observed a phenomenon I identified as the "ain't it great to be ignorant" syndrome. The dynamic worked like this: one spouse during a counseling session would make a request for more empathy, emotional disclosure or some expression of emotional support. The other spouse would respond by saying something like, "Gee, I'm sorry, but I don't know how to do that." Most often this would be accompanied by a self-indulgent smile.

I soon became more effective at pointing out the smile and suggesting that the smirking spouse might be taking up a kind of comfort in his or her ignorance. Spouses willing to let go of their smugness were able to learn how they were sacrificing their freedom in the name of being spared accountability. However, the question, "How willing are you to learn how to offer your partner emotional support?" would inevitably remove the smile and challenge the spouse into responsibility for his or her ignorance.

When the will of life (fate) sweeps through our lives like an intense storm our freedom will likely be seriously tested. The death of a loved one, a divorce, the loss of a job, a chronic illness, addiction, or a financial crisis all contain raging winds.

I experienced such a howling when my daughter Sarah was born with severe disability. When life presents such a powerful event, choices are limited. I could have placed Sarah in an institution, I could have left the family and Sarah, or I could have learned to live together.

Loyalty to my values eliminated two of the options, so there I was, learning to live with Sarah. I couldn't find a fourth, more palatable option, so I spent a good deal of time living in a crisis of freedom.

It took many years for me to move away from understanding my freedom as a measure of my choices. Over time, I became curious about how values might impact my experience of freedom. I realized that ignorance about our values can have a serious impact upon our freedom, as a net of confusion obscures what is really important.

We can see that a loss of options leading to a crisis of freedom can be a *proper time* for enlarging our spirits. We can bring significance to our choices by having curiosity about what life is asking of us. What are we to learn here? Is there a service we are being asked to perform?

The seminal studies of Katherine Briggs and Isabel Briggs-Myers expanded upon a particular element of Dr. Carl Jung's theory of choice. This helps to clarify diverse perspectives of choice and the ensuing crisis.

When those in the Judgment group are faced with making a decision, they are not terribly interested in the quantity of choices available. They are much more attracted to finalizing a choice by choosing one, since too many options, with none actually decided upon, creates a crisis. The strength of this group is to be very decisive; however, the group is prone to discontinuing its explorations of the alternatives prematurely and can exhibit a resistance to change.

Alternatively, those in the Perception group diminish the anxiety of making a decision by taking solace in the number of possible choices. This group enjoys keeping all options open and can feel restricted and anxious at the thought of making a choice, thus eliminating other alternatives. The strength of these people is their willingness to explore possibilities and their receptivity to change, but their lack of decisiveness brings about a crisis when a decision is actually needed.

The Judgment group deals with the anxiety of facing possible choices by gaining comfort when a choice is actually made, while the Perception group is challenged by making some choice real and eliminating others. It can be helpful to know which challenges we are most apt to be facing, so we might shamelessly hold the learnings that call to us. We can see that the Judgment group might need to learn more about change and remain open to exploring possibility, while the Perception group can deepen its capacity to let go of possibility and move into decisiveness.

We have been viewing the crisis of freedom from the perspectives of either too many choices or not enough. But what about the dilemma of making the wrong choice?

A wise teacher of mine once said, "Don't try to make the right choice; make the choice and make it right." He wasn't suggesting a cavalier attitude toward our choices, ignoring the consequences. Rather, he was offering an invitation to the mystery of choice where our power to be free might reside.

We cannot know all that our choices will bring. It's why true freedom calls for so much courage. We can see our choices as our wills being joined by the will of life (fate) and the two creating an unknown destiny. Even our best choices might be seriously challenged by circumstance. And choices we regret might ultimately be supported. We never quite know how fate will meet us. It is a powerful stranger who may be offering welcomed provisions or a nemesis appearing to impede our best efforts at being free.

Years ago I had a visitor to a class I was teaching. At the end, she approached me wide-eyed with enthusiasm. Just after the break, I had said something that would change her life significantly. My ego soared and I impatiently waited for her to repeat this cherished jewel. She went on to articulate something that was almost the exact opposite of my point. To make sure that my ears were not deceiving me, I asked her to repeat her comment. Sure enough, she was rejoicing over a clear contradiction of my statement. I took a deep breath and accepted her thanks.

I had an intended message in that class, but this woman had clearly come for something quite different. Fate had joined and, in this case, I had helped make her choice right for her.

My old teacher reminds us to let go of any attempt to penetrate the mystery of our choices and instead do what is in our power, "make the choice right." This means being bold enough to make a choice without the assuredness that the outcome will be favorable.

We can enlarge our spirit of freedom by separating from right-choice/wrong-choice thinking and accepting the mystery of how the will of life will impact our choices. And we should devote ourselves to minimizing the regret when unfavorable consequences result from our choices. We are more likely to be frightened about how we will treat ourselves in the wake of troublesome consequences than we are afraid of the consequences themselves.

Dedication to a vital life becomes a *proper time* to breathe a new robustness into our spirits. Devotion to owning our freedom starts with questioning where we come from. We carry our ancestors biologically and psychologically. Their strengths and wounds weave their way through the fabric of our attitudes and choices. It can be profoundly childish to think that we may have been the product of some pristine legacy, lacking in anything baneful or injurious. When we understand the psychological material of our ancestors, we can be free to interrupt the destructive elements of our legacies and create a new destiny.

The goal is not complete liberation from our legacies, but rather to create reverence for the forces that brought forth our own lives. We can choose to live either in accordance with a legacy or ramble down some untrodden path.

While we must remain committed to becoming freer, we may never know if we have actually achieved it. Our spiritual maturity is a reflection of this process and a crisis of freedom may herald the opportunity to cultivate a new dedication. Any account of a crisis of freedom needs to acknowledge the pivotal roles played by satisfaction and longing.

All choice is aimed at bringing about some level of satisfaction. To become satisfied is to reach contentment and gratification—settled—while longing keeps us aspiring, hungry and yearning. In a crisis of freedom we usually feel little or no satisfaction and an abundant amount of longing. However, the crisis is burdened by the culture's adoration of satisfaction and demonization of longing. We advertise and sell products on the promise that purchasers will gain the satisfaction they seek upon their acquisition. Such a mandate misses the sacred role of longing and its offering during a crisis of freedom.

Longing does not simply seek satisfaction, but rather has the power to guide us to who we are, perhaps leading us somewhere we've never been before. If we allow ourselves to see longing as a hunger then we might begin to understand how fitting it is for us to be wanting. Hunger calls us further into the mystery of ourselves when we eagerly seek our own unfolding by remaining curious about what will truly feed our souls.

Unlike hunger that sustains and supports our curiosity, greed is capable of marching like locusts swarming to an unencroachable fiat to annihilate and exterminate any expression of personal longing. Greed is an excessive form of hunger that devours our longing, separating us from our own mystery and the riddle that surrounds us. We are busy feeding an insatiable appetite, one where our soul's hunger to move closer to itself goes ignored. This craving for indulgence blinds us to our life's purpose and the beauty of our humanity, preventing us from noticing where we truly belong.

It may be that a crisis of freedom not only is filled with longing but it may also indicate a restlessness to travel closer to our true selves, not as an attainable goal but rather as a courageous participation in the divine journey. We will only find temporary solace in our attachment to a particular person or to a place. We must remember that our maturation seems to depend upon discovering the sacredness of our solitude and perhaps a unity that is meant to follow our earthly journey.

We end this look at a crisis of freedom with a blessing from John O'Donohue's book, *Eternal Echoes*:

A Blessing

Blessed be the longing that brought you here and that quickens your soul with wonder. May you have the courage to befriend your eternal longing. May you enjoy the critical and creative companionship of the question, "Who am I?" and may it brighten your longing. May a secret Providence guide your thought and shelter your feeling. May your mind inhabit your life with the same sureness with which your body belongs to the world. May the sense of something absent enlarge your life. May your soul be free as the ever-new waves of the sea. May you succumb to the danger of growth. May you live in the neighborhood of wonder.

May you belong to love with the wildness of dance.
May you know that you are ever embraced in the kind
circle of God.

Crisis of Power

More than any other spiritual crisis, a crisis of power invites us to leave our parents' house. It is appropriate to be confused about personal empowerment in childhood, but at some point we need to be able to step into a *proper time* for learning about genuine personal power. Relentless consumerism drives us toward defining real power as an ability to acquire whatever our hearts desire. And, as we have seen, it is greed that drives our need to possess an unlimited capacity to make acquisitions. We should not underestimate the power of greed. It is blindingly seductive.

Abdication of Power or Victimization

We typically experience a crisis of power when we feel that strength has been stripped from us, leaving us feeling helpless. If we view power as essentially existing somewhere outside of ourselves, we run the risk of living as a victim. Then we sit, waiting for a benevolent parent to save us from our fear of life. The passive posture of the victim diminishes our life energy and has us believing that if we reduce the number of risks we take, we will avoid making mistakes and failing. Of course, fate inevitably teaches that there will be no way to avoid or tame risks, failing is inevitable!

Many of the couples with whom I have worked come for help because they have stepped through the door of victimization into a crisis of power. They are waiting for their partners either to love them or take care of them, replacing what was missing in childhood—a love and care they are unwilling to give themselves. This hope is that they will discover that the partner is never going to be the parent they long for. What they seek can only come from inside. In possession of such awareness they might begin to own more of their own power and move toward right-sizing their souls.

People who undersize their souls often live with magical thinking. They live with a set of immature principles: If I'm kind to you, you'll be kind to me; As long as I am loving, I will be loved; I'll get my needs met as long as I'm not disruptive to others.

We can say that when we are living life with a victim's posture we are locked into childhood. We wait for the ideal parent to come and declare that we are lovable and deserving of love.

It's difficult to accept that we were not meant to receive all the blessings and love we needed as children, but this paves the way for a profound lesson about power. When we are tired of complaining that we are not getting enough love and exhausted from blaming others for our predicament, we may enter into a sacred crisis of power. Again, I use the word *sacred* here because of what will be sacrificed. In this case, some childhood belief or attitude must be forfeited.

Once we are agitated enough and sufficiently bothered by our inclination to be a victim, we can devote ourselves to four specific spirit-enriching lessons. I call these spirit lessons because they are not meant to be learned in a weekend workshop. They are both a life-long task and a call to the infinity of our spirits.

The first two were mentioned earlier. One is a devotion to generosity. When we characterize ourselves as generous, we acknowledge that we have something to give. By definition, a victim does not have much to give. Sometimes a victim exercises what seems like generosity, but it is not a real choice and often the only interaction available.

Generosity invites us to learn: Where can I make an offering of time and energy (including money)? Who might benefit from my offering? What offerings have I made today? Were there opportunities today to be generous that I missed? After living from a full spirit of generosity, we might be able to say in our last hours, "I offered much."

The second spirit-enriching lesson is about gratitude. Living amid gratitude demonstrates how much we are receiving. Victims live in a state of deprivation, unaware of what's being given to them. We instead can be mindful each day of what has been given and who has made offerings to us. Ask yourself: What gift is most difficult to recognize and who should I thank? The gifts are making their way to me. Am I open to receiving them? What a blessing to be able to say at the end of life, "I received much!"

The third lesson comes from learning to live from our desire. Victims are also thieves, but they only steal their own desire. Paramount in the thinking of victims is that their desire may interfere with the needs of others and cause conflict. Victims live by a mandate that they must be minimally disruptive to others. They are focused on pleasing everyone but themselves. This often leaves them prone to being passive aggressive.

Passive aggression is insidious and can be toxic. It is anger expressed indirectly and unconsciously. The actions of someone who is passive aggressive take many shapes—like violating agreements, forgetting simple instructions and important dates, being unable to apply simple lessons, and procrastinating. The behaviors almost always affect more that just the victim. Victims usually resist the thought that they could be capable of such deeds since their self-perception is that they are extremely accommodating. This however is the very breeding ground of passive aggression. It becomes apparent that one of the greatest gifts we have to offer others is our willingness to live with our desire.

When we are conscious of our desire, we remain close to what we want. How much do I want to eat? When and how hard do I want to play and when is the time I devote to other tasks? With whom do I want to engage and with whom do I want to avoid? From whom do I want to receive support and to whom do I wish to give support?

At any given moment, one of my favorite questions is: Whom do I want to be? It's the kind of curiosity that can help us live closer to integrity. Our responses might reflect what we value and believe in and keep us focused in the direction of our desire.

The final spirit lesson for anyone with an inclination for victimization is to learn effective boundaries. When we use effective boundaries we locate the responsibility and the power of our experiences within ourselves rather than with others. The issue becomes how effectively we have prevented ourselves from being injured by the behavior of others rather than look at the awful things others have been doing to us. Essentially, we are tapping into the control that is already available to us in order to consciously decide how much of others' beliefs, emotions and behavior we will allow in.

After identifying whose behavior we are allowing to negatively impact us, we might ask how prone are we to saying "yes" when the situation calls for a "no." How does that clear "no" frighten us?

Again, it is a testimony to a well-lived life if we can say in our final hours, "I took the power and responsibility for my own life by maintaining the best boundaries I could!"

In order to cultivate the power of our spirits in a larger way, there will need to be a moratorium on thievery, where we are determined to stop stealing our entitlement to desire and to protect ourselves. With that in place, the sacred restorative process can begin. Victims can let go of waiting for someone to take care of them and attend to their spirit lessons.

Crisis of Meaning

When we have little or no understanding of who we are, we are likely in a crisis of meaning and this has a profound impact upon identity. But this crisis can be seen as a turning point moving us away from a need to die and turning us toward demands for new life within us.

We can understand the notion of meaning in the ways we name ourselves, name our purpose, our beliefs, our values and the decisions we make about how we will expend our time and energy. In a crisis of meaning we don't know how to name our lives. We are lost.

In some circles—psychological as well as spiritual—a crisis of meaning would be seen as simply unfortunate or turned into a pathology. What gets missed is the understanding of the crisis as suggesting our willingness to maintain a relationship with the unknown. It implies that we are unwilling to continue to name our life experience in a way that feels incompatible with the yearning of our souls. We are willing to endure ambiguity, as disturbing as that might be, and allow its weight to nudge us closer to ourselves. This is an immense indication of spiritual maturity.

If we allow our crisis of meaning to be pathologized, we will not recognize how old ways which deaden our experience need to be sacrificed. Life loses its vitality and color, our vision is pale and the resonance of our voices no longer reflects the rhythm of our lives. We suppress the unlived life within us. Shame is also a likely consequence for someone who holds no compassion for one who has lost her way. Lastly, despair prevents us from listening to life. We can easily move into the depths of emotional isolation, cut off from ourselves and all that surrounds us.

As is often the case, by the time Theresa arrived at my office, she had already deeply pathologized her crisis of meaning. Our initial efforts focused on helping her strip the pathological judgments from her experience. Theresa had employed pathology as a way to fill the vacuum of meaning that permeated her life. Instead of tolerating the tension of the unknown, she decided she was crazy. Often repugnant definitions can be preferable to no names at all.

Initially, Theresa was certain her inner work was deciding whether to stay with her husband or leave him. She was the mother of three and was panic-stricken about the fracture of her family now in the same way it had happened to her at age ten when her parents divorced. Still, she could not tolerate life with her alcoholic husband and would seek an emotional respite with prescription drugs and multiple extramarital affairs. She would get her fix, literally and figuratively, and then return home to an existence she repeatedly defined as unbearable. Each time she named her task as whether or not to leave her husband, I intervened and explained that the real task was whether or not she would be willing to choose herself.

For months, my words meant little or nothing. But when Teresa began to acknowledge suicide as a possible exit from her pain, she came to understand the thinking that her desire to die was a powerful metaphor, bringing attention to something in her which needed to die.

Theresa began naming her life differently when she accepted that she had been attached to unavailable love. There was the love that could neither come from an alcoholic husband, nor from her lovers, nor from drugs. And she refused to recreate the fractured family she experienced at age ten. She was willing to name a major theme in her life without the pathological overtones. Although there was not much glamour in this new meaning, she was arousing a growing curiosity in herself as a person. She was beginning creatively to name her life and choose herself.

Her new purpose was to understand how she organized her life around the pursuit of unavailable love. She discovered a daughter in her who felt neither known nor chosen by her father. Theresa came to know the depth of her allegiance to the man who didn't know her and therefore in her estimation could not really love her. She would make sure that no man would know her, love her or choose her. In order to move forward in her life, she needed to let her extreme devotion to her father die.

Over several sessions, Theresa began to see more aspects of herself that needed to die. She realized that she relied on her physical beauty as a source of power. She also recognized that her tendency to engage in deception and secrecy was another old meaning seeking an honorable death. Authenticity and integrity would move from the unlived to the lived within her. Theresa decided to tell her husband the truth regarding her many affairs and began following a twelve-step program. She wanted a marriage that could be based upon trust and the creation of emotional intimacy. With the knowledge gained from her crisis, Theresa began living her life more authentically with greater ownership of her intelligence and intuition.

The Adventurous Life

Nothing facilitates the death of old meanings and the birth of the new more than adventure. It's an undertaking involving risks and a willingness to face the unexpected and the unknown and a venture that moves us away from the familiar and the convenient. An adventure is a way to agitate the meanings we attribute to our lives, bringing an attunement and refinement to our sensibilities.

Theresa went on an internal adventure that provoked both the death and birth of meaning in her life. I recently embarked on an adventure to Peru where I visited Machu Picchu and a remote beach town called Mancora. However, this external adventure was not simply a journey to novel and interesting sites. Toward the end of the trip I asked myself which voices spoke loudest to me. I recalled the myriad of stories I heard about the Spanish conquest of the Inca during our first week in Peru. Those accounts of the 16th century extinction of a rich culture called my attention to my own oppression.

I began to see how much I suppress the primitive and the instinctual within me. I saw that this exploration was asking me to reclaim my imagination.

Perhaps a little pretentiously, I expected some awakening

at Machu Picchu, generally viewed as an ancient spiritual center. However, it would be later, in another place, that I would receive a wake-up call.

On our third day of visiting the resort of Mancora, Connie and I decided to walk into town by way of the beach. After twenty-five minutes of rambling along soft white sand, with the smell of Pacific Ocean vapors permeating the air, we decided to make our way toward the main street of town. Our initial path took us down an alley bordered on each side by den-like hostels, housing visiting surfers. They had the feel of catacombs where secret religious rites might be held. Several moments later we encountered a stone wall preventing further progress. We retreated from the alley in search of another route to the street.

At this point we encountered an elderly Peruvian man shoveling dirt. Behind him a street ran parallel to a canal, but with no bridge in sight. Neither of us understood the other, but his using hand gestures and the word *agua* we comprehended that we were to walk adjacent to the canal until reaching a bridge that stretched over to the street. After walking some three hundred feet in the direction of the bridge, we encountered an eight-foot wooden fence with a hole stretching approximately two feet above the ground—the only way through.

Connie dropped to the ground and with her exceptionally lithe body scampered cat-like through the hole. I did not want to drag my entire body along the ground nor scrape my back on the fence. After all, we were on our way to breakfast. The trick would be to keep some distance from the turf while creating enough room to avoid contact with the fence.

As I felt my torso slip through the opening, I was filled with a confidence that my legs would easily follow. And so they did. I gleefully sprang to my feet only to be greeted by an unseen wire stretched across the path and I was instantly face-down in the dust of Mancora. I got to my feet, filled with an urgency to gather myself, more concerned about my damaged pride than any possible injury. I walked faster and faster as if my pace could somehow cancel the cosmic trick that had been played upon me.

It wasn't until breakfast, sipping my coffee and occasionally brushing dust off of my body in an attempt to clean the entire incident from my experience, that I allowed a new name to call to me. What had happened? As I whisked myself of Mancora's dust, images of typical Monday mornings back home filled my mind. I was sitting in my big red chair, comfortable and confident, facilitating someone's soul work. It was a familiar world, created from my vision and my values.

Sometimes a man must travel eight thousand miles away from home and look at himself away through a hole in a fence, face down, before he can rename his life as something larger. For the first time I saw how small my work is in my office. That is, how small within the context of all that is happening in the world. However, for the first time in my life I understood this smallness was worthy of my reverence. Until that moment, I had believed that either I am doing something magnificent, deserving to be honored, or something small that should be demeaned.

I made my way down the beach, as the morning sun in Mancora seemed to melt away an old meaning, replaced by naming what I do as small and yet still deserving of my respect.

A crisis of meaning is life's way of asking us to rename ourselves again, again, and again. We recognize that we are up to the task of creating, deconstructing, learning, risking, exploring, loving, etc. It often takes a great deal of disturbance in our lives before we are ready to allow old ways to die, making room for the new. We are reminded of how much our spiritual maturation is dependent upon our ability to endure turmoil, understanding that it is meant to give rise to an expanded spirit. This expansion is best exemplified when we shed cultural ideas and beliefs that don't really belong to us and develop a personal philosophy, allowing us to see whom we are more clearly.

Seeking Faces of the Self

Learning to endure and benefit from the four spiritual crises can mark the gestation of a quest to unveil faces of the self. We can say that a spiritual crisis is a *proper time* to begin to take on the challenge of creating a personal philosophy.

The word *philosophy* comes from the Greek, meaning "love of Sophia," with *Sophia* referring to personal wisdom. The first thing we might notice is that a personal philosophy is largely a love affair, an act of ardor and devotion to offer ourselves guidance through our interior worlds.

I have noticed that most modern references to wisdom are met with indifference, jocularity and even contempt. Curiously, we have found it valuable to demean what might be called one of the most profound expressions of the human condition. We might even say that this debased attitude toward wisdom is one of the great blasphemies of our time. So why have we turned our backs upon the honorable pursuit of wisdom?

Our society has a great admiration for the valuable contributions made by science. It is easy to be enthralled with computer technology and its ever-increasing capacity for data and speed. Modern technology offers us a useful distraction from our inner worlds. We do not have to visit the mysterious lagoons of the soul that stretch into eternity; instead we can remain comfortably at home, anonymous to ourselves. It's a frightening expedition and we might not like what we find there. It's far easier to view maturation as a reflection of the latest gadget we possess.

Knowledge reinforces the illusion that we live mostly in a visible world and points us outside of ourselves, focusing our attention on the external. Our reassuring role is that of the voyeur whose task it is to watch and observe rather than participate, although some contemporary physicists suggest that sub-atomic particles rearrange themselves depending on who is observing them, meaning that matter is having a relationship with us. We feel powerful when we master the machines. We gather data, measure it, draw implications for our measurements and pretend that we have some meaningful control over reality. Our thoughts, desires, loves, emotions, values and dreams are terrifying and we take great solace in running away.

Nothing seems more secure than the idea that we possess an answer. But what is an answer? We can say that an answer is a temporary way to comfort ourselves when we are exposed to the mystery of life. We decide that some line of inquiry has come to a satisfactory closure. We can then suspend our curiosity and wonder. Thomas Moore points out, "The emotions of uncertainty and the fever of wonder are essential components of the spiritual life."

It helps to know that we can offer ourselves comfort and respite when we accept this arduous journey of inquiry. The key is to resist pretending that our wonderment has actually reached completion and that we have accessed the essence of truth. Participation in the human condition suggests that we are condemned to only an approximation of the truth. We hurt our spirits when we believe we can achieve more.

A Living Philosophy

A love affair is vacuous and empty unless it lends itself to real action. Love cannot grow as a thought or a benevolent intention—devotional action is required. It can be extremely humbling to let go of acquiring endless amounts of data of the world around us and prioritize a faithful and reverent navigation of our own soulful waters.

Why commence an extensive exploration of our interior waters? For one, it can be a great way to die, which makes it a great way to live. If we can say in our final hours that we lived devotionally toward understanding our own souls, it should be a life well lived.

To conduct this exploration without love would mean that there is no way to maintain a creative and dynamic relationship with the self. My friend Henri Nouwen once wrote, "There is no truth without compassion." When I asked Henri what he meant by the statement, he replied, "Which of us would continue to troll the depths of ourselves if we did not hold what we find with compassion?"

Ultimately, we have no choice. We either learn to have a compassionate relationship with our self-discoveries or no relationship at all. It simply becomes too much to keep looking at ourselves under the burden of shame and self-loathing. However, there is an immense gift available to us when we are willing to internally navigate with compassion. Call it an abiding love affair. It is analogous to having a friend who bestows compassion upon us, upon hearing our stories. We visit this friend with an eagerness and anticipation of being the recipient of kindness and care. Such a friendship is built upon love and trust, and with that kind of love extended to the self, the love of wisdom can only intensify.

We might also say that our purpose here on earth becomes clearer, more authentic and more easily manifested through our love affair.

Philosophy as an Act of Personal Salvation

Beyond the deep reefs of our souls there are dark pools of water where a lighthouse beacon struggles to shine. Carl Jung's view on enlightenment can be summed up: "One doesn't become enlightened by imagining figures of light but by making darkness more conscious. The latter procedure, however, is disagreeable and therefore not popular."

Jung helps us see figures of light as those personal characteristics of which we are both aware and deem appropriate. The darkness we can understand as "shadow," or those elements of the self that are considered unacceptable and relegated to the unconscious. Under these terms, enlightenment seems to be more about wholeness, where we learn to welcome what we have abandoned and exiled about ourselves. What we banish may not necessarily be repugnant; it may simply be anything deemed unacceptable by our families or social groups. If a daughter believes that her father will be threatened by her intelligence then she may identify that characteristic as unsuitable and assign it to her unconscious. She then proceeds to live as if she is not bright.

What we judge as unacceptable and assign to the uncon-

scious remains unknown and yet active in our lives. Our choices
and attitudes are secretly impacted by "shadow" material. Essentially, we remain blind to the darker elements that accompany
some of our most noble intentions and actions. To describe them
as unconscious is to say that they lie deep within the mystery of
who we are and are not easily known or understood. Once these
traits are defined as undesirable, we don't want them. We discard
them in our psychological closet, hoping to forget about them.

We are reduced to being one-dimensional characters
when we attempt to purify ourselves of our blemishes. For example, we may try to see ourselves as purely selfless and altruistic, denying personal agendas that may also be motivating
our acts of kindness. These agendas may include a longing to
be needed or a desire to control people, holding them hostage
until they return the favor. Our magnanimity may also be a
competition, offering generosity in the hope of winning the
favor of family members.

Another example of a Shadow accompanying insidious
behavior is a situation where one person asks a friend not to
repeat what he is about to say and proceeds to explain how their
mutual friend has been making derogatory remarks about him.
This often leaves the receiver feeling stranded, hurt and helpless and suggests the speaker may have an unconscious need to
punish the listener.

Consider that a Shadow's relation to the self is like a child
who has been tagged as the troublemaker in his family. He is
scapegoated and marginalized. He might be punished by being
locked in a psychological closet. This child has three choices.
He can break out of the closet and run away, in which case, we
see him all over town. He can release himself and create havoc

within the family. Or he can come out and integrate into the family, becoming a part of the whole unit.

Such a child lives with restlessness and angst, always seeking greater acceptance and inclusion. Similarly, when we deny parts of ourselves, the energy of those unwanted aspects becomes turbulent and discontented. Ideally, these parts of us can be accepted into the self and achieve integration; but when this doesn't happen, these traits can either act out and take over the self (gotcha), or appear to us only as a trait in others who we deem as unfit but not within our own selves (projection).

When a lack of integration leads to projection, we view friends, family members and colleagues as selfish, arrogant, insensitive, self-righteous and uncooperative, attributing those characteristics to others so we don't have to acknowledge them in ourselves.

The question can certainly be asked if there is ever a negative perception of another that is not attributed to projection. Of course, an obvious indicator that we are likely projecting is the intensity of our disapproving perceptions of others.

Years ago when I was dating my wife, I arranged a session for the two of us with my therapist. When the therapist asked what we should focus on during the session, I eagerly suggested that Connie's intensity would be a worthwhile topic. Without waiting for a response to my suggestion from the therapist or Connie, I launched into passionate detail about why Connie should address the problem of her intensity.

"You offer an intensely convincing argument about Connie's need to do something about her intensity," the therapist responded with a smile. He and Connie both began to laugh.

"What's so funny?" I asked. I didn't see anything comical at all. Or intense.

"Well, it might be your intensity that is getting our attention but obviously not getting your attention," he pointed out to my surprise.

My self-perception as cool, calm and radiating serenity was severely shaken. It took some time to welcome my own intensity and come to understand that although Connie could be intense, my strong adverse reaction was testimony to the presence of my own Shadow.

Tony, a forty-two-year-old physical fitness trainer, took great pride in being gentle and encouraging. In one of our sessions he described how he was having very strong reactions to a fellow who regularly worked out at the gym.

"There's this guy. I mean I don't really like him. I get around him and feel pissed," Tony explained. He appeared embarrassed by his own, strong reaction.

"What's it about this guy that gets you going?"

"I know exactly what it is!" Tony exclaimed. "He's got answers for everybody! I mean, this guy walks around the gym giving a series of short lectures on topics he doesn't know shit about!" Tony showed more verve and hostility than I had ever heard from him.

"I hear that this guy is raising a powerful reaction in you," I offered. "I'm wondering if he might remind you of a part of yourself that also tends to enthusiastically generate answers." Could he be caught in a projection?

"Gee, I'm not sure I know that part of myself," he said, puzzled.

"Well, do you remember a time in your life when you were inclined to represent yourself as the answer-man?" I asked.

"In my twenties I tended to get into a know-it-all head, especially when I drank."

"How do you feel about the know-it-all guy who surfaced in your twenties?"

"I don't like him, not at all."

"Do you get what might be happening in the gym?"

"You mean this guy is reminding me of a part of myself that I'd rather forget," he said enthusiastically.

"Yes, I think he is reminding you of that part of yourself that you've sequestered to the backroom of your psyche. Do you know how you came to have so many answers back then?" I encouraged him to enlarge the story of the answer-man.

"Yes, I didn't feel that I was very bright," he said. "I guess I was trying to prove I was intelligent."

Projection places us in a precariously dependent relationship with others. It is as if we ask others to carry what we consider unacceptable in order that we might feel better about ourselves. As long as we see the unacceptable enacted by others, we can maintain the illusion that we are immune from such loathsome characteristics. Their inferiority guarantees us a superior position.

"Gotcha" is an expression I use when we are trapped by Shadow energy. It's analogous to a family with a disenfranchised child who acts out, making the other family members feel like they have been taken hostage. Anytime we are acting in a way that we don't understand or that seems contrary to how we see ourselves, it is likely that we are experiencing a gotcha, taken hostage by our Shadow material.

We have already seen the beginnings of a gotcha when we have strong repugnant reactions to the people or groups where we project. Our lack of compassion for these groups signals that we may be seeing what we have denied about ourselves in others. Acting in accord with our disparaging feelings and creating rationalizations aimed at justifying our choices perfect the gotcha.

We can identify a gotcha by recognizing when our thinking favors what we might otherwise find objectionable. We try to justify our actions by attributing our own unwanted characteristics to those we mistreat. For example, we convince ourselves that a certain ethnic or religious group is inferior and then treat them in a bigoted and contemptuous way. Or we get drunk and believe we have the right to do or say whatever we please; say something we know will be deeply hurtful to a person; rage because we believe someone deserves it; or choose to deceive those who trust us. Other examples might include exploiting the innocent and naïve and building a case for why it is good for them; taking pleasure in someone being physically or sexually assaulted; judging that it might be a good time to stop gambling and continuing anyway; and believing it would serve us to run away from all responsibilities.

By remaining conscious of projection, we can navigate the dark waters created by a Shadow and plot a course toward healthy self-awareness. The water is deep, but it is where we find the opportunity to make peace with ourselves by letting go of perfectionistic inclinations. When we integrate Shadow into consciousness, what Jung calls "individuation" or "undividedness" develops and our encounter with Shadow becomes a *proper time* of spiritual maturation. We can learn to welcome what we banished. We can move toward an authentic capacity to welcome ourselves and make us ready to sacrifice infantile impulses to live in small stories of ourselves.

It can be only too easy to look at exploring Shadow material as a better way to become a better person. We can ask: Better than what? Better than who we used to be? Better than the guy across the street? This idea that we are on the move toward a more exalted pristine state reflects the tenor of the heroic, feverishly devoted to improvement.

We might imagine this compulsion toward improvement as fallout from the encounters our ancestors had with the religious authorities of ancient times who would cite the celestial bounty awaiting those who followed their doctrine and insisted that they remained the intermediaries for spiritual evolution. It's not a bad way to secure power, since it guaranteed dependency while disciples labored toward an impossible goal.

The notion of getting better is best applied when we are attempting mastery over some very specific skill (i.e., baking bread, cutting wood, doing math, changing a flat tire, etc.). The idea of better understanding the relationship with ourselves is misguided. The core of any meaningful personal philosophy is a devotion to the mystery of the self which we never fully penetrate. We can, however, remain receptive, welcoming and invitational to the self, hoping to be granted glimpses.

Like any worthwhile philosophical endeavor, an abiding curiosity allows us to continue to stay engaged and reflects a spirit of maturity. Remaining conscious of projections and tendencies to see others as inferior while supporting our need to occupy the psychological high ground allows us to move closer to who we actually are. When we recognize both the positive and negative in us, we are empowered to be our true selves rather than a sanitized version of our identity. It also allows us to live with more compassion for ourselves and others, enhancing our freedom. Staying conscious imparts a chance to step into a larger story about ourselves. It will impact how we relate to others and impact the way we carry our fear.

An old Latin translation of the word *salvation* is "health and welfare." By committing to remaining conscious of our projections and gotcha, we can call a truce to the battle within ourselves that leaves us less separated from ourselves and from others. Our salvation becomes a kind of homecoming where we offer a welcome to our whole selves, thereby gaining a deeper acceptance of the humanity of others. We can commit to a willingness to forgive ourselves, again and again, learning to accept the limitations inherent in our own humanity.

Circling Back

We have been looking at maturity as being willing and able to identify that we are at a *proper time* for gaining some wisdom. We may be learning how to employ effective boundaries, how to steep our lives with authentic personal power, how to develop an intimate relationship or how to make peace with the inherent mysteries of our lives and eventually take responsibility for our own salvation.

Remember the quote by Rilke: "Every happiness is the child of a separation it did not think it could survive." The calculation of our maturity will greatly depend upon stepping right into the separations we believed we could not survive. How ironic that the buds of new life spring forth just when we're convinced we are going to die.

I want to end with a blessing for the reader who was bold enough to make this reading an event in his or her *proper time.*

A Blessing

May you possess both the patience and the eagerness
to allow yourself to be penetrated by a proper time
that has longed to join you.

May you refuse to be satisfied with being undersized or
caught in inflations that demean the rightful
size of your soul.

May your learnings rest easily in your body,
vitalizing your senses and allowing your heart
to welcome some forgotten part of yourself
that desires to come home.

May your stories grow, embellished by depictions
of grace, forgiveness, resolve and comfort.
Let these narratives find some small space where
the demons haunting your soul might dwell with
voices ever softening.

And when the inevitable aloneness of the journey
threatens to turn you against yourself,
remember those who came before you, your ancestors,
who prepared a place for you, long before your arrival.

May your betrothal to life be renewed by a single act
of generosity and a quiet moment of gratitude,
releasing the shackles of victimization.

May your heart exercise a fervent loyalty to the
beliefs that enliven your spirit, while holding your
views with a suppleness that allows you to greet a
fresh idea like the possibility of a new friendship.

Do not look at your life gravely through the eyes of

right and wrong, but rather reach more deeply,
beyond fear, to the place where wonder, curiosity
and awe dwell.

When you look at the distance that separates
who you are from whom you wish to be,
treat yourself kindly, for who you are is pregnant with
whom you wish to be.

Remember how fitting it is that you remain
engaged in a love affair with navigation of your inner
world.

And may your life possess enough peace and disturbance
to keep you enthralled with that love affair.